FACT
FINDER

Compiled by
Theodore Rowland-Entwistle and Jean Cooke
Contributors
David Lambert, Jill Thomas, Sean Connolly,
James Muirden, William Hemsley, Michael Chinery, Sue Reading
Editors
Cynthia O'Neill, Catherine Headlam, Jim Miles, Sally
Hamilton, Jennifer Justice, Julie Cairns, Kathy Gill (index)
Design
Sue Hall, Louise Jervis
Picture Research
Su Alexander

KINGFISHER BOOKS
Grisewood & Dempsey Inc.
95 Madison Avenue
New York, New York 10016

First American edition 1992

2 4 6 8 10 9 7 5 3 1

Library of Congress Cataloging-in-Publication Data
Factfinder/[compiled by Theodore Rowland-Entwistle and Jean Cooke:
contributors, David Lambert . . . et al.].
p. cm.
Includes Index.
Summary: Presents facts and figures about the universe, planet
earth, countries, animals, plants, the human body, science and
technology, arts and entertainment, sports, and history.
1. Children's encyclopedias and dictionaries. [1. Encyclopedias
and dictionaries.] I. Rowland-Entwistle, Theodore. II. Cooke, Jean
Isobel Esther, 1929- . III. Title: Factfinder.
AG5.F29 1992
031-dc20   92-53118 CIP AC
ISBN 1-85697-803-6

Printed in Hong Kong

FACT FINDER

Kingfisher Books

NEW YORK

ACKNOWLEDGMENTS

The publishers wish to thank the following for supplying photographs for this book:

Page 8 Zefa; 30–31 Zefa; 34 Nasa; 35 Zefa; 84 British Museum; 84–85 Town of Bayeux; 85 National Gallery of Art; 89 Rex Features; 91 South American Pictures; 93 & 94 National Portrait Gallery; 95 The Mansell Collection (top left), Camera Press (right); 96 & 97 Popperfoto; 98 & 99 Zefa; 102 Bibliothèque Nationale; 103 British Library; 104 Ancient Art and Architecture; 105 College of Arms, London; 107 Peter Newark; 108 The Mansell Collection; 109 Peter Newark; 110 Wellington Museum (bottom left), 110–111 The Mansell Collection (centre), 111 Benz; 112 Popperfoto; 118 Allsport; 128 Zefa; 160 The Hutchison Library; 169 Imitor; 171 Bibliothèque Nationale; 181 Philips; 183 Zefa; 215 TRH Pictures; 225 Zefa; 232 Giraudon; 233 National Gallery (bottom right), Bibliothèque Amrosiana (top left); 236 National Portrait Gallery (top left), The Mansell Collection (bottom right); 237 Victoria & Albert Museum (bottom left), Det Kongelige Bibliotek (top right); 238 Scala; 245 Dominic Photograph; 239, 244 The Mansell Collection; 246 Ronald Grant Archive; 247 Zefa; 248 National Portrait Gallery; 249 The Mansell Collection; 250 National Film Theatre; 252, 253 & 254 Ronald Grant Archive; 255 Rex Features; 256, 257 & 259 Allsport.

The publishers would like to thank the following artists for their contribution to this book:

Marion Appleton, Mike Atkinson, Craig Austin, Peter Bull, The Jillian Burgess Agency, Kuo Kang Chen, Jeane Colville, Mark Franklin, Jeremy Gower, Hardlines, Ron Hayward, Allan Hardcastle, John James, Linden Artists, Chris Lyon, Alan Male, Janos Marffy, David Wright.

Flags supplied by Lovell Johns, Oxford. Authenticated by the Flag Research Center, Winchester, Mass. 08190

Contents

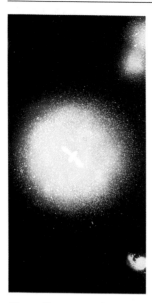

The Universe

The universe is still a mystery to people. Was it really formed 15 billion years ago in one gigantic "Big Bang"? Is the explosion still continuing as planets, asteroids, comets, moons, and billions upon billions of stars hurtle farther into deepest space?

Stars are vast spheres of gas that burn with different colored light. Our Sun is a star and planet Earth spins around it, kept in orbit by gravity. Other stars give off no light: these are the "black holes." Their gravitational force is so strong that even light waves can't escape.

All the stars, planets, and other bodies we see in the heavens are known as the universe. Stars are huge spheres of gas which give off light and heat. Our Sun is a typical medium-sized star. It looks so much larger than other stars because it is close to the Earth.

The distances between stars are so vast that the easiest way to measure them is in terms of the time it takes their light to reach us. The Sun's light takes 8 minutes 20

Above: *Quasars are the most distant objects we know. Each is about 100 times brighter than the brightest galaxies in our local star clusters. Quasar 3C273, about 600 million light years away, is one of the closest and brightest quasars known.*
Right: *How the Milky Way might appear from Earth if the solar system was a few hundred light years above the Galaxy's arms. In fact, the fierce energy waves from the blazing center would have prevented life from developing on Earth.*

seconds to travel to the Earth. The light from the next nearest star, called Proxima Centauri, takes 4 years 15½ weeks, or 4.3 light-years. The most distant stars are billions of light-years away.

The countless stars

Nobody knows for certain, but astronomers think there are at least 200 billion billion stars – that is 2 with twenty zeros after it. Some stars are much smaller than the Sun, and are known as dwarf stars. Others are between 100 and 1,000 times bigger, and are known as supergiants. Stars between 10 and 100 times the size of the Sun are giants.

All stars have one thing in common: the force known as gravitation. Every object has this force, and pulls other objects toward it.

The power of gravity depends on the mass of the object – that is, how much material it contains. On Earth, the effect of gravity is that if you let go of something, such as a ball, it falls to the ground, because the Earth's gravitational force is much stronger than that of the ball. A large star that is mostly gas may have less gravitational force than a small, more solid star.

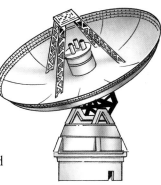

Astronomers use radio telescopes to collect signals from objects too far away to be seen through ordinary telescopes.

A pulsar, like this one in the Crab Nebula, is the spinning remains of a supernova, an exploding star. The beam of light and radio waves makes a pulse, like the circling beam of a lighthouse.

Halley's comet photographed from South Africa in 1910. It returns close to the Earth every 76 years.

Black holes, quasars, and pulsars

There are many different kinds of stars. They shine with different colored light, ranging from white through blue and yellow to red. Some white stars are called white dwarfs. Their gravitational force has shrunk them, making them small and dense. Some stars that give off no light at all are believed to exist. They are called black holes. Their gravitational force is so strong that even light waves cannot escape from them.

There are numbers of starlike bodies in the heavens that are still a mystery. Quasars – short for quasi (almost) starlike objects – give off strong radio waves. Pulsars are similar, but send out their radio waves in regular pulses. There are also stars which give off X rays, and others which emit heat rather than light.

Star clusters

Many stars are groups in clusters called constellations. A major group of stars, containing many millions, is called a galaxy. We are part of a galaxy called the Milky Way. It has that name because some of its stars form a vast, milky-looking band of light across the night sky. It is a huge, spinning disk made of stars, about 100,000 light years across. Our Sun is about 30,000 light years from the center of the disk. There are millions of galaxies – we just do not know how many.

Planets, asteroids, comets

A planet is a heavenly body that revolves around a star. Our Sun has nine major planets revolving around it, forming the Solar System. The Earth is one of the planets. A planet does not give off its own light, like a star, but shines with light reflected from the Sun.

There is also a group of small bodies, called the minor planets, or asteroids. They are found between the orbits of the major planets Mars and Jupiter. All but three of major planets – Mercury, Venus, and Pluto – have small, planet-like satellites revolving around them. They are called moons. The Earth has just one satellite, called the Moon, but other planets have several.

Finally, the solar system contains some wandering bodies called comets. They have very long, elliptical orbits, and shoot away into space after looping around the Sun. Some return after a few years, others not for thousands of years. Comets have been described as "dirty snowballs," consisting of a mixture of dust, gas, and particles of ice.

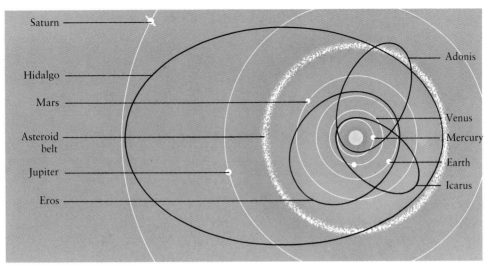

How old is the universe?

The universe is thought to be at least 15 billion years old. Many scientists think that before that time all matter was collected together in one large ball, a sort of super black hole. Then there was an explosion, called the "Big Bang." Matter was scattered in all directions.

From that matter all the stars were formed. According to one theory, the effects of the Big Bang are still going on, and stars and galaxies are still spreading out from the center of the explosion. Certainly, the galaxies are moving away from each other at high speed.

However, other astronomers believe there never was a Big Bang, and that the universe has always been roughly like it is today.

The Constellations

A constellation is a group of conspicuous stars that can be seen in a particular portion of the night sky. Altogether there are 88 constellations. Of these, 48 can be seen from the northern half of the Earth or from the lands around the equator.

Astronomers use the constellations as sky landmarks for fixing the position, not only of their own stars, but of any others that are detected with powerful telescopes.

The ancient Greeks gave the constellations the names of real and mythical beasts and their gods and heroes, because they fancied they saw patterns of stars that fitted these names. The patterns have changed since then.

The names are in Latin, because for centuries all scholarly books were written in that language.

The diagram above shows the orbits of the main asteroids. These minor planets are small and, though much closer to the Earth than the stars, are difficult to detect in the night sky.

THE CONSTELLATIONS

Latin name	English name	Latin name	English name
Andromeda	Andromeda	Chamaeleon	Chameleon
Antlia	Air Pump	Circinus	Pair of Compasses
Apus	Bird of Paradise	Columba	Dove
Aquarius	Water Bearer	Coma Berenices	Berenice's Hair
Aquila	Eagle	Corona Australis	Southern Crown
Ara	Altar	Corona Borealis	Northern Crown
Argo Navis	Ship Argo	Corvus	Crow
Aries	Ram	Crater	Cup
Auriga	Charioteer	Crux	Southern Cross
Boötes	Herdsman	Cygnus	Swan
Caelum	Chisel	Delphinus	Dolphin
Camelopardus	Giraffe	Dorado	Swordfish
Cancer	Crab	Draco	Dragon
Canes Venatici	Hunting Dogs	Equuleus	Little Horse
Canis Major	Great Dog	Eridanus	River Eridanus
Canis Minor	Little Dog	Fornax	Furnace
Capricornus	Sea-Goat	Gemini	Twins
Carina	Keel (of Argo)	Grus	Crane
Cassiopeia	Cassiopeia	Hercules	Hercules
Centaurus	Centaur	Horologium	Clock
Cepheus	Cepheus	Hydra	Sea-Serpent
Cetus	Whale	Hydrus	Watersnake

NORTHERN HEMISPHERE

1 Equuleus
2 Delphinus
3 Pegasus
4 Pisces
5 Cetus
6 Aries
7 Triangulum
8 Andromeda
9 Lacerta
10 Cygnus
11 Sagitta
12 Aquila
13 Lyra
14 Cepheus
15 Cassiopeia
16 Perseus
17 Camelopardus
18 Auriga
19 Taurus
20 Orion
21 Lynx
22 Polaris
23 Ursa Minor
24 Draco

25 Hercules
26 Ophiuchus
27 Serpens
28 Corona Borealis
29 Boötes
30 Ursa Major
31 Gemini
32 Cancer
33 Canis Minor
34 Hydra
35 Leo
36 Leo Minor
37 Canes Venatici
38 Coma Berenices
39 Virgo

The positions of the
constellations of the Northern
Hemisphere.

Latin name	English name	Latin name	English name
Indus	Indian	Piscis Austrinus	Southern Fish
Lacerta	Lizard	Puppis	Poop (of Argo)
Leon	Lion	Pyxis	Mariner's Compass
Leo Minor	Little Lion	Reticulum	Net
Lepus	Hare	Sagitta	Arrow
Libra	Scales	Sagittarius	Archer
Lupus	Wolf	Scorpius	Scorpion
Lynx	Lynx	Sculptor	Sculptor
Lyra	Lyre	Scutum	Shield
Mensa	Table	Serpens	Serpent
Microscopium	Microscope	Sextans	Sextant
Monosceros	Unicorn	Taurus	Bull
Musca	Fly	Telescopium	Telescope
Norma	Rule (straight-edge)	Triangulum	Triangle
Octans	Octant	Triangulum Australe	Southern Triangle
Orion	Orion (hunter)	Tucana	Toucan
Pavo	Peacock	Ursa Major	Great Bear (or Plough)
Pegasus	Pegasus (winged horse)	Ursa Minor	Little Bear
Perseus	Perseus	Vela	Sails (or Argo)
Pheonix	Phoenix	Virgo	Virgin
Pictor	Painter (or Easel)	Volans	Flying Fish
Pisces	Fishes	Vulpecula	Fox

SOUTHERN HEMISPHERE

1 Cetus
2 Sculptor
3 Aquarius
4 Piscis Austrinus
5 Capricornus
6 Grus
7 Phoenix
8 Fornax
9 Eridanus
10 Hydrus
11 Tucana
12 Indus
13 Sagittarius
14 Aquala
15 Corona Australis
16 Pavo
17 Octans
18 Dorado
19 Pictor
20 Columba
21 Lepus
22 Orion
23 Monoceros
24 Canis Major

25 Puppis
26 Carina
27 Volans
28 Chamaeleon
29 Apus
30 Triangulum Australe
31 Ara
32 Scorpio
33 Serpens
34 Ophiuchus
35 Lupus
36 Centaurus
37 Crux
38 Musca
39 Vela
40 Pyxis
41 Hydra
42 Sextans
43 Crater
44 Corvus
45 Libra
46 Virgo

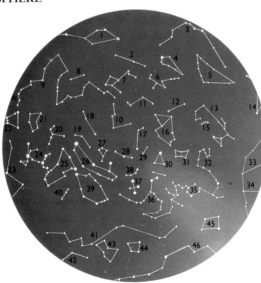

The positions of the constellations of the Southern Hemispheres.

STARS AND GALAXIES

You can tell stars from planets because their light seems to twinkle. Planets, which merely reflect the Sun's light, shine with a steady glow. The stars appear to move across the sky, but really this apparent motion is produced by the rotation of the Earth, just like the seeming movement of the Sun. Every star is a great glowing atomic furnace. It consists mainly of the two lightest gases, hydrogen and helium, which are burning all the time.

Galaxies are systems of stars. These are real systems, not apparent ones like the constellations. Galaxies have two main shapes, an ellipse or a spiral. Our own galaxy, the Milky Way, is a spiral galaxy. The galaxies are moving away from each other at ever-increasing speed. We know this because the lines of the spectrum of the light from each galaxy have moved toward the color red, a phenomenon that astronomers term red shift.

There are millions of spiral galaxies, like our own Milky Way Galaxy. Each one turns very slowly, like a vast wheel of stars in space. This photograph of a nearby spiral galaxy gives us a good idea of what our own galaxy must look like. The arms of this galaxy are more "open" than the arms of our own star system, however, and the central nucleus is smaller.

THE BRIGHTEST STARS

Name	Constellation	† Apparent magni-tude	Distance (light-years)
Sun	—	−26.74	—
Sirius	Canis Major	−1.45	8.7
Canopus	Carina	−0.73	1,200
Rigil Kent	Centaurus	−0.30	4.37
Arcturus	Boötes	−0.06	36
Vega	Lyra	0.04	26
Capella	Auriga	0.08	42
Rigel	Orion	0.11	900
Procyon	Canis Minor	0.38	11.4
Achernar	Eridanus	0.46	85
Hadar (Agena)	Centaurus	0.61	460
Altair	Aquila	0.77	16
Betelgeuse	Orion	0.80	310
Aldebaran	Taurus	0.85	68
Acrux	Crux	0.90	360
Spica	Virgo	0.96	261
Antares	Scorpius	1.00	330
Pollux	Gemini	1.14	36
Fomalhaut	Pisces Austrinus	1.16	22
Deneb	Cygnus	1.25	1,800
Mimosa	Crux	1.26	425
Regulus	Leo	1.35	85

† *A measure of brightness; the lower the number, the brighter the star.*

THE NEAREST STARS

Name	Distance (light-years
Proxima Centauri	4.28
Alpha-Centauri A	4.37
Alpha-Centauri B	4.37
Barnard's Star	5.80
Wolf 359	7.60
Lalande 21185	8.13
Sirius A	8.70
Sirius B §	8.70
Luyten 726–8 A	8.88
UV Ceti	8.88
Ross 154	9.44
Ross 248	10.28
Epsilon-Eridani	10.76
Luyten 789–6	10.76
Ross 128	10.83
61 Cygni A	11.09
61 Cygni B	11.09
Epsilon-Indi	11.20
Procyon A	11.40
Procyon B	11.40
Struve 2398 A	11.52
Struve 2398 B	11.52

§ *White dwarf*

Galaxies exist in groups. Our Milky Way Galaxy belongs to what scientists call the Local Group, of about 30 galaxies. This diagram shows the galaxies so far discovered, at their correct distances apart, although their sizes are not to scale. The Milky Way Galaxy and the Andromeda Galaxy are by far the largest members of the group. There is another smaller spiral galaxy, but the other galaxies are all elliptical dwarfs.

The Sun

During an eclipse of the Sun by the Moon, the glow of the Sun's corona can be seen.

The Sun provides us with light and heat, so it is extremely important to us. But it is really a very ordinary star, of the kind that astronomers call a "yellow dwarf." It has been shining for at least five billion years and it is certain to go on shining for at least five billion more.

Deep inside the Sun the temperature reaches millions of degrees. At such a temperature atoms of its main gas, hydrogen, join together to make the gas helium. This process is called fusion. Scientists are trying to make nuclear power plants here on Earth that will work in the same way.

The Sun's surface is seething as hot gases well up from underneath. On the surface we can see dark markings, known as sunspots. These spots come and go, and they appear to reach their maximum number every 11 years. The sunspots are about 3,600°F (2,000°C) cooler than the temperature of the rest of the Sun's surface.

Sun Statistics

Diameter at equator 865,000 mi. (1,392,000 km)
Volume 1,303,600 times Earth's volume
Mean density 1.41 (water = 1)
Mass 333,000 times Earth's mass
Gravity 28 times Earth's gravity.
Mean distance from Earth 92,960,000 mi. (149,600,000 km)
Escape velocity 384 mi./sec (618 km/sec.)
Surface temperature 10,800°F (6,000°C)

Core temperature circa 27,000°F (15,000,000°C)
Spins on axis in 25.38 days
Orbits galaxy in 225 million years
Distance from center of galaxy 30,000 light-years
† **Apparent magnitude** –26.74

† *A measure of brightness: the lower the number, the brighter the star.*

The Sun's daily path across the sky changes with the seasons of the year. The Sun is at its highest point in the sky at midsummer, and at its lowest point at midwinter. The Earth is tilted on its axis so that at different times of the year different parts of the Earth get stronger or weaker sunlight.

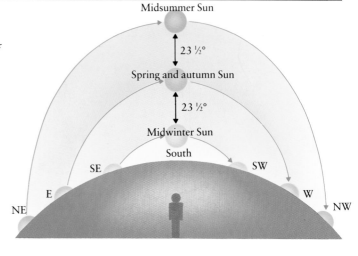

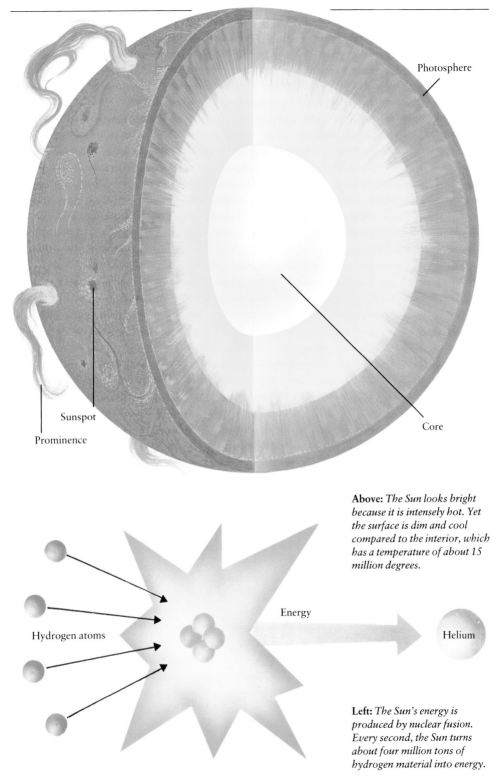

Photosphere

Sunspot

Prominence

Core

Above: *The Sun looks bright because it is intensely hot. Yet the surface is dim and cool compared to the interior, which has a temperature of about 15 million degrees.*

Hydrogen atoms

Energy

Helium

Left: *The Sun's energy is produced by nuclear fusion. Every second, the Sun turns about four million tons of hydrogen material into energy.*

New Moon

Crescent phase

Gibbous phase

Full Moon

Last quarter

Crescent phase

THE MOON

The Moon is a satellite of the Earth – that is, it circles around the Earth. It takes 27⅓ days to do so, slightly less than a calendar month. Its bright surface reflects the light of the Sun. When the Moon is directly between the Earth and the Sun we cannot see it. This is the new Moon. As the Moon moves on, a thin crescent of light appears. The first quarter is when half the surface is lit.

Later, we see all the surface – the full Moon. Up to this point we say the Moon has been "waxing." After this it starts to "wane." When half is lit again the Moon is in its

Sun

Left: *We call the varying appearance of the Moon its "phases." First comes the new Moon. As the Moon waxes, a thin crescent appears and gets bigger until half the surface is lit. We call this the Moon's first quarter. Next comes the gibbous Moon; then the full Moon. As the Moon wanes, the sunlit portion gets smaller, until it disappears at the next new Moon.*

Right: *We only ever see one face of the Moon. When the Moon was newly formed it was made of molten rock, spinning around once in a few hours. As it cooled, a hard skin or crust formed on the outside. The Earth's gravity, pulling at this crust, slowed the spin down and raised a "bulge" a few miles high on one side. Now this bulge is always turned inward, and the Moon keeps the same face toward the Earth.*

last quarter. The sunlit portion gets smaller until the Moon vanishes.

The diameter of the Moon is 400 times smaller than that of the Sun, but the Moon is 400 times closer to the Earth. As a result, we see the Moon and the Sun as about the same size. At certain times of the year, the Moon comes directly between us and the Sun and blots out the Sun from our sight for a few minutes. We say that an eclipse of the Sun has occurred. If the Earth's shadow comes between the Sun and the Moon, there is an eclipse of the Moon.

The tides are caused mainly by the Moon, because it is so close to the Earth. The Sun has some effect on the tides too, but the Moon's pull is more than twice that of the Sun's.

Below: An eclipse of the Sun, or solar eclipse, happens when the Moon blocks the Sun's light from reaching the Earth. A total eclipse can be seen only from within the umbra – a region of shadow a few hundred miles across. Around it is a less shadowy area, the penumbra.

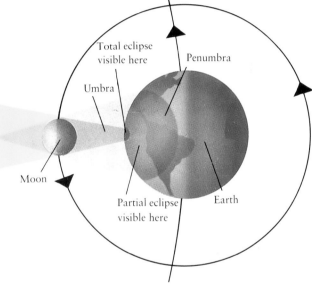

Total eclipse visible here

Penumbra

Umbra

Moon

Partial eclipse visible here

Earth

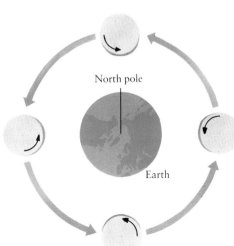

North pole

Earth

Moon Statistics

Diameter at equator 2160 mi. (3476 km)
Volume 1/49 Earth's volume
Density 3.34 (water = 1)
Mass 1/81 Earth's mass
Gravity 1/6 Earth's gravity
Closest distance from Earth 221,460 mi. (356,400 km)
Furthest distance from Earth 252,710 mi. (406,697 km)
Mean distance from Earth 238,860 mi. (384,400 km)
Spins on axis in 27⅓ days
Orbits Earth in (sidereal month) 27⅓ days
Synodic month (new Moon–new Moon) 29½ days

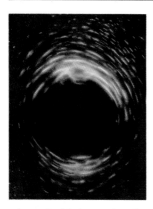

Above *Black holes are thought to be the final stage in a star's life.*

THE SOLAR SYSTEM

Nine plants orbit the Sun. We call the Sun's satellites the *Solar System*, "solar" meaning "of the Sun." The Earth is the third planet in distance from the Sun and – as far as scientists are aware to date – it is also the only planet on which there is life. The farther a planet is from the Sun, the longer its year – the time it takes to go once around the Sun. The Earth takes 365¼ days. Mercury, the nearest to the Sun, takes only 88 days. Pluto, the most distant planet, has a year more than 247 Earth-years long. The planets are all different. Jupiter, Saturn, Uranus, and Neptune are made mainly of gas. Pluto is probably made of ice and rock, and Mercury, Venus, and Mars are, like Earth, made of rock. Saturn is famous for its rings. The three major rings which can be seen through telescopes are in fact thousands of narrow ringlets made up of particles of ice varying in size from 3 to 30 feet (1 to 10 m) across. Uranus also has rings and Jupiter has a large red spot which is a vast swirling storm.

Earth is not the only planet to have a moon. Mars and Neptune have two, Uranus has at least five, and Jupiter and Saturn have at least 40 between them.

In between the orbits of two of the planets, Mars and Jupiter, are thousands of smaller bodies called the asteroids or minor planets. The largest of these minor planets, Ceres, is only 427 miles (687 km) across. Most of the asteroids are less than 60 miles (95 km) in diameter. We do not know if these little planets are debris that resulted from the breakup of a larger planet, or whether they just failed to form one body when the solar system began.

THE PLANETS AND THEIR STATISTICS

Name	Average distance from Sun, millions of miles	(km)	Diameter at equator miles	(km)	Circles Sun in:	Turns on axis in:
Sun	–	–	865,000	(1,392,000)	–	25⅓ days
Mercury	36	(58)	3,030	(4,876)	88 days	59 days
Venus	67	(108)	7,521	(12,104)	224 days	243 days
Earth	93	(150)	7,926	(12,756)	365¼ days	23:56 hours
Mars	142	(228)	4,222	(6,794)	687 days	24:37 hours
Jupiter	483	(778)	88,700	(142,700)	11.9 years	9:50 hours
Saturn	887	(1,427)	74,600	(120,000)	29.5 years	10:14 hours
Uranus	1,783	(2,870)	32,300	(52,000)	84 years	17 hours
Neptune	2,800	(4,500)	30,000	(48,000)	165 years	18 hours
Pluto	3,660	(5,900)	1,800	(3,000)	248 years	153 hours

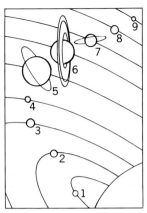

This view of the Sun and planets shows how small the Earth is compared with the four "giant planets." But even the giants are tiny compared with the Sun.
The nine planets of our system (in order from the Sun)
1. *Mercury*
2. *Venus*
3. *Earth*
4. *Mars*
5. *Jupiter*
6. *Saturn*
7. *Uranus*
8. *Neptune*
9. *Pluto*

NOTABLE COMETS

Comets are small heavenly bodies made up of dust and ice. They have been described as "dirty snowballs." They orbit the Sun in very long ellipses, and some take thousands of years to complete one circuit of their orbit.

Name	First observed	Orbital period (years)	Name	First observed	Orbital period (years)
Halley's Comet	240 B.C.	76	Schwassmann-		
Biela's Comet	1772	6.7	Wachmann 1 Comet	1925	15
Encke's Comet	1786	3.3	Arend-Roland Comet	1957	10,000
Great Comet of 1811	1811	3,000	Ikeya-Seki Comet	1965	880
Pons-Winnecke Comet	1826	6.3	Kouhoutek's Comet*	1975	–
Great Comet of 1843	1843	512.4	Comet West	1976	–
Donati's Comet	1858	2,040	*observed from Skylab and Soyuz spacecraft*		

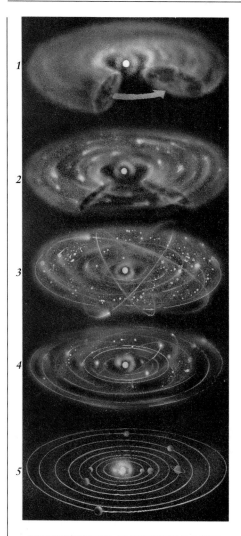

HOW THE PLANETS FORMED

1. *In the beginning, there was a spinning ring of gas and dust particles, circling the Sun.* **2.** *The solid particles began to stick together, forming larger bodies, made mostly of carbon and ice.* **3.** *The bodies became as big as planets, and began to "pull" against each other. Some of the very small ice bodies became comets.* **4.** *Eventually there were just nine large bodies going around the Sun in orbits: the major planets.* **5.** *In time, the planets' orbits stabilized.*

ASTRONOMY TERMS

asteroids Thousands of small bodies that orbit the Sun between the orbits of Mars and Jupiter.

astrobiology Study of life on other worlds.

astronomical unit (AU) Mean distance between Earth and Sun. About 93,000,000 miles or 150,000,000 km.

astrophysics Branch of astronomy concerned with physical nature of heavenly bodies.

aurora Phenomenon of the atmosphere seen around the polar regions, in form of colorful displays of light, attributed to sunspot activity. Northern Lights – Aurora Borealis; Southern Lights – Aurora Australis.

big bang theory See *universe*.

black holes Supposed regions of space of intense gravitational force caused by collapse of star.

celestial sphere Imaginary sphere in which heavenly bodies seem to be projected from point of observation.

chromosphere Layer of crimson gas around the Sun.

comet Heavenly body consisting of the head, a relatively small, star-like nucleus surrounded by *coma*, a glowing cloud, with, usually, a *tail* millions of miles long made up of dust and gas. Comets, visible near the Sun, orbit it with periods of a few to thousands of years.

constellation Apparent grouping of stars together within definite region of the sky; 88 officially recognized and designated.

corona Sun's pearly-white outer layer of gas, extending more than a million miles, visible only during eclipse.

eclipse Obscuration of one heavenly body by another.

equinox Instant when the Sun is directly over our equator, making equal day and night; occurs about 21 March and 23 September.

evening star Planet seen in western sky after sunset, especially Venus.

galaxy Vast system of stars (thousands of millions). Millions of galaxies exist, regular ones having spiral or elliptical forms.

halo (1) Luminous ring seen around Moon or Sun, caused by light refraction through high clouds. (2) Stars surrounding Milky Way in halo fashion.

insterstallar space Beyond the Solar System, among the stars.

light-year Distance traveled by light in 1 year, 5.88 million million miles or 9.46 million million km.

meridian Imaginary line in sky passing through poles of celestial sphere and directly over observer.

meteor Phenomenon caused by small body entering Earth's atmosphere and emitting light; estimated 100 million per day.

meteorite Meteor reaching Earth before burning up; lumps of stone (*aerolites*) or iron (*siderites*) up to a 50-ton specimen found near Grootfontein, Namibia.

Milky Way Our galaxy; contains estimated 200,000 million stars; spiral type.

moon Any natural satellite of planet.

morning star Planet seen in eastern sky before sunrise, especially Venus.

nebula (Lat. *mist*) Hazy mass of gases and particles in space.

Northern Lights See *aurora*.

orbit Path of one celestial body around another.

parsec Unit of distance equal to 3.258 light-years.

photosphere Visible surface of the Sun.

planetarium Projection instrument that demonstrates motions of heavenly bodies on domed ceiling.

planets The nine major bodies moving in orbit around the Sun.

quasar Quasi-stellar radio sources – mysterious distant objects in the universe, powerful sources of radio waves and light.

radio astronomy Branch concerned with study of radio energy emitted by stars or regions of space.

radio source A single source of radio emission in space.

radio telescope Instrument that collects radio waves from space.

red shift Spectra of galaxies shift toward the red, indicating receding of galaxies.

satellite A body, natural or artificial, that orbits a celestial body.

shooting star Common type of meteor, caused by objects smaller than one-sixteenth inch.

siderite See *meteorite*.

solar flare Eruption of radiation on the Sun.

Solar System The Sun and its satellites.

solar wind Permanent particle radiation from the sun.

solstice Instant when the Sun is farthest from Earth's equator, making longest or shortest day; occurs about 21 June and 22 December.

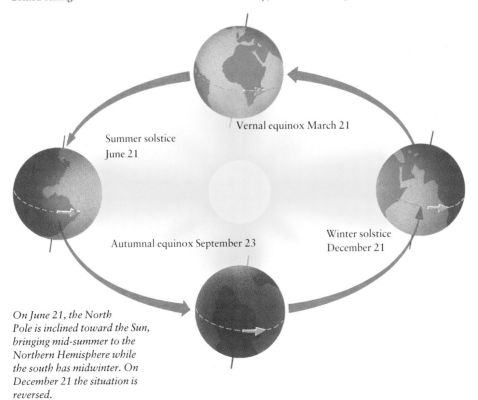

Vernal equinox March 21

Summer solstice
June 21

Autumnal equinox September 23

Winter solstice
December 21

On June 21, the North Pole is inclined toward the Sun, bringing mid-summer to the Northern Hemisphere while the south has midwinter. On December 21 the situation is reversed.

21

The Aurorae, or Northern and Southern Lights, are brilliant displays in the atmosphere.

Southern Lights See *aurora*.

star Heavenly body generating its own heat and light; nearest after Sun is Proxima Centauri (4.28 light-years); 5,000 stars are visible to the naked eye. Brightness is measured in terms of *star magnitude*.

steady-state theory See *universe*.

Sun Our star, basis of the Solar System, a glowing ball of gases, mainly hydrogen and helium. (See *chromosphere, corona, photosphere*).

sunspots Dark patches on the Sun, 3,600°F (2,000°C) cooler than normal; maximum actvity in 11-year cycles; origin unknown.

transit Passage of Mercury or Venus across the Sun's disk.

universe Everything that exists – matter, space, energy. Most astronomers set its age at 15 billion years; the universe seems to be expanding, like an inflating balloon. *Big bang theory* suggests explosion of "primeval atom" 100 million light-years in diameter – hence the expanding universe; *steady-state theory* suggests infinite universe, no beginning or end, matter continuously being created, changing, and "aging."

zenith Point in heavens directly above the observer.

STEPS INTO SPACE

1957 First artificial Earth satellite: Russians launch *Sputnik 1* on October 4, heralding Space Age; November 3, Russians launch *Sputnik 2*, containing dog Laika, first mammal in space.

1958 On January 31, Americans launch their first satellite, *Explorer 1*.

1959 Russians launch *Lunik 1* (first probe to go near Moon), *Lunik 2* (first to crash-land on Moon), and *Lunik 3* (first photographs of hidden side of Moon).

1960 U.S. launches *Tiros 1*, first Earth weather satellite (clear photographs of cloud cover).

1961 First man in space: Russian cosmonaut Yuri Gagarin makes one orbit in *Vostok 1* on April 12. First American astronaut Alan Shepard makes sub-orbital flight on May 5.

1962 First American in orbit, John Glenn makes 3 orbits in *Friendship 7* (Mercury craft). *Ranger 4* becomes first U.S. craft to reach Moon. First commercial communications satellite, *Telstar 1*, begins relaying TV programs across Atlantic.

1963 First woman in space is Russian comonaut Valentina Tereshkova.

1964 Russians launch *Voskhod 1* with Vladimir Komarov, Boris Yegorov, and Konstantin Feoktistov aboard, first craft with more than one spaceman (made 16 orbits).

1965 Alexei Leonov makes first space walk.

1966 Russia's *Luna 9* makes soft landing on Moon and returns TV pictures. Neil Armstrong and Dave Scott make first space docking with unmanned craft. First American soft landing on Moon by *Surveyor 1*.

1967 First space disasters: three U.S. astronauts and one Soviet cosmonaut die.

1968 First recovery of unmanned lunar probe, Russian *Zond 5*, from Indian Ocean on September 21. First manned lunar flight: *Apollo 8* (Frank Borman, James Lovell, William Anders) completes 10 orbits.

1969 First docking of two manned spacecraft, with exchange of cosmonauts by space walk (*Soyuz 4* and *5*). In July *Apollo 11* lands lunar module on Moon: American astronaut Neil Armstrong becomes first man to walk on Moon. Second landing (*Apollo 12*) in November.

1970 *Apollo 13* has narrow escape from disaster. Russians soft-land unmanned *Luna 17* on Moon and use 8-wheeled Lunokhod 1, first propelled vehicle on Moon. Russian probe *Venera 7* lands on Venus (Dec 15).

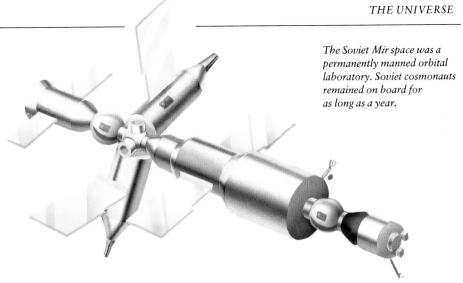

The Soviet Mir space was a permanently manned orbital laboratory. Soviet cosmonauts remained on board for as long as a year.

1971 *Apollo 14* makes third manned Moon landing. Three cosmonauts make longest space flight to date (23 days 17 hr 40 min) in *Soyuz 11*, but die on return. *Apollo 15* makes fourth Moon landing. U.S. probe *Mariner 9* becomes first artificial satellite of Mars.

1972 Americans launch *Pioneer 10* on 21-month mission to Jupiter. *Apollo 16* and *Apollo 17* make final Moon landings, bringing back lunar samples.

1973 Americans launch *Skylab 1*, unmanned portion of their first manned orbiting space station, including workshop and telescope mount. *Skylab 2, 3,* and *4* launched, each with three astronauts.

1974 *Mariner 10* (launched by U.S. in November 1973) passes Venus and flies close to Mercury (March 29) for Man's first close-up look.

1975 First joint Russian-American mission in space: *Soyuz 19* and *Apollo 18* dock while orbiting Earth. Astronauts and cosmonauts carry out exchange visits and experiments. Russian probes *Venera 9* and *Venera 10* soft-land on Venus.

1976 Soviet spacecraft *Luna 24* lands on the Moon and takes soil samples with an automatic scoop.

1977 The Soviet craft *Soyuz 24* docks successfully with orbiting *Salyut 5* space laboratory one day after launch. The U.S. launches two *Voyager* spacecraft to fly to Jupiter and Saturn.

1978 Two Soviet spacecraft dock with the orbiting *Salyut* space laboratory (Jan 11) thus achieving the first triple linkup in space.

1979 Western Europe's *Ariane* rocket makes first test flight.

1980 *Voyager 1* flies past Saturn. Its instruments reveal that Saturn's rings are more numerous and complex than thought.

1981 America's shuttle *Columbia* makes first test flight of 54½ hours, orbiting the Earth and gliding back to a perfect landing. *Voyager 2* flies near Saturn, before going on to visit Uranus and Neptune.

1983 U.S. launches space shuttle *Challenger* on a six-day mission. The crew includes a woman, Dr. Sally Ride.

1984 Three Soviet cosmonauts return to Earth after spending a record time in space of almost nine months. A Russian woman cosmonaut becomes the first woman to walk in space. The first repairs are carried out in space, using space shuttle *Challenger* to mend the Solar Max satellite.

1986 The *Challenger* tragedy causes a delay in the Shuttle programme. *Voyager 2* sends back detailed photographs of the moons of Uranus. Russians launch space station *Mir*.

1987 Russians send three more spacecraft to link up with space station *Mir*. U.S. and Soviet Union sign an agreement to cooperate on the exploration and use of space.

1988 U.S. shuttle *Discovery* makes successful flight in September, first since *Challenger* disaster. In November the Russians launch their first space shuttle, the unmanned *Buran*.

1990 Japan sends its first spacecraft to the Moon. *Voyager 2* photographs Neptune and its moons. *Magellan* spacecraft takes the first radar pictures of the surface of Venus.

Planet Earth

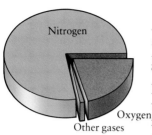

The two main gases in the atmosphere are nitrogen 78 percent and oxygen 21 percent. There is also an increasing amount of carbon dioxide and small quantities of other gases, water vapor, dust, and salt particles.

An atmosphere containing the element oxygen and an abundant supply of its compound, water, are found on planet Earth, and nowhere else in the solar system. These two ingredients are vital for life, which began here probably about 3½ billion years ago. During that unimaginable span of time, continents have formed and re-formed, ice ages have come and gone, and living things have evolved and some have become extinct.

Our Earth is one of nine planets that orbit the Sun. It ranks fifth in size. It is the only one with abundant water and an atmosphere containing oxygen – the two things necessary for life. Space probes have not detected any definite signs of life on the other planets.

Some form of life on Earth may have begun as long ago as 3½ billion years ago. But the abundant life we see today has been in existence for only about 600 million years. That is less than one-eighth of the Earth's age. During that time many species (kinds) of plants and animals have come into existence and died out again. Geologists divide the past 600 million years of Earth's history into periods. There is a chart showing these periods and the kinds of living things that flourished during them on pages 26–27.

Although the continents appear to have always been where they are now, this is not so. Millions of years ago, all the continents were part of one supercontinent known as Pangaea. About 200 million years ago this huge supercontinent began to break up, and the separate continents gradually moved to where they are now. This process is called continental drift. The continents are still moving. The Atlantic Ocean, for example, is growing wider by at least an inch (3 cm) a year, as America drifts to the west.

The continents rest on plates. There are about 20 covering the surface of the Earth's crust. As the plates move, some of them bump into one another. Such collisions happen very slowly. Some of them thrust up mountains, such as the ranges of western North and South America and the Himalayas of Asia. At such places, one plate may be sliding under another. New material is welling up under the oceans to replace the lost part of the plate, and to push the plates along. The plates also slide sideways against one another. One place where this is happening is the San Andreas Fault in California. The

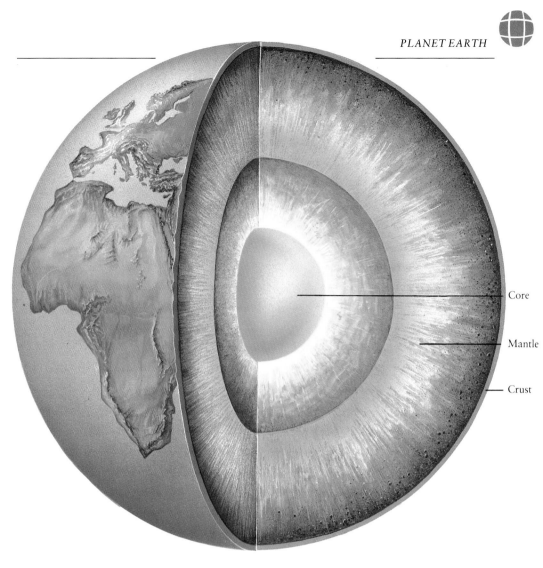

plates do not move smoothly, but in jerks. When a jerk happens, we get an earthquake.

Many factors influence the world's climate and weather. From time to time, large parts of the Earth's surface are covered with thick sheets of ice. Scientist think these Ice Ages – also called glacials – occur every few million years. We are now in one of the warmer periods, called interglacials. The most recent Ice Age lasted until about 10,000 years ago. During the Ice Age a large part of northern North America and Europe were covered with a sheet of ice up to 9,800 ft. (3,000 m) thick.

During the Ice Age there were a great many glaciers, ice rivers. As glaciers creep slowly over the land they wear it away, smoothing out mountains and gouging out deep valleys.

The Earth, with a slice cut out to show the different layers – the core 4,288 miles (6,900 km) thick, the mantle 1,740 miles (2,800 km) thick and the crust – only 5–19 miles (8 to 30 km) thick.

25

Earth's Long History

Era	Period	Millions of years ago
CENOZOIC	QUATERNARY	
	Epoch	
	Recent (Holocene)	0.01
	Pleistocene	0.01 – 2
	TERTIARY	
	Epoch	
	Pliocene	2 – 5
	Miocene	5 – 25
	Oligocene	25 – 35
	Eocene	35 – 60
	Paleocene	60 – 65
MESOZOIC		
	CRETACEOUS	65 – 145
	JURASSIC	145 – 210
	TRIASSIC	210 – 245
PALEOZOIC		
	PERMIAN	245 – 285
	CARBONIFEROUS	285 – 360
	DEVONIAN	360 – 410
	SILURIAN	410 – 440
	ORDOVICIAN	440 – 505
	CAMBRIAN	505 – 570
PRECAMBRIAN	Precambrian time stretches back to the formation of the Earth. About 4.6 billion years ago	570

Highlights of plant and
animal life

Recent (Holocene) Modern human beings emerged and
civilization began.
Pleistocene Ice Age in Northern Hemisphere, woolly mammals
survived the cold.

Pliocene "Ape-men" appeared. Many large mammals died out as
the weather got colder.
Miocene Many apes in Africa. Herds of mammals grazed on the
spreading grasslands.
Oliqocene Early apes appeared. Many modern mammals began
to evolve. Flowering plants increased.
Eocene Strange mammals, including early horses and elephants.
Plants mostly modern types.
Paleocene Mammals evolved rapidly after most reptiles had died
out.

Cretaceous Dinosaurs and many other reptiles died out at the
end of the period. Ammonites disappeared. First flowering plants.
Jurassic Dinosaurs ruled the land. Flying reptiles. First birds.
Ammonites common. Some small mammals.
Triassic First dinosaurs and large sea reptiles. First mammals.
Ammonites common. Cycads and Bennettitaleans evolved.
Conifers spread. Luxuriant forests.

Permiam Reptiles increased. Amphibians less important.
Trilobites died out. Primitive conifers and ginkgoes.
Carboniferous Amphibians increased. First reptiles. Clubmosses,
ferns and horsetails in coal-forming swamps.
Devonian The age of fishes (bony and cartilaginous).
Amphibians evolved. Land plants more common.
Silurian Giant armored fishes. First land/marsh plants. Large sea
scorpions – terrors of the seas.
Ordovician First vertebrates (jawless fishes). Graptolites and
trilobites abundant. Echinoderms and brachiopods spread.
Cambrian Fossils abundant. Graptolites, trilobites, primitive
shellfish, corals, crustaceans, etc.

Precambrian Life began about 3.5 billion years ago. Oldest
known fossils are organisms in Fig-Tree cherts (3.5 billion years)
and stromatolites (2.8 billion years). But fossils are rare –
probably because creatures were soft-bodied (e.g. jellyfish, worms).

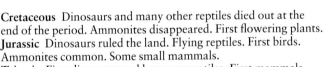

Earthquakes and Volcanoes

Earthquakes and volcanoes often seem to go together. They are most likely to occur in areas where two plates meet. Most of the world's active volcanoes occur in a band around the edge of the Pacific Ocean, called the "Ring of Fire," that continues north of Australia through New Guinea and Indonesia.

Volcanoes are also likely to occur over "hot spots," places in the Earth's crust where there are weaknesses. Many Pacific islands are the tops of old volcanoes that were once over such hot spots, before the plates moved on. Inside a volcano, lava (hot liquid rock) spouts up from a central vent. As the lava cools it forms solid rock again.

Low volcanoes (1) are made of liquid lava. This spreads out before it hardens. Cone volcanoes (2) are made from thick lava, which may form a plug. Pressure inside the volcano can blow out the plug (3) in a violent explosion.

THE EARTHQUAKE ZONES OF THE WORLD

MEASURING EARTHQUAKES

The intensity of an earthquake is measured on the Richter scale or the Modified Mercalli Scale (below). The numbers of this scale refer to the effects produced:

1. Very slight. Felt only by instruments.
2. Felt by people resting.
3. Feels like passing traffic.
4. Furniture and windows rattle.
5. Can be felt outdoors. Clocks stop. Doors swing.
6. Furniture moves about. Cracks appear in walls.
7. People knocked over. Masonry cracks and falls.
8. Chimneys and monuments fall. Buildings move on foundations.
9. Heavy damage to buildings. Large cracks open in ground.
10. Most buildings destroyed. Landslides occur. Water thrown out of canals and lakes.
11. Railroad lines badly bent.
12. No buildings left standing

FACTS ABOUT VOLCANOES

Active volcanoes There are about 535 of these, 80 below the sea.

Largest known eruption Tamboro, Indonesia, in 1815. The volcano threw out about 36 cubic miles (about 150 cubic km) of matter and lost 4,100 ft. (1,250 m) in height.

Greatest disaster 35,000 people were drowned by a giant wave unleashed when Krakatau, Indonesia, exploded in 1883.

Greatest volcanic explosion About 1470 B.C., Santorini in the Aegean Sea exploded with maybe 130 times the force of the greatest H-bomb.

Isoseismals

Epicenter

What happens during a volcanic eruption. Shock waves spread out from the epicenter of an earthquake. The source of an earthquake is called the focus.

Focus

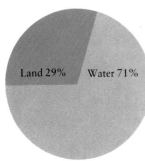

Most of the Earth's surface is watery, as this pie chart shows.

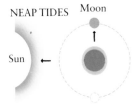

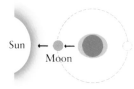

Spring tides are high because the Sun's gravitational pull is combined with the Moon's. Neap tides are low because the Moon and Sun are pulling at right angles to each other.

THE WORLD'S WATER

Nearly three-fourths of the Earth's surface is covered by water. The oceans are mostly very deep. Near land the seas are shallower, because part of each continent slopes down under the sea at what is called the continental shelf. Several parts of the oceans are very deep indeed. They are called ocean trenches, and they occur where one plate of the Earth's crust is sliding under another. The deepest of these trenches is the Marianas Trench, in the Pacific. It is 36,198 ft. (11,033 m) deep. The deepest trench in the Atlantic Ocean is the Puerto Rico Trench in the West Indies, which is 28,374 ft. (8,648 m) deep.

The water of the oceans is salty. It is always being evaporated by the heat of the Sun, forming clouds which eventually fall as rain. Rain collects on land to form ponds and lakes, and flows back down rivers to the sea. Some water collects in huge natural reservoirs deep underground. There are stores of such water under the dry Sahara desert. Much of it fell as rain thousands of years ago and it could not escape.

Right: *Five lakes make up North America's Great Lakes. They are Erie, Superior, Huron, Michigan, and Ontario. Shown here is Erie.*

LONGEST RIVERS

	Miles	Km
Nile (Africa)	4,160	6,695
Amazon (South America)	4,000	6,440
Chang Jiang (China)	3,964	6,380
Mississippi-Missouri-		
Red River (North America)	3,710	5,970
Ob-Irtysh (USSR)	3,362	5,410
Huang He (China)	2,903	4,672
Zaïre (Africa)	2,900	4,667
Amur (Asia)	2,744	4,416
Lena (USSR)	2,734	4,400
Mackenzie (Canada)	2,635	4,240
Mekong (Asia)	2,600	4,180
Niger (Africa)	2,590	4,170

LARGEST LAKES

	Sq. miles	Sq. km
Caspian Sea (Asia/Europe)	143,244	371,000
Superior (North America)	31,700	82,103
Victoria (Africa)	26,828	69,484
Huron (North America)	23,000	59,569
Michigan (North America)	22,300	57,757
Aral Sea (Asia; now shrinking)	15,500	40,000
Tanganyika (Africa)	12,700	32,893
Baykal (Asia)	12,162	31,499
Great Bear (North America)	12,096	31,328
Malawi (Africa)	11,150	28,878

SIZE OF THE OCEANS

	Sq. miles	Sq. km
Pacific Ocean	64,100,000	166,000,000
Atlantic Ocean	31,600,000	82,000,000
Indian Ocean	28,350,000	73,426,000
Arctic Ocean	4,700,000	12,173,000

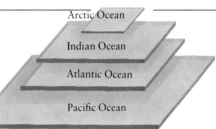

Arctic Ocean
Indian Ocean
Atlantic Ocean
Pacific Ocean

Above: *This diagram shows the relative sizes of the four major oceans.*

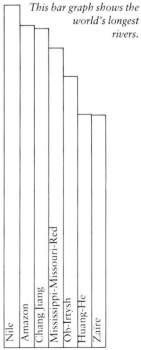

This bar graph shows the world's longest rivers.

Nile | Amazon | Chang Jiang | Mississippi-Missouri-Red | Ob-Irtysh | Huang-He | Zaïre

31

WORLD RECORD BREAKERS

Sand dunes in Colorado. The Earth's desert regions are the driest and most inhospitable environments for plants, animals, and people.

The world contains many natural features, such as deserts and mountains, which are outstanding in size. Here is a selection. It has proved very difficult to measure some of them. For example, several measurements have been made of Mount Everest, which do not quite agree. Several different ways of measuring the depth of the Marianas Trench have been tried, again giving slightly different readings. The figures given here are the best available.

NOTABLE WATERFALLS

	Drop (ft.)	(m)
AFRICA		
Tugela (South Africa)	2,014	614
ASIA		
Jog or Gersoppa (India)	830	272
AUSTRALASIA		
Sutherland (New Zealand)	1,904	580
Wallaman (Australia)	1,137	347
EUROPE		
Mardalsfossen, Southern (Norway)	2,149	655
Gavarnie (France)	1,385	422
NORTH AMERICA		
Yosemite (U.S.A., Cal.)	2,425	739
Della (Canada, B.C.)	1,443	440
SOUTHERN AMERICA		
Angel (Venezuela)†	3,212	979
Glass (Brazil)	1,325	404
† World's highest waterfall		

DEEP, LONG AND HIGH

Greatest ocean depth 36,198 ft (11,033 m), Marianas Trench, Pacific Ocean.

Deepest underwater gorge 5,900 ft (1,800 m), near Esperance, Western Australia.

Longest gorge 220 miles (350 km), Grand Canyon, Arizona.

Highest navigated lake Titicaca, Peru and Bolivia, 12,500 ft (3,810 m) above sea level.

Deepest lake Baykal, central Asia, 6,365 ft (1,940 m).

Largest ice sheet is the Antarctic Ice Sheet, covering 5 million square miles (13,000 square km).

Longest glacier is the Lambert-Fisher Ice Passage in Antarctica. It stretches over 300 miles (500 km).

Largest iceberg ever recorded was an Antarctic iceberg seen in 1956. It covered 12,000 square miles (31,000 square km).

LARGEST ISLANDS

	Sq. miles	Sq. km
Greenland	840,000	2,183,000
New Guinea	317,000	821,000
Borneo	280,100	727,900
Madagascar	226,658	589,081
Baffin Island	195,928	509,214
Sumatra	182,860	431,982
Honshu	87,805	228,204
Great Britain	84,200	218,800
Victoria Island	83,896	218,045
Ellesmere Island	75,767	196,917

GREATEST DESERTS

	Sq. miles	Sq. km
Sahara (Africa)	3,500,000	9,100,000
Australian Desert	600,000	1,550,000
Arabian Desert	500,000	1,300,000
Gobi (Asia)	500,000	1,300,000
Kalahari (Africa)	200,000	518,000
Chihuahuan (USA and Mexico)	140,000	363,900
Mojave (USA)	15,000	39,000

One of nature's most violent phenomena: an erupting volcano spews out lava.

EROSION FACTS

Weight of soil and rock removed by rivers is about 363 tons from each square mile (140 a year from each square kilometre) of the Earth's crust.

Thickness of land worn away by rivers is about 1 ft. (30 cm) a year as estimated for the United States.

Deepest gorges cut by rivers are those made by the rivers Indus, Brahamaputra, and Ganges in India–Pakistan; they are more than 3 miles (5 km) deep.

NOTABLE EARTHQUAKES

Shensi Province, China, 1556 Over 800,000 people perished.

Lisbon, Portugal, 1755 About 60,000 people died and shocks were felt in Norway.

San Francisco, California, 1906 City destroyed.

Kwanto Plain, Japan, 1923 Some 570,000 buildings collapsed. This was the costliest earthquake ever.

Tangshan China, 1976 About 242,000 people were reported killed in this industrial city.

Armenia, USSR, 1988 45,000 people died and 3 cities were destroyed.

HIGHEST MOUNTAINS

	feet	meters
ASIA		
Everest (Himalaya-Nepal/Tibet)	29,028	8,848
Godwin Austen (Pakistan/India)	28,250	8,611
Kanchenjunga (Himalaya-Nepal/India)	28,208	8,597
Makalu (Himalaya-Nepal/Tibet)	27,824	8,480
Dhaulagiri (Himalaya-Nepal)	26,810	8,170
Nanga Parbat (Himalaya-India)	26,660	8,126
Annapurna (Himalaya-Nepal)	26,504	8,078
SOUTH AMERICA		
Aconcagua (Andes-Argentina)	22,834	6,960
NORTH AMERICA		
McKinley (Alaska Range)	20,320	6,194
AFRICA		
Kilimanjaro (Tanzania)	19,340	5,895
EUROPE		
Elbruz (Caucasus-Russia)	18,481	5,633
Mont Blanc (Alps-France)	15,771	4,807
AUSTRALASIA		
Jaja (New Guinea)	16,500	5,029

THE WEATHER

The atmosphere – the layer of air around the Earth – is constantly moving because it is unevenly heated by the Sun. Huge masses of warm air from the Equator and cold air from the Poles flow around the world, meeting each other. The warm air rises and the cold air sinks, and this movement causes the winds.

A depression or cyclone is an area of low air pressure. This satellite photograph shows a hurricane, a severe tropical cyclone. Hurricane winds spiral at up to 210 mph (340 km/h).

The air picks up water vapor evaporated from the oceans, and rises, getting cooler. The vapor condenses into tiny droplets of water and forms clouds. If it cools further, the droplets form larger drops, which fall as rain. On very cold days the droplets form snowflakes. From storm clouds small pieces of ice may fall as hailstones.

WEATHER EXTREMES

Hottest shade temperature recorded 136°F (57.7°C) at Al'Aziziyah, Libya, on September 13, 1922.

Coldest temperature recorded –128.6°F (–89.2°C) at Vostock, Antarctica, on July 21, 1983.

Highest average annual rainfall 463 inches (11,770 mm) at Tutunendo, Colombia.

Driest place on earth: Arica, Chile, averages 0.030 inches(0.76 mm) of rain per year.

Greatest tides: 53.4 ft. (16.3 m) Bay of Fundy, Nova Scotia, Canada.

Strongest surface wind 231 mph (372 km/h) at Mt. Washington, New Hampshire, in 1934.

FACTS ABOUT STORMS

Most thundery region on Earth The tropics and nearby regions. More than 3,000 thunderstorms occur there every night of the year.

Fiercest storm winds Those whirling around in a tornado. They are thought to reach speeds of 500 mph (800 km/h).

Speed of lightning The fastest flashes move at 87,000 miles a second (140,000 km/sec).

Tornadoes A tornado is a storm that moves across the land at about 40 mph (65 km/h). It measures only about 650 ft. (200 m) across, but its whirling winds can cause severe damage.

Lighting is a huge electric spark. It happens when there is a sudden flow of electricity. This can be between two parts of a cloud, between two different clouds, or between a cloud and the ground. There are three kinds of lightning: Streak lightning, forked lightning, and sheet lightning. streak lightning is a flash in one line from a cloud to the ground. Forked lightning is when the lightning divides as it finds the quickest route to the ground. Sheet lightning is inside a cloud and it lights up the sky.

BEAUFORT SCALE

In 1805 Admiral Sir Francis Beaufort worked out a scale for measuring wind speed. The scale is from 1 to 12 and represents wind force out in the open, 10 metres (33 feet) above the ground.

No.	Wind force	mph	km/h	Observable effects
0	calm	<1.6	<1.6	smoke rises vertically
1	light air	1–3	1.6– 4.8	direction shown by smoke
2	slight breeze	4–7	6.4– 11.3	felt on face; wind vanes move
3	gentle breeze	8–12	12.9– 19.3	leaves, twigs move; flags extended
4	moderate breeze	13–18	20.9– 29.0	dust, paper, small branches move
5	fresh breeze	19–24	30.6– 38.6	small trees sway; flags ripple
6	strong breeze	25–31	40.2– 50.0	large branches move; flags beat
7	moderate gale	32–38	51.5– 61.2	whole trees sway; walking difficult
8	fresh gale	39–46	62.8– 74.0	twigs break off; walking hindered
9	strong gale	47–54	75.6– 86.9	slight damage to roofing
10	whole gale	55–63	88.5–101.4	severe damage; trees uprooted
11	storm	64–72	103.0–115.9	widespread damage
12	hurricane	>73	>117.5	devastation

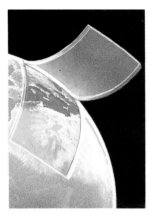

The atmosphere of the Earth acts like an insulating wrapping, stopping the planet from getting too hot or too cold.

Cirrostratus

Cirrus

Altostratus

Cirrocumulus

Altocumulus

Stratocumulus

Cumulonimbus

Cumulus

Stratus

Nimbostratus

TYPES OF CLOUDS

**Clouds consist of masses of water drops or ice crystals in the atmosphere.
They form when moisture in the air condenses.**

Altostratus A grayish sheet of cloud, with a hazy Sun above.

Altocumulus Fleecy bands of cloud with blue sky between.

Cirrus High, wispy clouds made of particles of ice.

Cirrocumulus Thin, high lines of cloud with rippled edges.

Cirrostratus Milky, thin, high cloud producing a halo around the Sun.

Stratus Low, gray, sheetlike cloud covering the sky.

Nimbostratus Low, grey, sheetlike cloud producing steady rain.

Stratocumulus Like a low, dark, heavy kind of altocumulus.

Cumulus A white heaped up cloud usually seen in fair weather.

Cumulonimbus A towering cloud that may give heavy showers.

SOME WEATHER TERMS

climate The average weather conditions of a place. Climate figures are averages of figures collected over a number of years, so extremes are hidden.

hurricane A severe tropical storm with spiraling winds and very low air pressure.

Mediterranean climate Summers are hot and dry; winters are warm and wet. Such a climate is found around the Mediterranean Sea and also in central California and Perth, Western Australia.

monsoon The word means season and usually refers to winds that bring an exceptionally wet season for part of the year. The most spectacular monsoon climates are in Asia.

temperate lands Those parts of the world between the tropics and the polar areas which have a cold season and a hot season. Places such as the Mediterranean which have warm winters may be called warm temperate.

precipitation When used of the weather, refers to rain and snow.

PLANET EARTH GLOSSARY

atmosphere The layer of moving air which surrounds the Earth. It consists of nitrogen, oxygen, water vapor, and other gases. The atmosphere becomes thinner away from the Earth.

axis An imaginary straight line around which a spinning object rotates. The Earth's axis goes from the North Pole, through the center of the Earth, to the South Pole.

block mountains Blocks of land raised up by vertical movements between faults in the Earth's crust.

canyon A deep, steep-sided valley, usually cut by a river in a *desert* area. The most famous is the Grand Canyon.

coral Coral is made by tiny creatures called polyps which live in warm sunny seas. They build skeletons outside their bodies. When they die new polyps build on the old skeletons to form coral reefs.

core The inner part of the Earth.

crust The outer layer of the Earth.

delta The Greek letter φ (delta) is used to describe an area of sediments deposited at the mouth of some rivers, such as the Mississippi and the Nile.

deserts A dry area where few plants grow. The Sahara is the largest desert; the Atacama is the driest.

dunes Mounds or ridges of sand. They are found on some sandy coasts and in sandy *deserts*.

earthquake A sudden movement within the Earth's *crust* which causes shock waves which make the Earth's surface shake.

estuary The mouth of a river where it enters the sea. Usually it is much wider than the rest of the river and it has tides.

fault A more or less vertical break in the Earth's crust, along which the rocks have moved. The rocks may move upward, downward or sideways.

fiord (fjord) A long, steep-sided inlet of the sea in a mountainous coastal area, as in Norway. Originally it was a valley eroded by a glacier. After the glacier melted, the valley was drowned as the sea level rose.

fold mountains Mountains formed by folding layers of rocks. When parts of the Earth's crust move together from each side, the rocks in between are folded.

geyser A hot spring which throws out a jet of hot water regularly or occasionally. The best-known geysers are in the U.S., Iceland, and New Zealand.

glacier A mass of ice which moves slowly downhill. It follows the easiest route – usually along a river valley which it deepens and straightens.

iceberg A lump of ice which has broken off from a glacier and floats in the sea. Only about one-tenth shows above water level.

latitude and **longitude** These are lines drawn on a globe. Lines which run through the poles north to south are called lines of longitude. The equator and lines parallel to it are lines of latitude.

meander A bend in a river, usually in soft, relatively flat ground.

oasis An area in a desert with water at or near the surface. Crops can be grown, and people can live there.

peninsula An area of land almost surrounded by water, but not completely cut off from the mainland.

plain A lowland area with a fairly level surface, though there may be hills. The North European Plain and the Great Plains of North America are examples of very large lowland plains.

plateau An upland area with a fairly level surface, though a plateau may have some hills and may be divided by deep valleys.

sedimentary rocks Rocks formed from sediments (small rock particles) which once accumulated on land or sea. Clay, sandstone, and limestone are examples of sedimentary rocks.

tropics Lines of latitude marking where the sun is directly overhead on Midsummer's Day. On June 21 the sun is overhead at the Tropic of Cancer. On December 21 it is overhead at the Tropic of Capricorn.

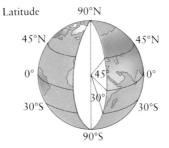

EARTH'S VITAL STATISTICS

Age About 4.6 billion years.

Diameter From Pole to Pole through the Earth's center, 7,900 miles (12,713 km); across the Equator through the Earth's center 7,927 miles (12,757 km).

Circumference Round the Poles 24,860 miles (40,007 km); round the Equator 24,900 miles (40,070 km)

Area Land 57,400,000 sq. miles (148,800,000 sq. km) = 29 percent; water 139,500,000 sq. miles (361,300,000 sq. km) = 71 percent.

Volume of the oceans 317 million cubic miles (1.3 billion cu km).

Average height of land 2,757 ft. (840 m) above sea level.

Average depth of oceans 12,450 ft. (3,795 m) below sea level.

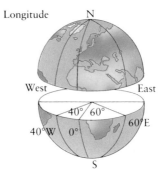

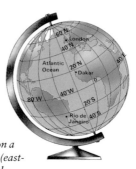

Fold mountains

Above: *The curved lines on a globe are lines of latitude (east-west) and lines of longitude (north-south).*

Below: *Fold mountains are formed when the Earth's crust squeezes rock layers upward.*

Faults

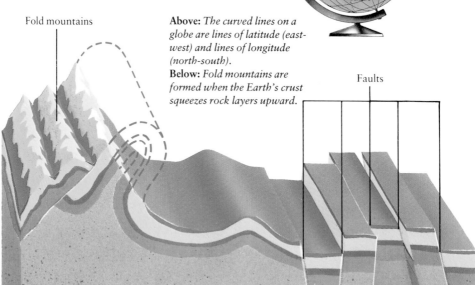

W·O·R·L·D

A·T·L·A·S

THE WORLD

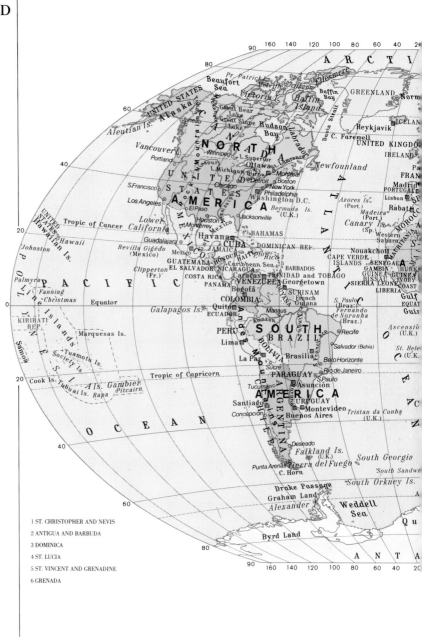

1 ST. CHRISTOPHER AND NEVIS

2 ANTIGUA AND BARBUDA

3 DOMINICA

4 ST. LUCIA

5 ST. VINCENT AND GRENADINE

6 GRENADA

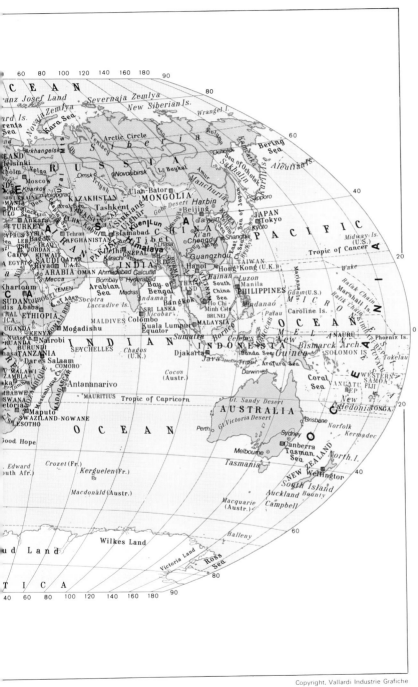

EUROPE

ASIA

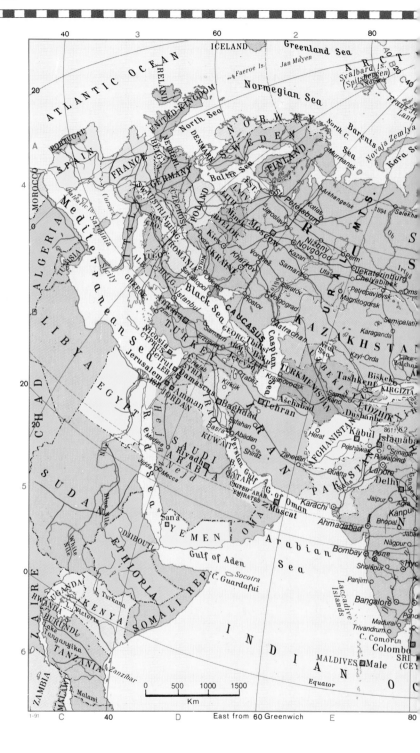

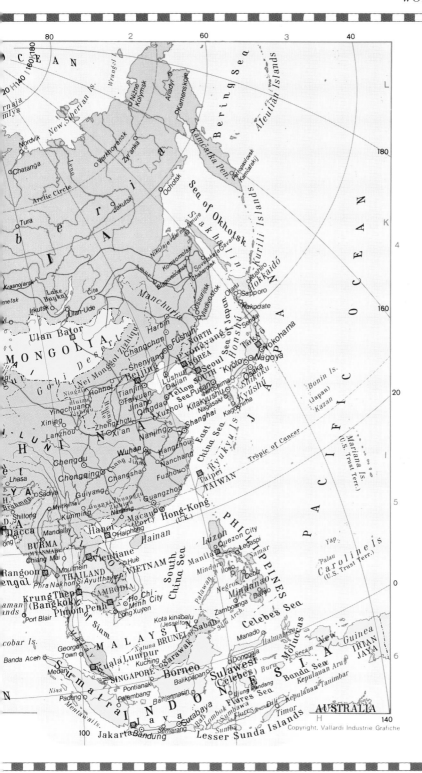

AFRICA

NORTH
AMERICA

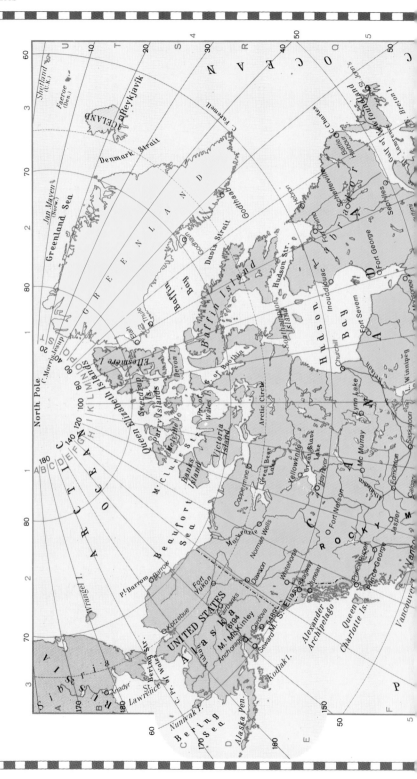

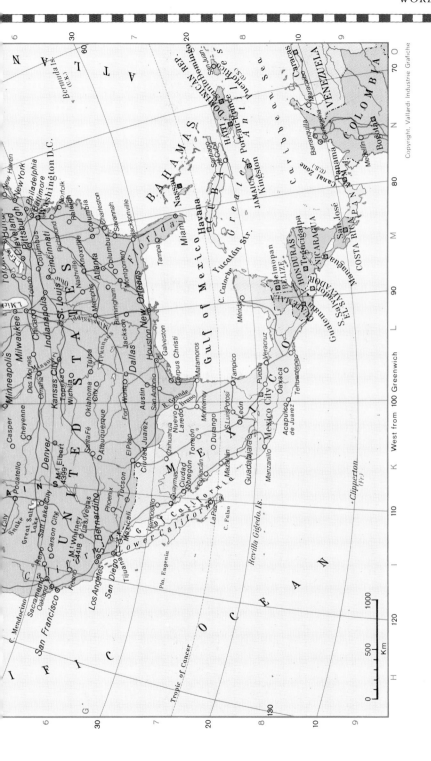

Copyright, Vallardi Industrie Grafiche

SOUTH AMERICA

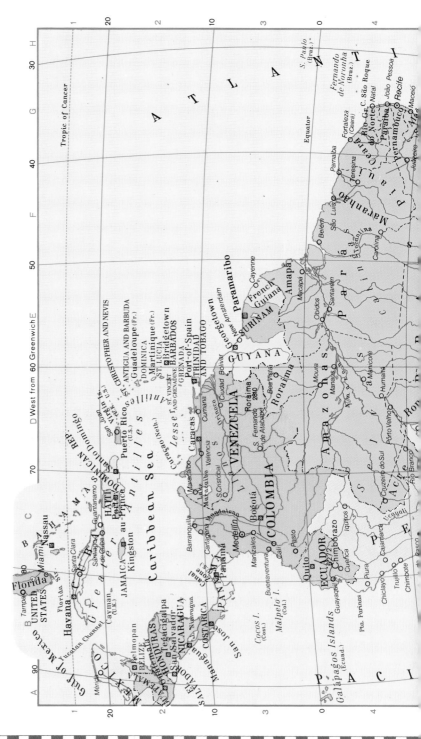

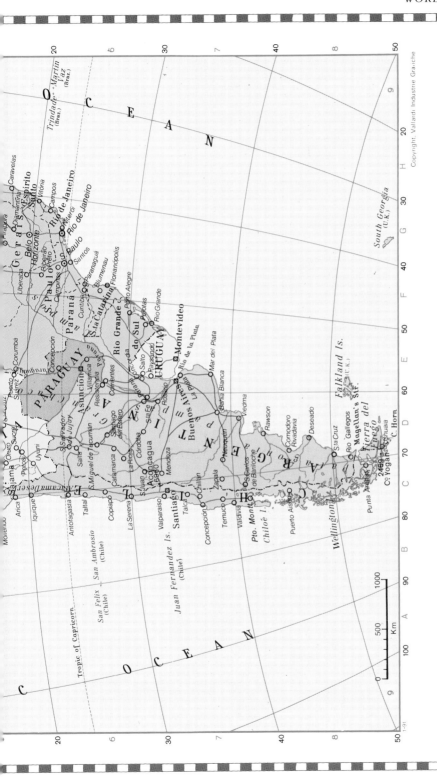

OCEANIA

120 · A · B · 140 · C · 160

CHINA
Hang chou
Nan chang
Chang sha
Fu chou
JAPAN
Kagoshima
East China Sea
Ryukyu Is.
Amami
Canton
Taipei
TAIWAN
Daito
Okinawa
Bonin Is.
(Ogasawara)
Tai nan
Hong Kong
(U.K.)
Macau (Port.)
Volcano Is.
(Kazan)
Marcus
(Minami Tori)
T
20
Lapag
Parece Vela
(Okino)
Agrihan
P   A   C
Wake
Luzon
Saipan
Mariana Is.
Manila
Quezon City
Batangas
Legaspi
Mindoro
Guam
(U.S.)
(U.S. Trust Terr.)
Marshall Isla
Ralik C
Samar
Iloilo
Yap · Ulithi Is.
Caroline Islands
Hall Is.
Eniwetok
Kwajalein
Palawan
Mindanao
Zamboanga
Davao
Palau Is.
Truk Is.
M   I   C
N
E
S
Jaluit
Sandakan
BRUNEI
Sulu Arch.
Nomoi Is.
Kusaie
Sarawak
Celebes
Sea
Manado
Halmahera
M   E   L
NAURU   Ocean
Borneo
Balikpapan
Pala
Sorong
Djajapura
Admiralty Is.
New Ireland
A
Sulawesi
(Celebes)
Sula
Bismarck
Archipelago
Bougainville
N
Bandjarmasin
Buru
Ambon
Seram
Irian Jaya
PAPUA
Madang
Rabaul
SOLOMON Is.
E
S
INDONESIA
Ujung
Pandang
Flores Sea
Banda Sea
New
Guinea
NEW GUINEA
New
Britain
Santa Isabel
Malaita
Surabaya
Aru Is.
Tanimbar
Port Moresby
Bairiki
Santa Cr
S
Bali
Lombok
Sumbawa
Lesser Sunda Islands
Flores
Dili
Timor
Merauke
Daru
Torres Strait
Samarai
Guadalcanal
S. Cristóbal
Sumba
Timor
Sea
Melville
Arafura Sea
Cape
York
Pen.
C. York
Coral
Sea
VANUATURE
Port Vila
Darwin
Arnhem
Land
Gulf of
Carpentaria
Great Barrier Reef
(France)
Wyndham
Newcastle
Waters
Normanton
New
Caledonia
Nouméa
Lo
Broome
Derby
NORTHERN
TERRITORY
Townsville
Mackay
Onslow
Great Sandy
Desert
Cloncurry
Rockhampton
QUEENSLAND
Barcaldine
20
N.W.
Cape
WESTERN
Gibson Desert
AUSTRALIA
Brisbane
C. Byron
Tasma
Carnarvon
AUSTRALIA
Gt. Victoria
Desert
Oodnadatta
L. Eyre
Broken
Hill
Bourke
NEW SOUTH
WALES
Newcastle
Sea
Norfolk I.
Geraldton
Kalgoorlie
SOUTH
AUSTRALIA
Sydney
Perth
Fremantle
Port Augusta
Adelaide
Murray
VICTORIA
Canberra
2228
Kosciusko
Melbourne
ZEA
Albany
Great Australian
Bight
Bass Strait
S.
AUSTRALIAN
BASIN
Launceston
TASMANIA
Hobart
Inverc
Stew
40   5
A   East from 120 Greenwich   B   140   C   160

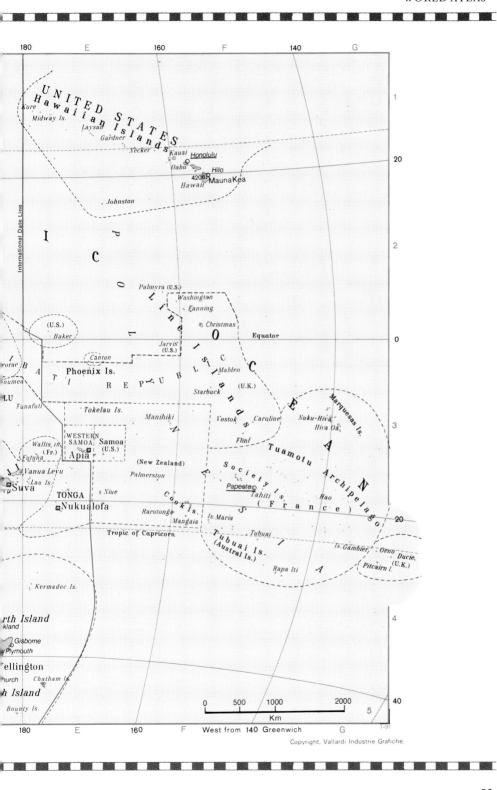

UNITED STATES
Hawaiian Islands
Kure
Midway Is.
Laysan
Gardner
Necker
Kauai Honolulu
Oahu
Hilo
4206 MaunaKea
Hawaii
Johnston

International Date Line

I
C
E
A
N

P
o
l
y
n
e
s
i
a

(U.S.)
Baker

Palmyra (U.S.)
Washington
Fanning
Christmas
Jarvis (U.S.)
Equator

L
i
n
e
I
s
l
a
n
d
s

O
C

Canton
Phoenix Is.
R E P U B L I C
Malden
(U.K.)
Starbuck

I
rorae B
numea
LU
Funafuti

T
I

Tokelau Is.
Manihiki
Vostok Caroline
Nuku-Hiva
Hiva Oa

Marquesas Is.

E
A
N

Wallis Is. (Fr.)
Futuna
WESTERN SAMOA
Samoa (U.S.)
Apia

Vanua Levu
Lau Is.
Suva

(New Zealand)
Palmerston

Flint

Tuamotu Archipelago

Society Is.
Papeete
Tahiti Hao

TONGA
Nukualofa

Niue
Cook Is.
Rarotonga
Mangaia
Is. Maria

(F r a n c e)

20

Kermadec Is.

Tropic of Capricorn
Tubuai
Tubuai Is.
(Austral Is.)
Rapa Iti
A

Is. Gambier Oeno
Ducie (U.K.)
Pitcairn I.

rth Island
kland
Gisborne
Plymouth
ellington
hurch Chatham I.
h Island
Bounty Is.

0   500   1000   2000
Km

West from 140 Greenwich

1-91

180   E   160   F   140   G
1
20
2
0
3
20
4
40
5

NORTH POLE/SOUTH POLE

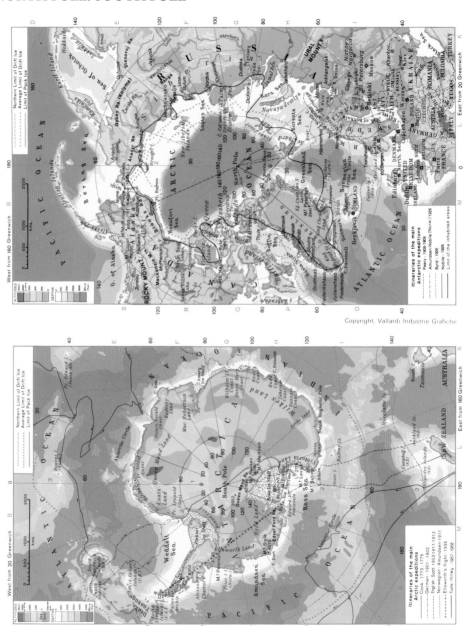

Copyright, Vallardi Industrie Grafiche

Copyright, Vallardi Industrie Grafiche

C O U N T R I E S

OF THE

W·O·R·L·D

ALGERIA

ANGOLA

BENIN

BOTSWANA

BURKINA FASO

BURUNDI

CAMEROON

AFRICA

ALGERIA
Republic of North Africa which borders the Mediterranean. The Sahara covers 85 per cent of the nation.
Area 919,600 sq.miles (2,382,000 sq.km).
Population 24,960,000.
Capital Algiers.

ANGOLA
Republic of west-Central Africa.
Area 481,000 sq.miles (1,247,000 sq.km).
Population 10,020,000.
Capital Luanda.

ASCENSION
Island in the South Atlantic, 500 miles (800km) south of the Equator, a dependency of St Helena.
Area 34 sq.miles (88 sq.km).
Population 1000.
Capital Georgetown.

BENIN
Republic on the Gulf of Guinea, West Africa.
Area 43,480 sq.miles (112,600 sq.km).
Population 4,736,000.
Capital Porto Novo.

BOTSWANA
Republic of Southern Africa, a member of the Commonwealth.
Area 232,000 sq.miles (600,400 sq.km).
Population 1,291,000.
Capital Gaborone.

BURKINA FASO
Republic of West Africa formerly called Upper Volta.
Area 105,900 sq.miles (274,200 sq.km).
Population 9,001,000.
Capital Ouagadougou.

BURUNDI
Republic of Central Africa; a small country sandwiched between Zaire, Tanzania, and Rwanda.
Area 10,750 sq.miles (27,800 sq.km).
Population 5,458,000.
Capital Bujumbura.

CAMEROON
Republic of West Africa.
Area 183,580 sq.miles (475,450 sq.km).
Population 11,834,000.
Capital Yaoundé.

CAPE VERDE
Republic, a number of islands in the North Atlantic.
Area 1560 sq.miles (4030 sq.km).
Population 370,000.
Capital Praia.

CENTRAL AFRICAN REPUBLIC
Republic of Equatorial Africa within the French Community.
Area 240,550 sq.miles (622,984 sq.km).
Population 3,039,000.
Capital Bangui.

CHAD
Republic of Equatorial
Africa within the French
Community.
Area 496,000 sq.miles
(1,284,000 sq.km).
Population 5,679,000.
Capital N'djamena.

COMOROS
Island republic in Indian
Ocean off Mozambique,
Africa. (*Flag not shown.*)
Area 838 sq.miles
(2170 sq.km).
Population 551,000.
Capital Moroni.

CONGO
Republic of Equatorial
Africa within the French
Community.
Area 132,000 sq.miles
(342,000 sq.km).
Population 2,271,000.
Capital Brazzaville.

CÔTE D'IVOIRE
Republic of West Africa.
Area 124,000 sq.miles
(322,500 sq.km).
Population 11,998,000.
Capital Abidjan.

DJIBOUTI
Republic of northeast
Africa within the French
Community, on the Red
Sea.
Area 8500 sq.miles
(22,000 sq.km).
Population 409,000.
Capital Djibouti.

EGYPT
Arab republic of northeast
Africa.
Area 387,000 sq.miles
(1,000,000 sq.km).
Population 53,153,000.
Capital Cairo.

EQUATORIAL GUINEA
Republic of West Africa.
Area 10,800 sq.miles
(28,000 sq.km).
Population 348,000.
Capital Malabo.

CENTRAL AFRICAN REPUBLIC

CHAD

CONGO

CÔTE D'IVOIRE

DJIBOUTI

EGYPT

EQUATORIAL GUINEA

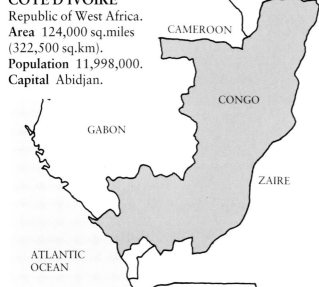
CAMEROON
CONGO
GABON
ZAIRE
ATLANTIC OCEAN
ANGOLA

ETHIOPIA

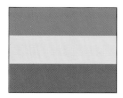

GABON

GAMBIA

GHANA

GUINEA

GUINEA-BISSEAU

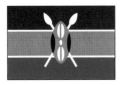

KENYA

ETHIOPIA
Republic of northeast Africa.
Area 472,000 sq.miles (1,222,000 sq.km).
Population 49,241,000.
Capital Addis Ababa.

GABON
Republic of Equatorial Africa within the French Community.
Area 103,000 sq.miles (268,000 sq.km).
Population 1,069,000.
Capital Libreville.

GAMBIA
Republic within the Commonwealth in West Africa.
Area 4300 sq.miles (11,300 sq.km).
Population 861,000.
Capital Banjul.

GHANA
Republic of West Africa, a member of the Commonwealth.
Area 92,000 sq.miles (239,000 sq.km).
Population 15,028,000.
Capital Accra.

GUINEA
Republic of West Africa.
Area 95,000 sq.miles (246,000 sq.km).
Population 5,756,000.
Capital Conakry.

GUINEA-BISSAU
Republic of West Africa which includes the Bijagós Islands.
Area 14,000 sq.miles (36,000 sq.km).
Population 965,000.
Capital Bissau.

KENYA
Republic of East Africa, a member of the Commonwealth.
Area 225,000 sq.miles (582,700 sq.km).
Population 24,032,000.
Capital Nairobi.

LESOTHO
Kingdom of Southern Africa surrounded by the country of South Africa.
Area 11,700 sq.miles (30,360 sq.km).
Population 1,774,000.
Capital Maseru.

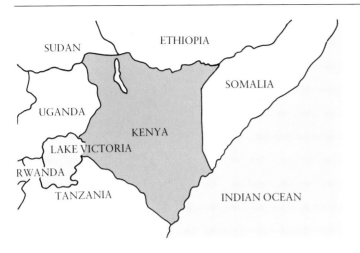

LESOTHO

LIBERIA

LIBYA

MADAGASCAR

MALAWI

MALI

MAURITANIA

LIBERIA
Republic of West Africa.
Area 38,200 sq.miles
(98,938 sq.km).
Population 2,607,000.
Capital Monrovia.

LIBYA
Republic of North Africa;
mostly desert.
Area 680,000 sq.miles
(1,760,000 sq.km).
Population 4,545,000.
Capital Tripoli.

MADAGASCAR
An island republic in Indian
Ocean about 250 miles
(400 km) east of Africa.
Area 226,700 sq.miles
(587,000 sq.km).
Population 11,197,000.
Capital Antananarivo.

MALAWI
Republic of Southern Africa
lying on the western shore
of Lake Nyasa.
Area 45,800 sq.miles
(118,500 sq.km).
Population 8,289,000.
Capital Lilongwe.

MALI
Republic of northwest
Africa.
Area 479,000 sq.miles
(1,240,000 sq.km).
Population 8,156,000.
Capital Bamako.

MAURITANIA
Republic of northwest
Africa.
Area 400,000 sq.miles
(1,030,700 sq.km).
Population 2,025,000.
Capital Nouakchott.

MAURITIUS
An independent state in the
Indian Ocean, made up of
two main islands.
Area 790 sq.miles
(2050 sq.km).
Population 1,075,000.
Capital Port Louis.

MAURITIUS

MOROCCO

MOZAMBIQUE

NAMIBIA

NIGER

NIGERIA

MAYOTTE
A French territory, an island in the Comoro Archipelago.
Area 145 sq.miles (374 sq.km).
Population 77,000.
Capital Dzaoudzi.

MOROCCO
A monarchy of northwest Africa.
Area 172,400 sq.miles (446,500 sq.km).
Population 25,061,000.
Capital Rabat.

MOZAMBIQUE
Republic of southeast Africa.
Area 309,000 sq.miles (800,310 sq.km).
Population 15,656,000.
Capital Maputo.

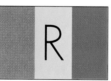
RWANDA

NAMIBIA
Republic in southwest Africa which became independent in 1990. Prior to this, Namibia's status had been in dispute. South Africa claimed control as it had been granted a mandate to govern the country after World War I by the League of Nations. However, the United Nations voted to end the mandate in 1966.
Area 318,000 sq.miles (824,000 sq.km).
Population 1,781,000.
Capital Windhoek.

NIGER
Republic of West Africa.
Area 489,000 sq.miles (1,267,000 sq.km).
Population 7,732,000.
Capital Niamey.

NIGERIA
Republic of West Africa.
Area 356,700 sq.miles (923,000 sq.km).
Population 108,542,000.
Capital Lagos (Abuja).

RÉUNION
A French overseas department in the Indian Ocean.
Area 969 sq.miles (2500 sq.km).
Population 575,000.
Capital St Denis.

RWANDA
Republic of Central Africa.
Area 10,000 sq.miles (26,400 sq.km).
Population 7,181,000.
Capital Kigali.

ST. HELENA

British colony, including the island of Ascension and the four islands of Tristan da Cunha, in the South Atlantic.
St. Helena **area** 47 sq.miles (122 sq.km).
Population 5200.
Capital Jamestown.

SÃO TOMÉ AND PRINCIPE

Island republic off the west coast of Africa.
Area 372 sq.miles (964 sq.km).
Population 121,000.
Capital São Tomé.

SENEGAL

Republic of West Africa. Mostly low-lying, and covered by savanna (open tropical grasslands).
Area 76,000 sq.miles (196,000 sq.km).
Population 7,327,000.
Capital Dakar.

SEYCHELLES

Island republic of the Indian Ocean, a member of the Commonwealth.
Area 171 sq.miles (443 sq.km).
Population 70,000.
Capital Victoria.

SIERRA LEONE

Republic of West Africa, an independent member of the Commonwealth.
Area 27,700 sq.miles (71,700 sq.km).
Population 4,151,000.
Capital Freetown.

SEYCHELLES

SOMALI REPUBLIC

Republic of Africa.
Area 246,000 sq.miles (637,700 sq.km).
Population 7,497,000,
Capital Mogadishu.

SOUTH AFRICA

Republic of Southern Africa.
Area 471,500 sq.miles (1,221,000 sq.km).
Population 35,282,000.
Capital Cape Town (legislative); Pretoria (Government); Bloemfontein (judicial).

SUDAN

Republic of northeast Africa.
Area 967,500 sq.miles (2,506,000 sq.km).
Population 25,204,000.
Capital Khartoum.

SWAZILAND

Kingdom of Southern Africa, a member of the Commonwealth.
Area 6700 sq.miles (17,400 sq.km).
Population 748,000.
Capital Mbabane.

TANZANIA

Republic of East Africa, a Commonwealth member.
Area 365,000 sq.miles (945,000 sq.km).
Population 25,635,000.
Capital Dodoma.

SENEGAL

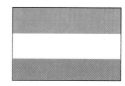

SIERRA LEONE

SOMALIA

SOUTH AFRICA

SUDAN

SWAZILAND

TANZANIA

TOGO

TUNISIA

UGANDA

ZAIRE

ZAMBIA

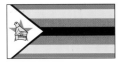

ZIMBABWE

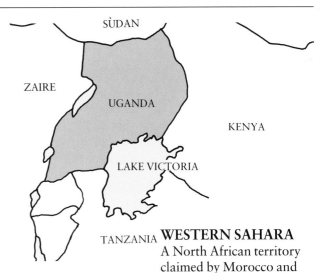

TOGO
Republic of West Africa
Area 21,600 sq.miles
(56,000 sq.km).
Population 3,531,000.
Capital Lomé.

TRISTAN DA CUNHA
Island in the South Atlantic
Ocean, a dependency of St.
Helena.
Area 38 sq.miles
(98 sq.km).
Population 320.
Capital Edinburgh.

TUNISIA
Republic of North Africa.
Area 63,000 sq.miles
(163,000 sq.km).
Population 8,180,000.
Capital Tunis.

UGANDA
Republic of east-central
Africa. A member of the
Commonwealth.
Area 91,000 sq.miles
(236,000 sq.km).
Population 18,795,000.
Capital Kampala.

WESTERN SAHARA
A North African territory
claimed by Morocco and
local nationalists.
Area 102,700 sq.miles
(266,000 sq.km).
Population 76,000.
Capital El Aiun.

ZAIRE
Republic of west-central
Africa.
Area 905,600 sq.miles
(2,345,400 sq.km).
Population 35,562,000.
Capital Kinshasa.

ZAMBIA
Republic in south-central
Africa. A member of the
Commonwealth.
Area 290,600 sq.miles
(752,600 sq.km).
Population 8,073,000.
Capital Lusaka.

ZIMBABWE
Republic of Southern
Africa. A member of the
Commonwealth.
Area 150,800 sq.miles
(390,600 sq.km).
Population 9,369,000.
Capital Harare.

ASIA

AFGHANISTAN
Republic of southwestern Asia.
Area 250,000 sq.miles (650,000 sq.km).
Population 16,121,000.
Capital Kabul.

BAHRAIN
Island group off Saudi Arabia forming a state.
Area 240 sq.miles (622 sq.km).
Population 503,000.
Capital Manama.

BANGLADESH
Republic in Southeast Asia. A member of the Commonwealth.
Area 55,600 sq.miles (144,000 sq.km).
Population 115,594,000.
Capital Dacca.

BHUTAN
Kingdom of the Himalayas.
Area 18,000 sq.miles (47,000 sq.km).
Population 1,517,000.
Capital Thimphu.

BRUNEI
Sultanate of Borneo. Commonwealth member.
Area 2230 sq.miles (5760 sq.km).
Population 266,000.
Capital Bandar Seri Begawan.

CAMBODIA (Kampuchea)
Republic of Southeast Asia.
Area 70,000 sq.miles (181,000 sq.km).
Population 8,246,000.
Capital Phnom Penh.

CHINA
Republic of east Asia. China contains about 20 percent of the world's total population.
Area 3,706,000 sq.miles (9,597,000 sq.km).
Population 1,070,600,000.
Capital Beijing (Peking).

AFGHANISTAN

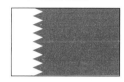

BAHRAIN

BANGLADESH

BHUTAN

BRUNEI

CAMBODIA

CHINA

MONGOLIA

CHINA

PACIFIC OCEAN

INDIA

INDIA

INDONESIA

IRAN

IRAQ

ISRAEL

JAPAN

JORDAN

HONG KONG
British dependency on the south coast of China.
Area 410 sq.miles (1061 sq.km).
Population 5,801,000.
Capital Victoria, usually called Hong Kong.

INDIA
Republic of Asia. A member of the Commonwealth.
Area 1,269,345 sq.miles (3,287,590 sq.km).
Population 827,057,000.
Capital New Delhi.

INDONESIA
Republic of Southeast Asia.
Area 735,003 sq.miles (1,903,650 sq.km).
Population 179,300,000.
Capital Djakarta.

IRAN
Islamic Republic of southwest Asia. It is one of the Gulf States.
Area 636,296 sq.miles (1,648,000 sq.km).
Population 54,608,000.
Capital Tehran.

IRAQ
Republic of southwest Asia.
Area 168,000 sq.miles (435,000 sq.km).
Population 18,920,000.
Capital Baghdad.

ISRAEL
Republic of the Middle East.
Area 8000 sq.miles (20,700 sq.km).
Population 4,659,000.
Capital Jerusalem.

JAPAN
Constitutional monarchy of the Far East.
Area 143,800 sq.miles (372,300 sq.km).
Population 123,537,000.
Capital Tokyo.

JORDAN
Kingdom of the Middle East.
Area 37,700 sq.miles (97,740 sq.km).
Population 4,009,000.
Capital Amman.

KOREA, NORTH
Republic of the Far East bordering on northeast China.
Area 46,500 sq.miles (120,500 sq.km).
Population 21,773,000.
Capital Pyongyang.

KOREA, SOUTH
Republic of the Far East.
Area 38,000 sq.miles (98,000 sq.km).
Population 42,793,000.
Capital Seoul.

KUWAIT
An Emirate on the Persian Gulf in southwest Asia.
Area 6900 sq.miles (17,800 sq.km).
Population 2,143,000.
Capital Kuwait.

LAOS
Republic of Southeast Asia lying in the Mekong Basin.
Area 91,400 sq.miles (236,800 sq.km).
Population 4,139,000.
Capital Vientiane.

LEBANON
Republic of the Middle East at the eastern end of the Mediterranean Sea.
Area 4000 sq.miles (10,400 sq.km).
Population 2,701,000.
Capital Beirut.

MACÃO
An overseas territory of Portugal on the southeast coast of China.
Area 6 sq.miles (16 sq.km).
Population 430,000.
Capital Macão.

MALAYSIA
A state of Southeast Asia. A member of the Commonwealth. Ruled by a sultan and a prime minister. Forested mountains cover large areas.
Area 127,300 sq.miles (330,000 sq.km).
Population 17,861,000.
Capital Kuala Lumpur.

MALDIVES
An island republic of the Indian Ocean southwest of India, with about 2000 islands. A member of the Commonwealth.
Area 115 sq.miles (300 sq.km).
Population 215,000.
Capital Malé.

KOREA, NORTH

KOREA, SOUTH

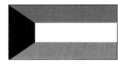
KUWAIT

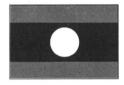
LAOS

LEBANON

MALAYSIA

MALDIVES

MONGOLIA

MYANMAR (Burma)

NEPAL

OMAN

PAKISTAN

PHILIPPINES

QATAR

MONGOLIA
Republic of central Asia.
Area 604,300 sq.miles
(1,565,000 sq.km).
Population 2,000,000.
Capital Ulan Bator.

MYANMAR (Burma)
Republic of Southeast Asia.
Area 261,230 sq.miles
(676,500 sq.km).
Population 41,675,000.
Capital Yangon
(Rangoon).

NEPAL
A monarchy of the
Himalayas between China
and India.
Area 54,000 sq.miles
(140,800 sq.km).
Population 18,916,000.
Capital Katmandu.

OMAN
A sultanate at the eastern
end of the Arabian
peninsula.
Area 82,000 sq.miles
(212,400 sq.km).
Population 1,502,000.
Capital Muscat.

PAKISTAN
Republic of southern Asia.
Member of the
Commonwealth.
Area 310,400 sq.miles
(804,000 sq.km).
Population 112,050,000.
Capital Islamabad.

PHILIPPINES
Republic of many islands in
Southeast Asia.
Area 116,000 sq.miles
(330,000 sq.km).
Population 62,000,000.
Capital Manila.

QATAR
An Emirate, a peninsula in
the Persian Gulf.
Area 4000 sq.miles
(11,000 sq.km).
Population 368,000.
Capital Doha.

SAUDI ARABIA
Kingdom of the Arabian
peninsula.
Area 840,000 sq.miles
(2,175,600 sq.km).
Population 14,870,000.
Capital Riyadh.

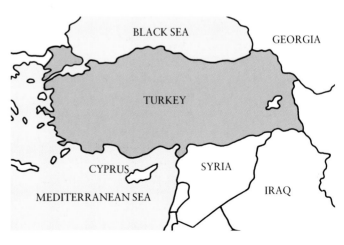

SINGAPORE

Island republic of Southeast Asia, a member of the Commonwealth.
Area 224 sq.miles (580 sq.km).
Population 3,003,000.
Capital Singapore.

SRI LANKA

Island republic of south Asia, a member of the Commonwealth.
Area 25,000 sq.miles (65,600 sq.km).
Population 16,993,000.
Capital Colombo.

SYRIA

Republic of the Middle East.
Area 71,5000 sq.miles (185,000 sq.km).
Population 12,116,000.
Capital Damascus.

TAIWAN

(Republic of China).
Republic about 90 miles (140 km) off mainland China.
Area 14,000 sq.miles (36,000 sq.km).
Population 20,280,000.
Capital Taipei.

THAILAND

Kingdom of Southeast Asia.
Area 198,000 sq.miles (514,000 sq.km).
Population 55,000,000.
Capital Bangkok.

TURKEY

Republic partly in Europe, partly in Asia.
Area 301,400 sq.miles (780,000 sq.km).
Population 58,687,000.
Capital Ankara.

UNITED ARAB EMIRATES

A federation of seven independent emirates in the Persian Gulf. They are: Abu Dhabi, Ajman, Dubai, Fujairah, Ras al Khaimah, Sharjah, Umm al Qaiwain.
Area 32,300 sq.miles (83,600 sq.km).
Population 1,589,000.
Capital Abu Dhabi.

UNITED ARAB EMIRATES

SAUDI ARABIA

SINGAPORE

SRI LANKA

SYRIA

TAIWAN

THAILAND

TURKEY

VIETNAM

YEMEN

ALBANIA

ANDORRA

AUSTRIA

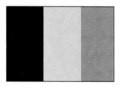

BELGIUM

ESTONIA

VIETNAM
Republic of Southeast Asia
bordering on south China.
Area 127,250 sq.miles
(330,000 sq.km).
Population 66,710,00.
Capital Hanoi.

YEMEN
Republic in the Arabian
peninsula.
Area 203,900 sq.miles
(528,000 sq.km).
Population 9,430,000.
Capital San'a.

--- *EUROPE* ---

ALBANIA
Republic of Europe in the
Balkans.
Area 11,100 sq.miles
(28,700 sq.km).
Population 3,250,000.
Capital Tirana.

ANDORRA
Tiny landlocked country of
the Pyrenees: sovereignty
divided between France and
the Spanish Bishop of Urgel.
Area 175 sq.miles
(453 sq.km).
Population 52,000.
Capital Andorra la Vella.

AUSTRIA
Republic of central Europe.
Area 32,376 sq.miles
(83,850 sq.km).
Population 7,712,000.
Capital Vienna.

LATVIA

LITHUANIA

THE BALTIC STATES
Northeast Europe. Once
part of the former USSR,
now republics with
independent status. Low-
lying, coastal plains.

ESTONIA
Area 17,375 sq.miles
(45,000 sq.km).
Population 1,573,000.
Capital Tallinn.

LATVIA
Area 24,711 sq.miles
(64,000 sq.km).
Population 2,681,000.
Capital Riga.

LITHUANIA
Area 25,097 sq.miles
(65,000 sq.km).
Population 3,690,000.
Capital Vilnius.

BELGIUM
Kingdom of northern
Europe, sandwiched
between France, Germany,
and Holland.
Area 11,800 sq.miles
(30,500 sq.km).
Population 9,845,000.
Capital Brussels.

BULGARIA
Republic of Europe in the Balkans.
Area 42,855 sq.miles (111,000 sq.km).
Population 9,011,000.
Capital Sofia.

CYPRUS
Island republic in the Mediterranean. In 1974 Turkish forces occupied the North; member of the Commonwealth.
Area 3600 sq.miles (9250 sq.km).
Population 702,000.
Capital Nicosia.

CZECHOSLOVAKIA
Republic of central Europe.
Area 50,000 sq.miles (128,000 sq.km).
Population 15,662,000.
Capital Prague.

DENMARK
Kingdom of northern Europe.
Area 17,400 sq.miles (45,000 sq.km).
Population 5,140,000.
Capital Copenhagen.

FINLAND
Republic of northeast Europe.
Area 130,000 sq.miles (337,000 sq.km).
Population 4,986,000.
Capital Helsinki.

FRANCE
Republic of western Europe.
Area 213,000 sq.miles (547,000 sq.km).
Population 55,000,000.
Capital Paris.

GERMANY
Republic of western Europe.
Area 96,000 sq.miles (356,755 sq.km).
Population 79,070,000.
Capital Bonn.

GIBRALTAR
British colony at tip of southern Spain. A rocky peninsula.
Area $2\frac{1}{2}$ sq.miles (6.5 sq.km).
Population 31,000.
Capital Gibraltar.

BULGARIA

CYPRUS

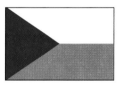

CZECHOSLOVAKIA

DENMARK

FINLAND

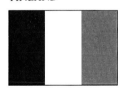

FRANCE

GERMANY

BALTIC SEA

NORTH SEA

NETHERLANDS

BELGIUM

LUXEMBOURG

FRANCE

GERMANY

POLAND

CZECHOSLOVAKIA

AUSTRIA

GREECE

HUNGARY

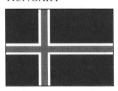

ICELAND

IRELAND

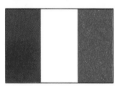

ITALY

LIECHTENSTEIN

LUXEMBOURG

GREECE
Republic of southeast
Europe which includes
many islands.
Area 51,000 sq.miles
(132,000 sq.km).
Population 10,048,000.
Capital Athens.

GREENLAND
Self-governing part of
Denmark in the North
Atlantic.
Area 840,000 sq.miles
(2,176,000 sq.km).
Population 57,000.
Capital Godthaab.

HUNGARY
Republic of central Europe.
Area 36,000 sq.miles
(93,000 sq.km).
Population 10,553,000.
Capital Budapest.

ICELAND
Island republic of the
northern Atlantic.
Area 40,000 sq.miles
(103,000 sq.km).
Population 255,000.
Capital Reykjavik.

IRELAND Republic of
Republic of northern
Europe.
Area 27,000 sq.miles
(70,200 sq.km).
Population 3,557,000.
Capital Dublin.

ITALY
Republic of southern
Europe.
Area 116,000 sq.miles
(301,000 sq.km).
Population 57,663,000.
Capital Rome.

LIECHTENSTEIN
A principality of western
Europe.
Area 62 sq.miles
(157 sq.km).
Population 29,000.
Capital Vaduz.

LUXEMBOURG
A Grand Duchy of western
Europe. Low mountains
with large forests.
Area 1000 sq.miles
(2600 sq.km).
Population 373,000.
Capital Luxembourg City.

MALTA

An island republic of the Mediterranean, a member of the Commonwealth.
Area 122 sq.miles (316 sq.km).
Population 354,000.
Capital Valetta.

MONACO

A principality on the Mediterranean coast, in southeast France.
Area 467 acres (1.9 sq.km).
Population 29,000.
Capital Monaco.

NETHERLANDS

Kingdom of northwest Europe.
Area 15,770 sq.miles (40,844 sq.km).
Population 14,700,000.
Capital Amsterdam.

NORWAY

Kingdom of northern Europe.
Area 125,182 sq.miles (324,219 sq.km).
Population 4,242,000.
Capital Oslo.

POLAND

Republic of eastern Europe.
Area 120,725 sq.miles (312,677 sq.km).
Population 38,186,000.
Capital Warsaw.

PORTUGAL

Republic in southwest Europe; part of the Iberian peninsula. Much mountainous countryside.
Area 35,553 sq.miles (92,082 sq.km).
Population 10,525,000.
Capital Lisbon.

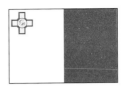

MALTA

MONACO

NETHERLANDS

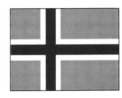

NORWAY

POLAND

PORTUGAL

FRANCE

PORTUGAL

SPAIN

ATLANTIC OCEAN

MEDITERRANEAN SEA

ALGERIA

MOROCCO

71

ROMANIA

SAN MARINO

SPAIN

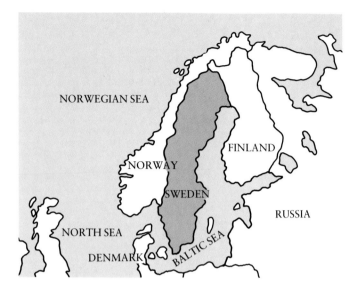

ROMANIA
Republic in eastern Europe.
Area 91,699 sq.miles
(237,500 sq.km).
Population 23,200,000.
Capital Bucharest.

SAN MARINO
Republic in the Apennines,
Italy.
Area 24 sq.miles
(61 sq.km).
Population 24,000.
Capital San Marino.

SPAIN
Kingdom of Europe.
Area 195,000 sq.miles
(504,700 sq.km).
Population 38,959,000.
Capital Madrid.

SWEDEN
Kingdom of northern
Europe.
Area 173,700 sq.miles
(450,000 sq.km).
Population 8,559,000.
Capital Stockholm.

SWITZERLAND
Republic of western
Europe.
Area 16,000 sq.miles
(41,000 sq.km).
Population 6,500,000.
Capital Bern.

COUNTRIES OF THE WORLD

FORMER UNION OF SOVIET SOCIALIST REPUBLICS

Previously, the world's largest nation spanning Europe and Asia. Formally ended 1991.
Total Area 8,650,000 sq.miles (22,402,200 sq.km).
Population 229,000,000.
Capital Moscow.

Individual republics:
Armenia; Azerbaijan; Byelorussia; Georgia; Kazakhstan; Kirgizia; Moldavia; Russian SFSR; Tadzhikistan; Turkmenistan; Ukraine; Uzbekistan.

UNITED KINGDOM

Kingdom of northwest Europe.
Area 94,232 sq.miles (244,046 sq.km).
Population 57,237,000.
Capital London.
The United Kingdom consists of the following:

ENGLAND
Area 50,336 sq.miles (130,363 sq.km).
Population 49,000,000.
Capital London.

SCOTLAND
Area 30,416 sq.miles (78,772 sq.km).
Population 5,094,000.
Capital Edinburgh.

WALES
Area 8017 sq.miles (20,736 sq.km).
Population 2,857,000.
Capital Cardiff.

NORTHERN IRELAND
Area 5463 sq.miles (14,148 sq.km).
Population 1,600,000.
Capital Belfast.

ISLE OF MAN
Area 227 sq.miles (588 sq.km).
Population 62,000.
Capital Douglas.

CHANNEL ISLANDS
Area 75 sq.miles (195 sq.km).
Jersey
Area 45 sq.miles (116 sq.km).
Population 73,000.
Capital St. Helier.
Guernsey
Area 24½ sq.miles (63 sq.km)
Dependencies: Alderney, Hern, Brechou, Jethou, Lithou.
Total population 131,000.
Capital St. Peter Port.

VATICAN CITY
State in northwest Rome, Italy, in which is located the government of the Roman Catholic Church.
Area 108.7 acres (44 hectares).
Population 1000.

YUGOSLAVIA
A federal republic on the Adriatic. Formerly included Slovenia, Croatia, Bosnia and Hercegovina, and Macedonia; these are now independent republics. Serbia and Montenegro make up the present Yugoslavia.

SWEDEN

SWITZERLAND

UNITED KINGDOM

VATICAN CITY

YUGOSLAVIA

ANTIGUA
AND BARBUDA

BAHAMAS

BARBADOS

BELIZE

CANADA

COSTA RICA

NORTH AND CENTRAL AMERICA

ANGUILLA
British colony of the Leeward Islands, West Indies.
Area 35 sq.miles (90 sq.km).
Population 6500.
Capital The Valley.

ANTIGUA and BARBUDA
State of the West Indies within the Commonwealth.
Area 170 sq.miles (440 sq.km).
Population 77,000.
Capital St. John's.

BAHAMAS
An independent Commonwealth member in the West Atlantic.
Area 5380 sq.miles (14,000 sq.km).
Population 253,000.
Capital Nassau.

BARBADOS
Independent Commonwealth member in the West Indies.
Area 166 sq.miles (430 sq.km).
Population 255,000.
Capital Bridgetown.

BELIZE
State on the east coast of Central America, a member of the Commonwealth.
Area 8860 sq.miles (22,960 sq.km).
Population 188,000.
Capital Belmopan.

BERMUDA
British dependent territory in the West Atlantic.
Area 20 sq.miles (53 sq.km).
Population 62,000.
Capital Hamilton.

CANADA
Independent member of the Commonwealth in the north of North America.
Area 3,582,000 sq.miles (9,976,000 sq.km).
Population 26,522,000.
Capital Ottawa.
Canada has 12 provinces listed below:

PROVINCE	CAPITAL
Alberta	Edmonton
British Columbia	Victoria
Manitoba	Winnipeg
New Brunswick	Fredericton
Newfoundland	St. John's
Northwest Terr.	Yellowknife
Nova Scotia	Halifax
Ontario	Toronto
Prince Edward Is.	Charlottetown
Quebec	Quebec
Saskatchewan	Regina
Yukon Territory	Whitehorse

CAYMAN ISLANDS
British colony, a number of islands in the West Indies.
Area (100 sq.miles) 260 sq.km
Population 23,000.
Capital George Town.

COSTA RICA
Republic of Central America.
Area 19,600 sq.miles (50,700 sq.km).
Population 2,994,000.
Capital San José.

CUBA

DOMINICA

DOMINICAN REPUBLIC

EL SALVADOR

CUBA
West Indian republic.
Area 44,220 sq.miles
(114,500 sq.km).
Population 10,609,000.
Capital Havana.

DOMINICA
Republic within the
Commonwealth in the
Windward Islands, West
Indies.
Area 290 sq.miles
(751 sq.km).
Population 83,000.
Capital Roseau.

DOMINICAN
REPUBLIC
Republic of the West Indies,
occupying two-thirds of the
island of Hispaniola.
Area 18,800 sq.miles
(49,000 sq.km).
Population 7,170,000.
Capital Santo Domingo.

EL SALVADOR
Republic of Central
America.
Area 8000 sq.miles
(21,000 sq.km).
Population 5,000,000.
Capital San Salvador.

GRENADA

GUATEMALA

HAITI

HONDURAS

JAMAICA

GRENADA

An independent country within the Commonwealth, one of the Windward Islands.
Area 133 sq.miles (344 sq.km).
Population 85,000.
Capital St. George's.

GUADELOUPE

A French overseas department in the West Indies.
Area 688 sq.miles (1780 sq.km).
Population 332,000.
Capital Basse-Terre.

GUATEMALA

Republic of Central America. A land of dense jungles, volcanoes, dry deserts, and sparkling lakes.
Area 42,000 sq.miles (108,900 sq.km).
Population 9,197,000.
Capital Guatemala City.

HAITI

Republic of the West Indies, occupying one third of the island of Hispaniola.
Area 10,700 sq.miles (28,000 sq.km).
Population 6,486,000.
Capital Port-au-Prince.

HONDURAS

Republic of Central America. A mountainous country, which has a long coastline with the Caribbean Sea and a short one with the Pacific.
Area 43,000 sq.miles (112,000 sq.km).
Population 5,105,000.
Capital Tegucigalpa.

JAMAICA

An independent member of the Commonwealth in the West Indies.
Area 4200 sq.miles (11,000 sq.km).
Population 2,420,000.
Capital Kingston.

MARTINIQUE

A French overseas department in the West Indies.
Area 426 sq.miles (1100 sq.km).
Population 117,000.
Capital Fort-de-France.

MEXICO

Republic of North America. Much of the country is hilly, with fertile uplands.
Area 761,000 sq.miles (1,970,000 sq.km).
Population 86,154,000.
Capital Mexico City.

MONTSERRAT
British colony in the Leeward Islands, West Indies.
Area 38 sq.miles (98 sq.km).
Population 12,000.
Capital Plymouth.

NETHERLANDS ANTILLES (Dutch West Indies)
Two groups of Dutch islands in the Caribbean, with internal autonomy.
Area 370 sq.miles (960 sq.km).
Population 187,000.
Capital Willemstad.

NICARAGUA
Republic of Central America. A line of high mountains runs down the center, with some active volcanoes.
Area 50,000 sq.miles (130,000 sq.km).
Pouplation 3,871,000.
Capital Managua.

PANAMA
Republic of Central America.
Area 29,000 sq.miles (75,700 sq.km).
Population 2,418,000.
Capital Panama.

PUERTO RICO
A United States self-governing Commonwealth in the West Indies.
Area 3435 sq.miles (8900 sq.km).
Population 3,599,000.
Capital San Juan.

ST. KITTS-NEVIS
A state in the Leeward Islands of the West Indies within the Commonwealth.
Area 100 sq.miles (260 sq.km).
Population 44,000.
Capital Basseterre.

ST. LUCIA
An independent state within the Commonwealth; one of the Windward Islands.
Area 238 sq.miles (616 sq.km).
Population 151,000.
Capital Castries.

ST. PIERRE AND MIQUELON
A French overseas department; eight islands off Newfoundland, Canada.
Area 93 sq.miles (242 sq.km).
Population 6000.
Capital St. Pierre.

MEXICO

NICARAGUA

PANAMA

ST. KITTS-NEVIS

ST LUCIA

ST VINCENT AND
GRENADINES

TRINIDAD AND
TOBAGO

UNITED STATES OF
AMERICA

ST. VINCENT AND THE GRENADINES

An independent member of the Commonwealth in the Windward Islands, West Indies.
Area 150 sq.miles (388 sq.km).
Population 116,000.
Capital Kingstown.

TRINIDAD AND TOBAGO

Island Republic of the West Indies within the Commonwealth.
Area 2000 sq.miles (5000 sq.km).
Population 1,300,000.
Capital Port-of-Spain.

TURKS AND CAICOS ISLANDS

British colony in the Caribbean.
Area 166 sq.miles (430 sq.km).
Population 7200.
Capital Cockburn Town.

UNITED STATES OF AMERICA

Federal republic of North America.
Area 3,615,319 sq.miles (9,363,123 sq.km).
Population 249,975,000.
Capital Washington, District of Columbia. The United States is made up of 50 states. These are listed below:

STATE	CAPITAL
Alabama	Montgomery
Alaska	Juneau
Arizona	Phoenix
Arkansas	Little Rock
California	Sacramento
Colorado	Denver
Connecticut	Hartford
Delaware	Dover
Florida	Tallahassee
Georgia	Atlanta
Hawaii	Honolulu
Idaho	Boise
Illinois	Springfield
Indiana	Indianapolis
Iowa	Des Moines
Kansas	Topeka
Kentucky	Frankfort
Louisiana	Baton Rouge
Maine	Augusta
Maryland	Annapolis
Massachusetts	Boston
Michigan	Lansing
Minnesota	St. Paul
Mississippi	Jackson
Missouri	Jefferson City
Montana	Helena
Nebraska	Lincoln
Nevada	Carson City
New Hampshire	Concord
New Jersey	Trenton
New Mexico	Santa Fé
New York	Albany
North Carolina	Raleigh
North Dakota	Bismarck
Ohio	Columbus
Oklahoma	Oklahoma City
Oregon	Salem
Pennsylvania	Harrisburg
Rhode Island	Providence
South Carolina	Columbia
South Dakota	Pierre
Tennessee	Nashville
Texas	Austin
Utah	Salt Lake City
Vermont	Montpelier
Virginia	Richmond
Washington	Olympia
West Virginia	Charlestown
Wisconsin	Madison
Wyoming	Cheyenne

VIRGIN ISLANDS
(British)
Group of 36, West Indies.
Area 59 sq.miles
(153 sq.km).
Population 11,500.
Capital Road Town.

VIRGIN ISLANDS (U.S.)
A territory near Puerto Rico
in the West Indies.
Area 133 sq.miles
(344 sq.km).
Population 119,000.
Capital Charlotte Amalie.

ARGENTINA

BOLIVIA

--- *SOUTH AMERICA* ---

ARGENTINA
Republic lying on the east
coast of South America.
Area 1,068,360 sq.miles
(2,766,890 sq.km).
Population 32,322,000.
Capital Buenos Aires.

BRAZIL
Republic, largest country of
South America.
Area 3,286,670 sq.miles
(8,512,000 sq.km).
Population 150,368,000.
Capital Brasilia.

BRAZIL

CHILE

BOLIVIA
Landlocked republic at the
center of South America.
Area 424,000 sq.miles
(1,093,500 sq.km).
Population 7,400,000.
Capital La Paz (seat of
government); Sucre (legal
capital).

CHILE
Republic lying on the
western coast of South
America. Andes Mountains
lie to its east.
Area 292,274 sq.miles
(757,000 sq.km).
Population 13,173,000.
Capital Santiago.

COLOMBIA

ECUADOR

FRENCH GUIANA

GUYANA

COLOMBIA
Republic of South America.
Area 440,000 sq.miles
(1,139,000 sq.km).
Population 32,987,000.
Capital Bogota.

ECUADOR
Republic of South America.
Area 109,500 sq.miles
(283,600 sq.km).
Population 10,782,000.
Capital Quito.

FALKLAND ISLANDS
British colony in the South
Atlantic.
Area 4700 sq.miles
(12,200 sq.km).
Population 2000.
Capital Stanley.

FRENCH GUIANA
A French overseas
department in northeast
South America.
Area 35,000 sq.miles
(91,000 sq.km).
Population 92,000.
Capital Cayenne.

GUYANA
Republic of northeast South
America, a member of the
Commonwealth.
Area 83,000 sq.miles
(215,000 sq.km).
Population 796,000.
Capital Georgetown.

PARAGUAY
Landlocked republic at the
center of South America.
Area 157,000 sq.miles
(406,700 sq.km).
Population 4,277,000.
Capital Asunción.

PERU
Republic lying on the western coast of South America.
Area 496,000 sq.miles (1,285,000 sq.km).
Population 22,332,000.
Capital Lima.

SURINAM
Small republic of the north-east coast of South America.
Area 63,000 sq.miles (163,300 sq.km).
Population 422,000.
Capital Paramaribo.

URUGUAY
Republic of South America.
Area 68,000 sq.miles (176,200 sq.km).
Population 3,094,000.
Capital Montevideo.

VENEZUELA
Republic of South America. Flat-topped mountains cover much of south.
Area 352,000 sq.miles (912,000 sq.km).
Population 19,735,000.
Capital Caracas.

PARAGUAY

PERU

SURINAM

URUGUAY

VENEZUELA

AUSTRALIA

OCEANIA

AUSTRALIA
An independent Commonwealth member, occupying the continent of Australia and outlying islands.
Area 2,968,000 sq.miles (7,686,800 sq.km).
Population 17,086,000.
Capital Canberra.
States and territories include:
Australian Capital Territory, New South Wales, Northern Territory, South Australia, Western Australia, Queensland, Tasmania, Victoria.

COOK ISLANDS
Self-governing territory of New Zealand in the South Pacific.
Area 90 sq.miles (234 sq.km).
Population 18,000.
Capital Avarua.

FIJI
Republic in southwest Pacific. Made up of hundreds of islands, the biggest of which is Viti Levu.
Area 7050 sq.miles (18,300 sq.km).
Population 765,000.
Capital Suva.

FIJI

NEW GUINEA
SOLOMON ISLANDS
PACIFIC OCEAN
 FIJI
AUSTRALIA

KIRIBATI

NAURU

NEW ZEALAND

PAPUA NEW GUINEA

WESTERN SAMOA

FRENCH POLYNESIA

A French overseas
department in the Eastern
Pacific.
Area 1550 sq.miles
(4000 sq.km).
Population 166,000.
Capital Papeete.

GUAM

A territory of the United
States in the Marianas
archipelago in the North
Pacific. The people are self-
governing.
Area 212 sq.miles
(549 sq.km).
Population 119,000.
Capital Agana.

KIRIBATI

Island republic of the
Central Pacific, a member
of the Commonwealth. It
includes Ocean (Banaba)
island, the sixteen Gilbert
Islands, eight of the eleven
Line Islands, and the eight
Phoenix islands.
Area 360 sq.miles
(930 sq.km).
Population 66,000.
Capital Tarawa.

NAURU

An island republic in the
Western Pacific, with
special status within the
Commonwealth.
Area 8 sq.miles (21 sq.km).
Population 10,000.
Capital Nauru.

NEW ZEALAND

An independent member of
the Commonwealth in the
southwest Pacific.
Area 103,700 sq.miles
(268,000 sq.km).
Population 3,346,000.
Capital Wellington.

NIUE

A self-governing territory of
New Zealand in the Cook
Islands, South Pacific.
Area 100 sq.miles
(260 sq.km).
Population 4000.
Capital Alofi.

NORFOLK ISLAND

An Australian territory in
the southwest Pacific.
Area 14 sq.miles (36 sq.km).
Population 2000.
Capital Kingstown.

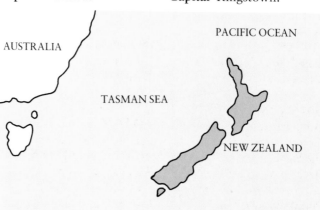

PACIFIC ISLANDS TRUST TERRITORY

Group of islands, including the Marianas, Caroline and Marshall Islands, governed by the United States.
Area 687 sq.miles (1780 sq.km).
Population 149,000.
Capital Saipan.

PAPUA NEW GUINEA

An independent Commonwealth state in the southwest Pacific. Hot and wet, with swampy river valleys and active volcanoes in the north.
Area 178,200 sq.miles (461,700 sq.km).
Population 3,699,000.
Capital Port Moresby.

PITCAIRN ISLAND

British colony in the South Pacific.
Area 2 sq.miles (5 sq.km).
Population 63.
Capital Adamstown.

SAMOA, AMERICAN

Group of eight islands in the South Pacific, governed by the United States.
Area 76 sq.miles (197 sq.km).
Population 35,000.
Capital Pago Pago.

SAMOA, WESTERN

An independent Commonwealth member in the Pacific.
Area 1090 sq.miles (2900 sq.km).
Population 200,000.
Capital Apia.

SOLOMON ISLANDS

An independent state, a member of the Commonwealth, in the southwest Pacific.
Area 11,000 sq.miles (28,500 sq.km).
Population 321,000.
Capital Honiara.

TONGA

Island kingdom in the South Pacific within the Commonwealth. Tonga is also known as the "Friendly Islands."
Area 270 sq.miles (700 sq.km).
Population 95,000.
Capital Nuku'alofa.

TUVALU

An independent member of the Commonwealth, a group of islands in the South Pacific.
Area 3 sq.miles (8 sq.km).
Population 10,000.
Capital Fongafale.

VANUATU

Island republic in the southwest Pacific, a member of the Commonwealth.
Area 5700 sq.miles (14,800 sq.km).
Population 147,000.
Capital Port Vila.

WALLIS AND FUTUNA ISLANDS

A French overseas territory in the southwest Pacific.
Area 77 sq.miles (200 sq.km).
Population 9000.
Capital Mata-Uta.

SOLOMON ISLANDS

TONGA

TUVALU

VANUATU

History

The colorful pageant of history tells of the conflicts and achievements of the human race, of bloody wars and milestones of civilization. It is studded with the names of statesmen and conquerors, explorers, inventors, and artists; it also records the way ordinary people lived in times past. Records of daily life and world events have been kept since writing was invented 5,500 years ago.

Alexander the Great (356–323 B.C.) was the greatest conqueror of the ancient world. He became ruler of Macedon at the age of 20.
Right: *The Bayeux tapestry tells the story of the Norman conquest of England. At the battle of Hastings in 1066 William of Normandy defeated Harold Godwinnsson, his rival for the English crown, and established Norman rule over England.*

History is the story of people and what they did in the past. For most people, the life they led was very ordinary. Like the newspapers you read today, writers who chronicled the events of their time tended to write down only the outstanding events. For some periods of history, we have only the sketchiest idea of everyday life.

However, it is the important events that distinguish one period of history from another. Rulers exerted an enormous influence on their people. They could declare wars, negotiate peace settlements, exact taxes, control finances, and make laws.

Some rulers have had much more influence than others. The most notorious have been the conquerors. Alexander the Great set out to conquer the whole world, as it was known in his day. From Macedonia, in Greece, he extended his empire over the Middle East, including Egypt, Persia (modern Iran), and Afghanistan as far as the Indus River valley, now in Pakistan.

Another conqueror was the French general Napoleon

At the battle of Austerlitz in 1805, the French emperor Napoleon won his greatest victory, defeating a combined army of Austrian and Russian troops.

Bonaparte, who, at the height of his power, ruled most of Europe. Neither his career nor that of Alexander lasted long: Alexander died of fever at the age of 33; Napoleon was sent into exile at 46. By contrast, a third great general, George Washington, lived to be 67. He fought not to conquer but to liberate his country from colonial rule, and went on to become the first president of the United States.

The history of the whole world shows that people

MAJOR WARS

Name	Date	Won by	Against
Peloponnesian War	431–404 BC	Peloponnesian League, led by Sparta, Corinth	Delian League, led by Athens
Punic Wars	264–146 BC	Rome	Carthage
Hundred Years' War	1337–1453	France	England
Wars of the Roses	1455–1485	House of Lancaster	House of York
Thirty Years' War	1618–1648	France, Sweden, the German Protestant states	The Holy Roman Empire, Spain
Civil War, English	1642–1651	Parliament	Royalists
Spanish Succession, War of the	1701–1713	England, Austria, Prussia, the Netherlands	France, Bavaria, Cologne, Mantua, Savoy
Austrian Succession, War of the	1740–1748	Austria, Hungary, Britain	Bavaria, France, Poland, Prussia, Sardinia, Saxony, Spain
Seven Years' War	1756–1763	Britain, Prussia, Hanover	Austria, France, Russia, Sweden
American Revolutionary War	1775–1783	Thirteen Colonies	Britain
Napoleonic Wars	1792–1815	Austria, Britain, Prussia, Russia, Spain, Sweden	France
War of 1812	1812–1814	United States	Britain
Mexican-American War	1846–1848	United States	Mexico
Crimean War	1853–1856	Britain, France, Sardinia, Turkey	Russia
Civil War, American	1861–1865	23 Northern States (The Union)	11 Southern States (The Confederacy)
Franco-Prussian War	1870–1871	Prussia and other German states	France
Chinese-Japanese War	1894–1895	Japan	China
Spanish-American War	1898	United States	Spain
Boer (South African) War	1899–1902	Britain	Boer Republics
Russo-Japanese War	1904–1905	Japan	Russia

Lord Protector of England and brilliant military strategist, Oliver Cromwell. He died in 1658.

developed at very different times, and that great events in one part of the world were completely unknown to people living in other places. For example, while Roman soldiers were defending Hadrian's Wall in northern Britain against attacks from the Picts and Scots, across the Atlantic the Maya were beginning to build huge temple pyramids in Central America.

At the time Leif Ericsson discovered the land he called Vinland, in North America, the ancient Empire of Ghana was flourishing in West Africa, Polynesians were colonizing New Zealand, and in England the Saxon king Ethelred the Unready was paying Danish invaders large

Name	Date	Won by	Against
World War I	1914–1918	Belgium, Britain and Empire, France, Italy, Japan, Russia, Serbia, United States	Austria-Hungary, Bulgaria, Germany, Ottoman Empire
Chinese-Japanese War	1931–1933	Japan	China
Abyssinian War	1935–1936	Italy	Abyssinia (Ethiopia)
Civil War, Spanish	1936–1939	Junta de Defensa Nacional (Fascists)	Republican government
Chinese-Japanese War	1937–1945	China	Japan
World War II	1939–1945	Australia, Belgium, Britain, Canada, China, Denmark, France, Greece, Netherlands, New Zealand, Norway, Poland, South Africa, Soviet Union, United States, Yugoslavia	Bulgaria, Finland, Germany, Hungary, Italy, Japan, Romania
Korean War	1950–1953	South Korea and United Nations forces	North Korea and Chinese forces
Vietnam War	1954–1975	North Vietnam	South Vietnam, United States
Six-Day War	1967	Israel	Egypt, Syria, Jordan, Iraq
Civil War, Nigerian	1967–1970	Federal government	Biafra
Civil War, Pakistani	1971	East Pakistan (Bangladesh) and India	West Pakistan
October War	1973	Ceasefire arranged by UN: fought by Israel against Egypt, Syria, Jordan, Iraq, Sudan, Saudi Arabia, Lebanon	
Iran–Iraq War	1980–1988	Ceasefire arranged with UN help	
Gulf War	1991	UN coalition of countries	Iraq

sums in gold to go away.

Human beings have lived on Earth for about two million years. The first humans appear to have lived in eastern Africa. By 100,000 years ago they had spread over most of Africa and Europe, and large parts of Asia. People migrated from Asia into North America less than 40,000 years ago, when they traveled across a huge ice sheet where the Bering Strait now is. The Native American people spread south to all parts of the continent. Archaeological finds show that 15,000 years ago there were agricultural settlements in the Middle East, where skills such as weaving and metallurgy were developed.

Above: *Over the centuries there have been hundreds of wars. Even in times of apparent peace, people have been fighting in some area of the world. These are a few of the most important conflicts.*

87

MAJOR BATTLES

BC

490 Marathon Force of 10,000 Athenians and allies defeated 50,000 Persian troops, crushing a Persian invasion attempt.

AD

732 Tours The Franks under Charles Martel defeated the Muslims, halting their advance in western Europe.

1066 Hastings About 8,000 troops under Duke William of Normandy defeated an equal force under Saxon king Harold II. England came under Norman rule.

1415 Agincourt Henry V of England with 10,000 troops defeated 30,000 Frenchmen, and recaptured Normandy.

1453 Siege of Constantinople Ottoman Turkish army captured the city and destroyed the Byzantine Empire. The Turks gained a foothold in Europe.

1571 Lepanto Allied Christian fleet of 208 galleys under Don John of Austria defeated Ali Pasha's Turkish fleet of 230 galleys; last great battle with galleys.

1588 Armada Spanish invasion fleet of 130 ships was defeated by 197 English ships.

1757 Plassey Robert Clive with an Anglo-Indian army of 3,000 defeated the Nawab of Bengals army of 60,000 setting Britain on the road to domination in India.

1777 Saratoga British troops under John Burgoyne surrendered to American colonial forces. Defeat led France to join war against Britain.

1781 Yorktown Charles Cornwallis with 8,000 British troops surrendered to a larger force under George Washington, ending the American Revolutionary War.

1798 Nile Horatio Nelson commanding a British fleet of 15 ships destroyed a 17-ship French fleet in Aboukïr Bay, cutting off Napoleon Bonaparte's French army in Egypt.

1805 Trafalgar British fleet of 27 ships under Horatio Nelson shattered Franco-Spanish fleet of 33 ships, ending Napoleon's hopes of invading England.

1805 Austerlitz Emperor Napoleon I with 65,000 French troops defeated an 83,000-strong Austro-Russian army under the Austrian and Russian emperors.

1813 Leipzig Napoleon I with 190,000 French troops was surrounded and crushed by an allied force of 300,000 Austrian, Prussian, Russian, and Swedish troops.

1815 Waterloo A British, Dutch, and Belgian force of 67,000 fought off 74,000 French troops under Napoleon I until the arrival of the Prussian army.

1863 Gettysburg Federal forces under George Meade defeated Robert E. Lee's Confederate army, a turning point in the American Civil War.

1914 Marne French and British armies halted German forces invading France.

1916 Verdun In a six-month struggle, French forces held a major attack by German armies. French losses were 348,000 men, the German losses 328,800.

1917 Passchendaele British forces launched eight attacks over 102 days in heavy rain and through thick mud, gaining five miles and losing 400,000 men.

1940 Britain German air force launched an attack lasting 114 days. The smaller Royal Air Force defeated the attack.

1942 Midway A 100-ship Japanese fleet led by Isoruku Yamamoto aiming to capture Midway Island was defeated by American fleet half the size, under Raymond Spruance.

1942 El Alamein British Eighth Army under Bernard Montgomery drove German Afrika Korps under Erwin Rommel out of Egypt and deep into Libya.

1942–3 Stalingrad Twenty-one German divisions tried to capture Stalingrad (now Volgograd), but siege was broken and Friedrich von Paulus had to surrender with more than 100,000 German troops.

1944 Normandy Allied forces under Dwight D. Eisenhower invaded German-held northern France in biggest-ever sea-borne attack.

1944–5 Ardennes Bulge Last German counter-attack in west through Ardennes Forest failed; Germans lost 100,000 casualties and 110,000 prisoners.

1954 Dien Bien Phu Vietnamese forces defeated French army, signaling the end of the French hold on its former colony.

People were unable to record the events of their times until the invention of writing, a mere 5,500 years ago. So we have to piece together the events before that from what ancient peoples have left behind, such as their cave dwellings, or the ruins of buildings such as Stonehenge in England or the temples of Malta. Today science helps the archaeologist who carries out this work with radiocarbon dating which helps tell us when objects were made, and with infrared and X-ray photography, which will make out the design under the surface on a rotted bronze bowl. Modern diving equipment can explore sunken wrecks and other remains of the past.

In the Chronology of World History on pages 128–148 we deal only with events within the time of written history. We owe our present knowledge of the world to a number of brave men – and a few women – who had the urge to explore distant lands that were unknown to them. Because people knew so little about the shape and size of the Earth, the earliest explorers needed real courage. For example, many of the Portuguese navigators trying to find a sea route to India thought the Earth was flat, and were afraid that if they ventured too far they might fall off the edge of the world.

The president of the United States is one of the most powerful people in the world. Not only is he the country's head of state, but he is also the chief executive, whose duty is to make sure the law of the land is carried out, and the

In the 1991 Gulf War the American Stealth bomber was almost invisible to radar because of its unusual "flying wing" shape.

EXPLORATION AND DISCOVERY

Place	Achievement	Explorer or discoverer	Date
Pacific Ocean	discovered	Vasco Núñez de Balboa (Sp.)	1513
World	circumnavigated	Ferdinand Magellan and Juan Sebastian del Cano (Port. for Sp.)	1519–1521
AFRICA			
Congo (river)	discovered	Diogo Cão (Port.)	c. 1483
Cape of Good Hope	sailed around	Bartolomeu Dias (Port.)	1488
Niger (river)	explored	Mungo Park (Scot.)	1795
Zambezi (river)	discovered	David Livingstone (Scot.)	1851
Sudan	explored	Heinrich Barth (Germ. for GB)	1852–1855
Victoria Falls	discovered	Livingstone	1855
Lake Tanganyika	discovered	Richard Burton & John Speke (GB)	1858
Congo (river)	traced	Sir Henry Stanley (GB)	1877
ASIA			
China	visited	Marco Polo (Ital.)	c. 1272
India (Cape route)	visited	Vasco da Gama (Port.)	1498
Japan	visited	St. Francis Xavier (Sp.)	1549
China	explored	Ferdinanad Richthofen (Germ.)	1868
NORTH AMERICA			
North America	discovered	Leif Ericsson (Norse)	c. 1000
West Indies	discovered	Christopher Columbus (Ital. for Sp.)	1492
Newfoundland	discovered	John Cabot (Ital. for Eng.)	1497
Mexico	conquered	Hernando Cortés (Sp.)	1519–1521
St. Lawrence (river)	explored	Jacques Cartier (Fr.)	1534–1536
Mississippi (river)	discovered	Hernando de Soto (Sp.)	1541
Canadian interior	explored	Samuel de Champlain (Fr.)	1603–1609
Hudson Bay	discovered	Henry Hudson (Eng.)	1610
Alaska	discovered	Vitus Bering (Dan. for Russ.)	1741
Mackenzie (river)	discovered	Sir Alexander Mackenzie (Scot.)	1789
SOUTH AMERICA			
South America	visited	Columbus	1498
Venezuela	explored	Alonso de Ojeda (Sp.)	1499
Brazil	discovered	Pedro Alvares Cabral (Port.)	1500
Río de la Plata	discovered	Juan de Solis (Sp.)	1516
Tierra del Fuego	discovered	Magellan	1520
Peru	conquered	Francisco Pizarro (Sp.)	1532–1538
Amazon (river)	explored	Francisco de Orellana (Sp.)	1541
Cape Horn	discovered	Willem Schouten (Dut.)	1616
AUSTRALASIA, POLAR REGIONS, etc.			
Greenland	visited	Eric the Red (Norse)	c. 986
Australia	discovered	unknown	1500s
Spitsbergen	discovered	Willem Barents (Dut.)	1596
Australia	visited	Abel Tasman (Dut.)	1642
New Zealand	sighted	Tasman	1642
New Zealand	visited	James Cook (Eng.)	1769
Antarctic Circle	crossed	Cook	1773
Antarctica	sighted	Nathaniel Palmer (U.S.)	1820
Antarctica	circumnavigated	Fabian von Bellingshausen (Russ.)	1819–1821
Australian interior	explored	Charles Sturt (G.B.)	1828
Antarctica	explored	Charles Wilkes (U.S.)	1838–1842
Australia	crossed (S–N)	Robert Burke (Ir.) & William Wills (Eng.)	1860–1861

A modern painting representing the Conquest of Mexico *by Hernando Cortés during the years 1519–1521. Cortés' horses and guns helped convince the Aztecs he was a god.*

Place	Achievement	Explorer or discoverer	Date
Greenland	explored	Fridtjof Nansen (Nor.)	1888
Arctic	explored	Abruzzi, Duke of the (Ital.)	1900
North Pole	reached	Robert Peary (U.S.)	1909
South Pole	reached	Roald Amundsen (Nor.)	1911
Antarctica	crossed	Sir Vivian Fuchs (Eng.)	1957–1958

commander-in-chief of the armed forces. Forty-one men have held this office since the first, George Washington, took the oath in 1789.

Past rulers of Britain held immense power, and were effectively dictators. After the Civil Wars of 1642–1651 they lost much of their power, and the rest was removed during the next hundred years. However, although the present Queen's duties are largely ceremonial; the government is carried on in her name. The monarch provides continuity, no matter which political party is in power.

Assassination is the murder of a political leader or any other public figure. These killings are carried out for revenge, to remove a tyrant or a political opponent, or

Above: *Ronald Reagan was succeeded as U.S. President by his two-term Vice-President, George Bush.*
Right: *George Washington (1732–99)*
Far right: *Thomas Jefferson (1743–1826)*

AMERICAN PRESIDENTS

President (party)	Term
1 Geroge Washington (F)	1789–1797
2 John Adams (F)	1797–1801
3 Thomas Jefferson (DR)	1801–1809
4 James Madison (DR)	1809–1817
5 James Monroe (DR)	1817–1825
6 John Quincy Adams (DR)	1825–1829
7 Andrew Jackson (D)	1829–1837
8 Martin Van Buren (D)	1837–1841
9 William H. Harrison* (W)	1841
10 John Tyler (W)	1841–1845
11 James K. Polk (D)	1845–1849
12 Zachary Taylor* (W)	1849–1850
13 Millard Fillmore (W)	1850–1853
14 Franklin Pierce (D)	1853–1857
15 James Buchanan (D)	1857–1861
16 Abraham Lincoln† (R)	1861–1865
17 Andrew Johnson (U)	1865–1869
18 Ulysses S. Grant (R)	1869–1877
19 Rutherford B. Hayes (R)	1877–1881
20 James A. Garfield† (R)	1881
21 Chester A. Arthur (R)	1881–1885
22 Grover Cleveland (D)	1885–1889
23 Benjamin Harrison (R)	1889–1893
24 Grover Cleveland (D)	1893–1897
25 William McKinley† (R)	1897–1901
26 Theodore Roosevelt (R)	1901–1909
27 William H. Taft (R)	1909–1913
28 Woodrow Wilson (D)	1913–1921
29 Warren G. Harding* (R)	1921–1923
30 Calvin Coolidge (R)	1923–1929
31 Herbert C. Hoover (R)	1929–1933
32 Franklin D. Roosevelt* (D)	1933–1945
33 Harry S. Truman (D)	1945–1953
34 Dwight D. Eisenhhower (R)	1953–1961
35 John F. Kennedy† (D)	1961–1963
36 Lyndon B. Johnson (D)	1963–1969
37 Richard M. Nixon (R)	1969–1974
38 Gerald R. Ford (R)	1974–1977
39 James E. Carter (D)	1977–1981
40 Ronald Reagan (R)	1981–1989
41 George H.W. Bush (R)	1989–

*Died in office. †Assassinated in office.
F = Federalist. DR = Democratic-Republican.
D = Democratic. W = Whig. R = Republican. U = Union.

BRITISH RULERS

Rulers of England

SAXONS

Egbert	827–839
Ethelwulf	839–858
Ethelbald	858–860
Ethelbert	860–866
Ethelred I	866–871
Alfred the Great	871–899
Edward the Elder	899–924
Athelstan	924–939
Edmund	939–946
Edred	946–955
Edwy	955–959
Edgar	959–975
Edward the Martyr	975–978
Ethelred II the Unready	978–1016
Edmund Ironside	1016

DANES

Canute	1016–1035
Harold I Harefoot	1035–1040
Hardicanute	1040–1042

SAXONS

Edward the Confessor	1042–1066
Harold II	1066

HOUSE OF NORMANDY

William I the Conqueror	1066–1087
William II	1087–1100
Henry I	1100–1135
Stephen	1135–1154

HOUSE OF PLANTAGENET

Henry II	1154–1189
Richard I	1189–1199
John	1199–1216
Henry III	1216–1272
Edward I	1272–1307
Edward II	1307–1327
Edward III	1327–1377
Richard II	1377–1399

HOUSE OF LANCASTER

Henry IV	1399–1413
Henry V	1413–1422
Henry VI	1422–1461

HOUSE OF YORK

Edward IV	1461–1483
Edward V	1483
Richard III	1483–1485

HOUSE OF TUDOR

Henry VII	1485–1509
Henry VIII	1509–1547
Edward VI	1547–1553
Jane	1553
Mary I	1553–1558
Elizabeth I	1558–1603

Henry VIII, painted by Holbein.

Rulers of Scotland

Malcolm II	1005–1034
Duncan I	1034–1040
Macbeth (usurper)	1040–1057
Malcolm III Canmore	1057–1093
Donald Bane	1093–1094
Duncan II	1094
Donald Bane (restored)	1094–1097
Edgar	1097–1107
Alexander I	1107–1124
David I	1124–1153
Malcolm IV	1153–1165
William the Lion	1165–1214
Alexander II	1214–1249
Alexander III	1249–1286
Margaret of Norway	1286–1290
(*Interregnum* 1290–1292)	
John Balliol	1292–1296
(*Interregnum* 1296–1306)	
Robert I (Bruce)	1306–1329
David II	1329–1371

HOUSE OF STUART

Robert II	1371–1390
Robert III	1390–1406
James I	1406–1437
James II	1437–1460
James III	1460–1488
James IV	1488–1513
James V	1513–1542
Mary	1542–1567
James VI*	1567–1625

*Became James 1 of Great Britain in 1603.

Rulers of Great Britain

HOUSE OF STUART

James I	1603–1625
Charles I	1625–1649
(*Commonwealth* 1649–1659)	

HOUSE OF STUART (restored)

Charles II	1660–1685
James II	1685–1688
William III ⎱ jointly	1689–1702
Mary II ⎰	1689–1694
Anne	1702–1714

HOUSE OF HANOVER

George I	1714–1727
George II	1727–1760
George III	1760–1820
George IV	1820–1830
William IV	1830–1837
Victoria	1837–1901

HOUSE OF SAXE-COBURG

Edward VII	1901–1910

HOUSE OF WINDSOR

George V	1910–1936
Edward VIII	1936
George VI	1936–1952
Elizabeth II	1952–

Queen Victoria (1819–1901) was to become Britain's longest-reigning monarch.

BRITISH PRIME MINISTERS

Prime Minister (party)	Term
Sir Robert Walpole (W)	1721–42
Earl of Wilmington (W)	1742–43
Henry Pelham (W)	1743–54
Duke of Newcastle (W)	1754–56
Duke of Devonshire (W)	1756–57
Duke of Newcastle (W)	1757–62
Earl of Bute (T)	1762–63
George Grenville (W)	1763–65
Marquess of Rockingham (W)	1765–66
Earl of Chatham (W)	1766–67
Duke of Grafton (W)	1767–70
Lord North (T)	1770–82
Marquess of Rockingham (W)	1782
Earl of Shelburne (W)	1782–83
Duke of Portland (Cln)	1783
William Pitt (T)	1783–1801
Henry Addington (T)	1801–04
William Pitt (T)	1804–06
Lord Grenville (W)	1806–07
Duke of Portland (T)	1807–09
Spencer Perceval (T)	1809–12
Earl of Liverpool (T)	1812–27
George Canning (T)	1827
Viscount Goderich (T)	1827–28
Duke of Wellington (T)	1828–30
Earl Grey (W)	1830–34
Viscount Melbourne (W)	1834
Sir Robert Peel (T)	1834–35
Viscount Melbourne (W)	1835–41
Sir Robert Peel (T)	1841–46
Lord John Russell (W)	1846–52
Earl of Derby (T)	1852
Earl of Aberdeen (P)	1852–55
Viscount Palmerston (L)	1855–58
Earl of Derby (C)	1858–59
Viscount Palmerston (L)	1859–65
Earl Russell (L)	1865–66
Earl of Derby (C)	1866–68
Benjamin Disraeli (C)	1868
William Gladstone (L)	1868–74
Benjamin Disraeli (C)	1874–80
William Gladstone (L)	1880–85
Marquess of Salisbury (C)	1885–86
William Gladstone (L)	1886
Marquess of Salisbury (C)	1886–92
William Gladstone (L)	1892–94
Earl of Rosebery (L)	1894–95
Marquess of Salisbury (C)	1895–1902
Arthur Balfour (C)	1902–05
Sir Henry Campbell-Bannerman (L)	1905–08
Herbert Asquith (L)	1908–15
Herbert Asquith (Cln)	1915–16

William Ewart Gladstone (1809–98), four times British prime minister.

Prime Minister (party)	Term
David Lloyd-George (Cln)	1916–22
Andrew Bonar Law (C)	1922–23
Stanley Baldwin (C)	1923–24
James Ramsay MacDonald (Lab)	1924
Stanley Baldwin (C)	1924–29
James Ramsay MacDonald (Lab)	1929–31
James Ramsay MacDonald (Cln)	1931–35
Stanley Baldwin (Cln)	1935–37
Neville Chamberlain (Cln)	1937–40
Winston Churchill (Cln)	1940–45
Winston Churchill (C)	1945
Clement Atlee (Lab)	1945–51
Sir Winston Churchill (C)	1951–55
Sir Anthony Eden (C)	1955–57

Prime Minister (party)	Term
Harold Macmillan (C)	1957–63
Sir Alec Douglas-Home (C)	1963–64
Harold Wilson (Lab)	1964–70
Edward Heath (C)	1970–74
Harold Wilson (Lab)	1974–76
James Callaghan (Lab)	1976–79
Margaret Thatcher (C)	1979–90
John Major (C)	1990–

W = *Whig.* T = *Tory.* Cln = *Coalition.*
P = *Peelite.* L = *Liberal.* C = *Conservative.*
Lab. = *Labor*

John Major's first months as British Prime Minister were dominated by the Gulf War.

AUSTRALIAN PRIME MINISTERS

Edmund Barton	1901–1903	Joseph A. Lyons	1932–1939
Alfred Deakin	1903–1904	Robert Gordon Menzies	1939–1941
John C. Watson	1904	Arthur William Fadden	1941
George Houston Reid	1904–1905	John Curtin	1941–1945
Alfred Deakin	1905–1908	Joseph Benedict Chifley	1945–1949
Andrew Fisher	1908–1909	Robert Gordon Menzies	1949–1966
Alfred Deakin	1909–1910	Harold Edward Holt	1966–1967
Andrew Fisher	1910–1913	John Grey Gorton	1968–1971
Joseph Cook	1913–1914	William McMahon	1971–1972
Andrew Fisher	1914–1915	Edward Gough Whitlam	1972–1975
William M. Hughes	1915–1923	John Malcolm Fraser	1975–1983
Stanley M. Bruce	1923–1929	Robert James Hawke	1983–1991
James H. Scullin	1929–1931	Paul Keating	1991–

PRIME MINISTERS OF NEW ZEALAND

Henry Sewell	1856
William Fox	1856
Edward William Stafford	1856–1861
William Fox	1861–1862
Alfred Domett	1862–1863
Frederick Whitaker	1863–1864
Frederick Aloysius Weld	1864–1865
Edward William Stafford	1865–1869
William Fox	1869–1872
Edward William Stafford	1872
George Marsden Waterhouse	1872–1873
William Fox	1873
Julius Vogel	1873–1875
Daniel Pollen	1875–1876
Julius Vogel	1876
Harry Albert Atkinson	1876–1877
George Grey	1877–1879
John Hall	1879–1882
Frederick Whitaker	1882–1883
Harry Albert Atkinson	1883–1884
Robert Stout	1884
Harry Albert Atkinson	1884
Robert Stout	1884–1887
Harry Albert Atkinson	1887–1891
John Ballance	1891–1893
Richard John Seddon	1893–1906
William Hall-Jones	1906
Joseph George Ward	1906–1912
Thomas Mackenzie	1912
William Ferguson Massey	1912–1925
Francis Henry Dillon Bell	1925
Joseph Gordon Coates	1925–1928
Joseph George Ward	1928–1930
George William Forbes	1930–1935
Michael J. Savage	1935–1940
Peter Fraser	1940–1949
Sidney J. Holland	1949–1957
Keith J. Holyoake	1957
Walter Nash	1957–1960
Keith J. Holyoake	1960–1972
Sir John Marshall	1972
Norman Kirk	1972–1974
Wallace Rowling	1974–1975
Robert Muldoon	1975–1984
David Lange	1984–1989
Geoffrey Palmer	1989–1990
Michael Moore	1990
James Bolger	1990–

CANADIAN PRIME MINISTERS

Sir John MacDonald	1867–1873
Alexander Mackenzie	1873–1878
Sir John MacDonald	1878–1891
Sir John Abbott	1891–1892
Sir John Thompson	1892–1894
Sir Mackenzie Bowell	1894–1896
Sir Charles Tupper	1896
Sir Wilfred Laurier	1896–1911
Sir Robert L. Borden	1911–1920
Arthur Meighen	1920–1921
W. L. Mackenzie King	1921–1930
R. B. Bennett	1930–1935
W. L. Mackenzie King	1935–1948
Louis St Laurent	1948–1957
John G. Diefenbaker	1957–1963
Lester B. Pearson	1963–1968
Pierre Elliott Trudeau (below)	1968–1979
Joe Clark	1979–1980
Pierre Elliott Trudeau	1980–1984
John Turner	1984
Brian Mulroney	1984–

In 1984 Brian Mulroney of the Progressive Conservative Party achieved a landslide victory to become Canada's Prime Minister.

CIVIL RIGHTS LEADERS

Ralph D. Abernathy	1926–
James Baldwin	1924–1987
Stokely Carmichael	1941–
Jesse L. Jackson	1941–
Mahalia Jackson	1911–1972
Martin Luther King Jr.	1929–1968
Rosa Lee Parks	1913–
Malcolm X	1925–1965

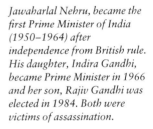

Assassination is the murder of a political leader or any other public figure. These killings are carried out for revenge, to remove a tyrant or a political opponent, or sometimes for financial gain. The word "assassin" originally meant an eater of hashish (a drug). A group of such drug-takers carried out many murders in Persia in the 1100s.

Assassinations have been a tragic feature all through history. One, the murder of Archduke Franz Ferdinand of Austria in 1914, sparked off World War I. Four U.S. presidents – Lincoln, Garfield, McKinley, and Kennedy – have been assassinated.

Perhaps the three most famous people to have been assassinated since the end of World War II are President Kennedy; Rev. Martin Luther King Jr., Black civil rights leader; and former Beatle, John Lennon.

Jawaharlal Nehru, became the first Prime Minister of India (1950–1964) after independence from British rule. His daughter, Indira Gandhi, became Prime Minister in 1966 and her son, Rajiv Gandhi was elected in 1984. Both were victims of assassination.

President Anwar El Sadat of Egypt worked for a peace treaty with Israel. He is shown here with former Israeli prime minister Yitzhak Rabin. Sadat was assassinated in 1981.

97

CHRONOLOGY OF WORLD HISTORY

BC

*c.***3500** Sumerians develop flourishing civilization along Euphrates River.

*c.***3400** Upper and Lower Egypt united to form one nation.

*c.***2100** Abraham migrates from Ur.

*c.***2000** Bronze Age begins in northern Europe.

*c.***1750** Hammurabi of Babylon draws up first known legal code.

1500s Shang Dynasty of China founded.

*c.***1020** Saul becomes first king of Israel.

*c.***1000** Chou dynasty founded in China.

1000–961 David king of Israel.

922 Death of David's son Solomon: kingdom divided into Judah and Israel.

700s Homer composes the *Iliad* and the *Odyssey* in ancient Greece.

776 Earliest known Olympic Games.

753 Traditional date of founding of Rome.

750 Phoenicians found Carthage.

1570 Hyksos invaders of Egypt defeated.

1450 Minoan civilization flourishes in Crete: begins to decline soon after.

1410 Reign of Amenhotep III of Egypt: golden age of nation at height.

1400 Beginning of Iron Age in India and Asia Minor (Turkey)

1358 Tutankhamen becomes pharaoh of Egypt: restores old religion destroyed by his predecessor Akhenaton.

1290–1224 Rameses II pharaoh of Egypt; Abu Simbel temple built.

1230–1200 Israelites leave Egypt and make their way to Canaan (Palestine).

*c.***1100** Assyrian empire founded in Mesopotamia.

The discovery of Tutankhamen's tomb in 1922 revealed the incredible wealth of the Egyptian Pharaohs.

722 Assyrians conquer Israel.

689 Assyrians capture and destroy Babylon.

670 Assyrians ravage Egypt; destruction of Thebes and Memphis.

626 Nabopolassar liberates Babylon from Assyrian rule and becomes king.

612 Babylonians, Medes, and Scythians overthrow Assyrian empire, destroying capital, Nineveh.

586 Nebuchadnezzar of Babylon seizes Jerusalem and takes people of Judah into captivity.

563 Siddhartha Gautama, later the Buddha, born at Lumbini, Nepal.

559–530 Reign of Cyrus the Great, founder of Persian empire.

551 Birth of K'ung Fu-tzu – Confucius, Chinese philosopher.

539 Jews allowed to return to Jerusalem; rebuilding of city begins.

525–404 Persians rule Egypt.

510 Last king of Rome, Tarquin, deposed; city becomes republic.

500 Ionian war (Persian War): Greek revolt against Persian rule.

494 Thirty cities of Latium form Latin League against Etruscans.

492 First Persian expedition against Athens ends when storm destroys Persian fleet.

490 Athenians crush second Persian expedition at Battle of Marathon.

486 Xerxes king of Persia.

480 Persian fleet defeated by Greeks at Battle of Salamis.

479 Greek soldiers rout Persians at Battle of Plataea; end of Persian attempt to subdue Greece.

460 Pericles becomes leader of Athenians.

431–421 Great Peloponnesian War between Athens and Sparta.

420–404 Second Peloponnesian War, ending with Spartan capture of Athens.

403 Thirty Tyrants seize power in Athens.

399 Philosopher Socrates put to death for teaching heresies to the young.

395–387 Corinthian War: coalition of Argos, Athens, Corinth, Thebes against Sparta.

391 Romans conquer Etruscans.

390 Gauls under Brennus sack Rome.

352–336 Philip II king of Macedon; rise of Macedon to power in Greece.

350 Persians suppress revolt of Jews.

338 Philip of Macedon conquers Greece.

336–323 Reign of Alexander III, the Great.

335 Alexander destroys Thebes.

332 Alexander conquers Egypt and Jerusalem, destroys Tyre.

331 Alexander overthrows Persian empire, defeating Darius III and capturing Babylon.

326 Greeks under Alexander extend empire to Indus river in what is now Pakistan.

323 Death of Alexander; birth of Euclid.

320 Egyptians under Pharaoh Ptolemy Soter capture Jerusalem.

305 Seleucus I Nicator founds Seleucid dynasty in Syria, Persia and Asia Minor.

305 Romans extend their rule over southern Italy.

301 Egyptians conquer Palestine.

295–294 Demetrius captures Athens and makes himself master of Greece.

290 Romans finally defeat Samnite attempt to usurp Roman power in Italy.

280 Achaean League of 12 Greek city-states formed.

274 Pyrrhus of Epirus conquers Macedonia; killed two years later.

264–241 First Punic War between Rome and Carthage; Carthage defeated ·

221 Ch'in dynasty (to 207); founded by Shih Huang-te, who builds the Great Wall.

The Great Wall of China runs for 1,500 miles (2,400 km) and is up to 30 ft. (9.1 m) high.

218–201 Second Punic War.

218 Carthaginians under Hannibal cross Alps to invade Italy; defeat Romans at Trebbia.

216 Hannibal defeats Romans at Cannae.

206 Romans under Scipio drive Carthaginians out of Spain.

202 Carthaginians defeated at Zama.

202 Han dynasty founded in China.

200–197 Romans drawn into war against Macedonia; Philip V of Macedon defeated.

192 Rome defeats Sparta.

182 Suicide of Hannibal to avoid capture by Romans.

171–168 Perseus of Macedonia attacks Rome and is defeated; Roman rule in Macedonia.

167 Antiochus IV Epiphanes of Syria persecutes Jews and desecrates Temple in Jerusalem.

166 Revolt of Jews under Judas Maccabeus against Antiochus.

153 Jews win independence from Syrian rule.

149–146 Third Punic War ends in destruction of Carthage.

88–82 Civil war in Rome; Lucius Cornelius Sulla emerges victor.

The most famous Roman – Julius Caesar (100–44 B.C.).

87 Sulla defeats attack by Mithradates, King of Pontus, and captures Athens.

86 Civil war in China.

82 Sulla dictator of Rome.

73–71 Revolt of gladiators and slaves under Spartacus; defeated by consuls Gnaeus Pompeius (Pompey) and Licinius Crassus.

65 Roman armies under Pompey invade Syria and Palestine.

63 Romans occupy Jerusalem.

61 Gaius Julius Caesar becomes Roman governor of Spain.

60 Pompey, Crassus, and Caesar form First Triumvirate to rule Rome.

58–51 Caesar conquers Gaul and invades Britain; British pay tribute to Rome.

53 Death of Crassus in battle.

52 Pompey appointed sole consul in Rome.

49 Caesar crosses Rubicon river in Italy to challenge Pompey for power.

48 Pompey, defeated at Pharsalus, flees to Egypt and is assassinated.

47 Caesar appoints Cleopatra and her brother Ptolemy XII joint rulers of Egypt; Cleopatra disposes of Ptolemy.

45 Caesar holds supreme power in Rome.

44 Brutus, Cassius, and others murder Caesar.

43 Mark Antony, Marcus Lepidus, and Caesar's nephew Octavian form Second Triumvirate.

43 Cleopatra queen of Egypt.

37 Mark Antony joins Cleopatra; prepares to attack Octavian.

31 Battle of Actium: Octavian's fleet defeats Antony and Cleopatra, who commit suicide. Rome conquers Egypt.

27 Octavian emperor of Rome, with title of Augustus.

6 Romans seize Judaea.

4 Birth of Jesus Christ at Bethlehem (probable date).

A.D.

9 Battle of Teutoburg Forest: German leader Arminius wipes out three Roman legions.

14 Augustus dies; succeeded by stepson Tiberius.

26 Pontius Pilate appointed Procurator of Judaea.

27 Baptism of Jesus by John the Baptist.

30 Jesus crucified on Pilate's orders on charge of sedition.

32 Saul of Tarsus converted; baptized as Paul.

37–41 Caligula emperor of Rome; orders Romans to worship him as god.

41–54 Claudius emperor of Rome.

43–51 Roman conquest of Britain under Aulus Plautius.

54–68 Reign of Emperor Nero.

64 Fire destroys Rome; Christians persecuted; St. Paul and St. Peter put to death.

65 Gospel of St. Mark probably written.

66–70 Revolt of Jews; subdued by Vespasian and his son Titus.

68 Suicide of Nero; Galba becomes Emperor of Rome.

69–79 Reign of Vespasian.

77–84 Roman conquest of northern Britain.

79 Vesuvius erupts, destroying Pompeii, Herculaneum, and Stabiae.

98–117 Reign of Trajan; Roman empire at greatest extent.

122 Emperor Hadrian (ruled 117–138) visits Britain; orders building of wall to keep out Picts and Scots.

132–135 Jewish revolt led by Simon Bar-Cochba suppressed; Romans disperse Jews from Palestine (*Diaspora*).

161–180 Marcus Aurelius emperor: Roman empire at its most united.

177 Increased persecution of Christians in Rome.

205–211 Revolts and invasions in Britain suppressed by Emperor Septimus Severus.

212 Emperor Caracalla (211–217) gives Roman citizenship to all free men in the empire.

220 Han dynasty in China ends; China frequently invaded over three centuries.

226 Artaxerxes founds new Persian empire.

249 Emperor Decius (249–251) inaugurates first general persecution of Christians.

253–259 Franks, Goths, and Alamanni cross empire's frontiers and invade Italy.

268 Goths sack Sparta, Corinth, Athens.

284–305 Reign of Diocletian.

285 Empire divided into West (based on Rome) and East (based on Nicomedia in Bythnia).

300–900 Maya empire flourishes in Central America.

*c.*300 Buddhism spreading throughout China.

303–313 New persecution of Christians.

306–337 Constantine the Great emperor of Rome.

313 Edict of Milan proclaims toleration for Christians throughout the Roman empire.

314 Council of Arles: meeting of Christian leaders at which Constantine presides.

320 Gupta empire founded in India.

324 Eastern and Western empires reunited under Constantine's rule.

325 First world council of Christian Church at Nicaea in Asia Minor.

330 Foundation of Constantinople on site of village of Byzantium, as capital of Roman Empire.

360 Huns invade Europe; Picts and Scots cross Hadrian's Wall to attack north Britain.

369 Picts and Scots driven out of Roman province of Britain.

378 Battle of Adrianople: Visigoths defeat and kill Emperor Valens, and ravage Balkans.

379–395 Reign of Theodosius the Great; on his death, Roman Empire is again split up.

407 Roman troops leave Britain to fight Barbarians in Gaul.

410 Goths under command of Alaric sack Rome.

425–450 Jutes, Angles, and Saxons invade Britain.

451 Battle of Châlons: Franks and allies defeat Attila the Hun.

476 Goths depose Emperor Romulus Augustus, ending western Roman empire; date generally regarded as beginning of Middle Ages.

481 Clovis king of Franks.

493 Theodoric the Ostrogoth conquers Italy.

496 Clovis converted to Christianity; increases Frankish power.

527–565 Justinian the Great, Byzantine (eastern Roman) emperor.

529–565 Justinian has Roman laws codified.

534 Franks conquer Burgundy.

534 Eastern Empire reconquers northern Africa from Vandals.

535 Byzantine troops occupy southern Italy.

550 St. David introduces Christianity into Wales.

552 Buddhism introduced into Japan.

554 Byzantine armies complete conquest of Italy

563 St. Columba preaches Christianity to the Picts in Scotland.

568 Lombards conquer north and central Italy.

570 Prophet Muhammad born at Mecca.

581 Sui dynasty founded in China.

590 Gregory the Great becomes pope.

597 St. Augustine converts southeastern England to Christianity for Rome.

611–622 Persians conquer Palestine and Egypt; Jerusalem sacked.

618 T'ang dynasty founded in China.

621 Visigoths drive Romans from Spain.

622 The Hegira: Muhammad flees from Mecca to Yathrib, afterward called Medina.

624 Japan adopts Buddhism.

625 Muhammad begins dictating material later gathered into the *Koran*.

622–630 Byzantine emperor Heraclius drives Persians from Egypt and Palestine.

628 Muhammad enunciates principles of Islamic faith.

632 Death of Muhammad.

An ivory chesspiece fashioned during the reign of Charlemagne, first ruler of the Holy Roman Empire (c. 742–814).

634–641 Muslim Arabs conquer Syria, Jerusalem, Mesopotamia, Egypt, and overthrow Persian empire.

634–642 Oswald, king of Northumbria, introduces Celtic Christian Church to northern England.

646 Taikwa, Japanese edict of reform; Japanese begin to copy Chinese culture.

664 Synod of Whitby: Oswy, king of Northumbria, joins England to Church of Rome.

711–715 Spain conquered by Moors.

712 Islamic state set up in Sind, now part of Pakistan.

717–718 Arab siege of Constantinople fails.

720 Moors invade France.

732 Charles Martel of Franks defeats Moorish invaders at Poitiers.

752 Pepin the Short elected king of Franks.

756 Donation of Pepin: Franks agree to pope's controlling central Italy.

771–814 Reign of Charlemagne, king of Franks.

773–774 Charlemagne conquers Lombardy.

778 Moors defeat Franks at Roncesvalles.

781 Christian missionaries reach China.

786–809 Rule of Harun Al-Raschid as Caliph of Baghdad.

787 First attacks by the Northmen (Vikings) on England.

800 Pope Leo III crowns Charlemagne as Roman Emperor of the West.

814 Division of Charlemagne's empire following his death.

827–839 Egbert, first Saxon king claiming to rule all England.

832 Muslims capture Sicily.

*c.*850 Jainism and Hinduism established as main religions of northern India.

871–899 Reign of Alfred the Great in southern England

874 Northmen begin settling in Iceland.

878 Treaty of Wedmore divides England between Saxons and Danes.

885 Paris besieged by Vikings.

896 Magyar tribes conquer Hungary.

906 Magyars begin invasion of Germany.

907 End of T'ang dynasty in China; civil war breaks out.

919–936 Reign of Henry I (the Fowler) of Germany.

926 Athelstan, king of England, conquers Wales and southern Scotland.

929 Wenceslaus of Bohemia – "good King Wenceslaus" – murdered by brother.

936–973 Reign of Otto I, the Great, of Germany.

955 Battle of the Lechfeld: Otto the Great repulses Magyars.

960 Sung dynasty founded in China.

962 Revival of Roman empire in West: Pope John XII crowns Otto of Germany as Holy Roman Emperor.

970 Foundation of Al-Azhar University in Cairo.

978 Ethelred II, the Redeless, becomes king of England.

986 Eric the Red founds colonies in

Greenland.

987 Hugh Capet elected king of Franks; Capetian dynasty founded.

994 London besieged by Olaf Trygvason of Norway and Sweyn of Denmark.

c.1000 Polynesian settlers reach New Zealand.

c.1000 Ancient Empire of Ghana flourished in west Africa.

c.1000 Leif Ericsson of Norway discovers Vinland in North America.

1004–1013 Danish attacks on England, bought off by Ethelred II.

1016 Canute also becomes king of England, deposing Ethelred.

1018 Canute (Cnut) becomes king of Denmark and Norway.

1040 Macbeth murders Duncan, king of Scots, and becomes king.

1042–1066 Edward the Confessor, son of Ethelred, king of England.

1048 Henry I wrests Normandy from elder brother Robert.

1057 Malcolm III Canmore becomes king of Scots, having killed Macbeth in 1057 in battle near Aberdeen.

1066 Harold II chosen king of England; invasion of England by William of Normandy, who seizes throne.

1075–1122 Struggle between popes and German emperors over right to appoint bishops.

1076 Pope Gregory VII excommunicates German Emperor Henry IV.

1077 Penance at Canossa: Henry submits to the Pope.

1084 Normans under Robert Guiscard sack Rome.

1096–1099 First Crusade to free Holy Land (Palestine) from Muslim rule; capture of Jerusalem.

1100 William II (Rufus) of England shot while hunting; brother Henry I becomes king.

1113 Order of the Knights of St. John founded.

1119 Order of Knights Templars founded.

1122 Concordat of Worms ends disputes between emperors and popes.

1147–1149 Second Crusade: Christian armies disagree and crusade fails.

1152–1190 Frederick I (Barbarossa) king of Germany and Holy Roman Emperor.

1154–1189 Reign of Henry II of England; much of France under English rule.

1174–1193 Rule of Saladin as Sultan of Egypt and Syria.

1180s Persecution of Jews in France.

1187 Saladin captures Jerusalem.

1189–1192 Third Crusade, led by Frederick Barbarossa, Philip II of France, and Richard I of England; Acre and Jaffa captured.

1192–1194 Richard of England prisoner of Leopold of Austria and Emperor Henry VI.

1197–1212 Civil war in Germany following death of Emperor Henry VI; ends with election of Frederick II (*Stupor Mundi*).

c.1200 Settlement of Mexico by Aztecs; Incas found their first kingdom in Peru.

1200–1669 German cities form Hanseatic League to promote their trade.

1202–1204 Fourth Crusade: Crusaders, in debt to Venice, capture Constantinople for Venetians.

1206 Mongol leader Temujin proclaimed *Genghis Khan* (Emperor within the seas).

1210 Francis of Assisi founds Franciscan order of monks.

1211–1222 Mongol invasion of China.

1212 Children's Crusade: 30,000 children from France and Germany set off to free Holy Land; many die.

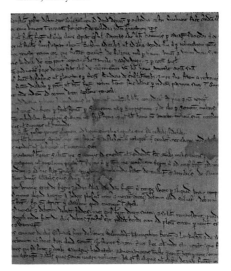

In 1215 King John was forced to sign the Magna Carta by his barons.

1215 King John of England agrees to Magna Carta, statement of the rights of his subjects.

1215 St. Dominic founds Dominican order of friars.

1217–1221 Fifth Crusade fails to liberate Holy Land.

1223 Mongol invasion of Russia.

1224 Carmelite order of friars founded.

1228–1229 Sixth Crusade led by Emperor Frederick II regains Jerusalem.

1238 Mongol warriors capture Moscow.

1240 Russian hero Alexander Nevsky defeats Swedish force at River Neva.

1241 "Golden Horde" Mongol kingdom established on banks of River Volga.

1244 Muslims recapture Jerusalem.

1249 St. Louis (Louis IX of France) leads Seventh Crusade; captured by Muslims and ransomed in 1254.

1256 Foundation of Augustinian order.

1260–1294 Kublai Khan becomes ruler of Mongol Empire and founds Yüan dynasty in China.

1268 Egyptians capture Antioch, held by Christians.

1270 Eighth and last Crusade, led by St. Louis, who dies during it.

1271–1295 Marco Polo visits court of Kublai Khan, travels in Asia, and returns to Venice.

1273 Rudolf I of Habsburg becomes Holy Roman Emperor, founding Habsburg dynasty.

1282 Edward I of England conquers Wales.

1290 Expulsion of Jews from England.

1295 First truly representative parliament summoned in England.

1301 Edward I of England creates his son Edward as the first Prince of Wales.

1302 Papal Bull *Unam sanctam* proclaims papal superiority over national rulers.

1306 Robert Bruce leads Scottish revolt against English rule.

1309–1378 Avignonese Papacy: seven popes based at Avignon in France because of unrest in Italy.

1314 Scotland becomes independent after Bruce defeats English at Battle of Bannockburn.

1325 Aztecs found Tenochtitlán, now Mexico City.

1332–1351 The Black Death (bubonic plague) ravages Europe, killing one in four.

1337 Hundred Years' War between England and France starts when Edward III of England takes title of King of France.

1339 English invasion of France begins.

1346 Edward III defeats French army at Battle of Crécy: long-bow proved to be the most formidable weapon.

1356 English under Edward the Black Prince capture John II of France at Battle of Poitiers.

1360 First part of Hundred Years' War ended by Treaty of Bretigny.

1368 Ming Dynasty begins in China.

1369 War breaks out again between England and France.

1369–1405 Reign of Tamerlane, Mongol ruler of Samarkand, and conqueror of much of southern Asia.

1371 Robert I becomes first Stuart king of Scotland.

1374 Peace between England and France, England having lost nearly all its French possessions.

1378–1417 The Great Schism: rival lines of popes elected, splitting the Church.

1384 Death of religious reformer John Wyclif.

1396 Bulgaria conquered by Ottoman Turks.

1397 Union of Kalmar: Denmark, Norway and Sweden united under one king.

1400 Welsh revolt led by Owen Glendower.

1414 Lollards (heretics) revolt against persecution in England.

1414–1417 Council of Constance called to heal Great Schism; Martin V elected pope.

1415 Henry V of England renews claim to French throne, and defeats French at Battle of Agincourt.

1420 Treaty of Troyes: Henry V acknowledged as heir to French throne.

1422 Deaths of Henry V and of Charles VI of France; renewed struggle for French throne.

During the War of the Roses the red rose was the badge of the Lancastrian side.

1429 Joan of Arc raises English siege of Orléans; Charles VII crowned king at Rheims.

1431 Joan of Arc burned as witch.

1437 Portuguese naval institute founded by Prince Henry the Navigator.

c.1450 Invention of printing from moveable type by Johannes Gutenberg.

1453 Hundred Years' War ends, leaving England with Calais as only French possession.

1453–1476 Inca empire in Peru at its height.

1453 Ottoman Turks capture Constantinople, ending Byzantine Empire; taken as the end of the Middle Ages.

1455–1485 Wars of the Roses: civil wars in England between rival families of York and Lancaster.

1461–1485 House of York triumphant in England.

1475 Edward IV of England invades France; bought off by Louis XI.

1479 Crowns of Castile and Aragon united, making Spain one country.

1480 Ivan III, first tsar (emperor) of Russia, makes himself independent of Mongols.

1483 Boy king Edward V of England deposed – possibly killed by uncle, Richard III.

1485 Richard III killed at Battle of Bosworth; Henry Tudor brings Lancastrians back to power as Henry VII.

1488 Bartolomeu Dias, Portuguese navigator, becomes first European to sail round Cape of Good Hope.

The Westminster Tournament Roll is a painting which commemorates a tournament held by Henry VIII in 1511 in honor of Catherine of Aragon. The illustration here shows the young King jousting.

1492 Spaniards finally drive Moors out of Granada, last Muslim province.

1492 Christopher Columbus discovers West Indies while searching for westward route to eastern Asia.

1497 John Cabot discovers Newfoundland; claims it for England.

1498 Vasco da Gama of Portugal discovers sea route to India by way of Cape of Good Hope.

1506 Work begins on St. Peter's Basilica, Rome; Donato Bramante, chief architect.

1508–1512 Michelangelo paints ceiling of Sistine Chapel in Vatican.

1516 African slave traffic to Americas begins.

1517 Beginning of Reformation: monk Martin Luther publishes *95 Theses* at Wittenberg, Germany.

1519–1555 Reign of Holy Roman Emperor Charles V, who has become king of Spain two years earlier.

1519–1521 First voyage around world; expedition led by Ferdinand Magellan, who dies during journey.

1519–1521 Conquest of Mexico by Spanish adventurer Hernán Cortés.

1520 Field of Cloth of Gold: meeting between Francis I of France and Henry VIII of England.

Luther nailed his arguments against the Church's practices to a church door in Wittenburg.

1521 Diet of Worms (church conference) condemns doctrines of Martin Luther.

1524–1525 Peasants' War: revolt of German peasants. Peasants defeated and punished.

1525 Battle of Pavia: Imperial forces defeat and capture Francis I of France.

1527 Sack of Rome by imperial forces; Pope Clement VII taken prisoner.

1529 Turkish armies advancing through Hungary besiege Vienna.

1530 Baber, founder of Mogul Empire in India, dies.

1532–1537 Spaniards under Francisco Pizarro conquer the Incas of Peru.

1533 Henry VIII of England excommunicated by pope for divorcing Catherine of Aragon.

1534 Act of Supremacy: Henry VIII assumes leadership of the Church in England, and breaks with Rome.

1534 Society of Jesus (Jesuits) founded by Ignatius Loyola.

1541 John Calvin takes Reformation movement to Geneva.

1545–1563 Council of Trent marks beginning of Counter-Reformation.

1549 Book of Common Prayer introduced in England.

1553–1558 Reign of Mary I brings England into reconciliation with Rome.

1558 French capture Calais, last English possession in France.

1558–1603 Reign of Elizabeth I in England; return to Protestantism.

1562–1598 Religious Wars in France between Roman Catholics and Huguenots (Protestants).

1567 Foundation of Rio de Janeiro.

1568 Mary, Queen of Scots, driven into exile; imprisoned by Elizabeth I of England.

1571 Battle of Lepanto: allied Christian fleet defeats Turkish fleet.

1572 Massacre of St. Bartholomew's Day in France; thousands of Huguenots killed.

1572 Active rebellion of the Netherlands against Spain begins.

1575 Bengal conquered by Akbar the Great.

1577–1580 Sir Francis Drake of England sails around the world.

1582 Pope Gregory XIII introduces reformed Gregorian calendar, which most Roman Catholic countries adopt.

1586–1589 War of the Three Henrys in France–Henry III, Henry of Navarre, Henry of Guise.

1587 Elizabeth I of England orders execution of Mary, Queen of Scots, found guilty of treason.

1587 Sir Francis Drake destroys Spanish fleet at Cádiz.

1588 Spanish Armada sets sail to invade England; defeated by English fleet.

1589 Assassination of Henry III of France;

1607 John Smith founds Colony of Virginia.

1609 Netherlands win independence from Spain.

1610 Henry IV of France assassinated; succeeded by Louis XIII, aged nine.

1610–1611 Henry Hudson discovers Hudson Bay; set adrift by his crew, following a mutiny.

1611 English and Scottish colonists begin settlement in Ulster.

1611 Publication of Authorized (King James) Version of the Bible.

1616 Dutch navigator Willem Schouten makes first ever voyage around Cape Horn.

1618–1648 Thirty Years War in Europe; begins with revolt by Protestants in Prague.

1620 Pilgrim Fathers sail to America in *Mayflower*.

1625–1649 Reign of Charles I in England.

1626 Dutch colony of New Amsterdam (now New York) founded.

1629 Massachusetts colony founded.

1631 First colonists settle in Maryland.

1631 Sack of Magdeburg by Tilly; defeat of Tilly by Gustavus Adolphus of Sweden at Battle of Leipzig.

1633 Colonists settle in Connecticut.

1638 Japanese massacre Christians, and stop all foreign visitors to country.

1639 Colonists settle in New Hampshire and Maine.

1640 Financial crisis in England: Charles I summons Long Parliament.

1641 French colonize Michigan.

Above: *Gustavus Adolphus of Sweden.*
Below: *In 1588 the Spanish Armada was heavily defeated at the hands of the British.*

1642–1646 Civil War in England; Parliament in revolt against Charles I.

1642 Abel Tasman discovers New Zealand.

1643–1715 Reign of Louis XIV of France.

1643 Manchu dynasty founded in China.

1647 Charles I flees to Isle of Wight.

1648 Peace of Westphalia: end of Thirty Years' War.

1648 Second Civil War in England; crushed by Parliamentary forces.

1649 Charles I tried and executed for treason; England a republic.

1650–1651 Charles II tries to regain throne, but is defeated by Oliver Cromwell.

1652 Dutch pioneer Jan van Riebeeck founds first European settlement in South Africa.

Peter the Great (1672–1725). He created a Russian navy, and under his rule Russia rose to be a power in western Europe.

1652–1654 War between Dutch and English.

1653 Oliver Cromwell becomes Lord Protector of England, Scotland, Ireland.

1660 Charles II restored to thrones of England and Scotland.

1665–1667 Second Anglo-Dutch War.

1665 New Jersey colony founded.

1665 Great Plague ravages London.

1666 London destroyed by fire.

1667–1668 War of Devolution between France and Spain.

1668 Spain recognizes Portuguese independence.

1672–1674 Third Anglo-Dutch War; France allied to England.

1685 Louis XIV of France revokes Edict of Nantes; Huguenots flee from France.

1688–1689 Glorious Revolution in England: Roman Catholic James II deposed; Parliament offers throne to William III of Orange and his wife, James's daughter Mary II. Bill of Rights defines liberties established by Glorious Revolution.

1689 France declares war on Spain and England.

1690 Battle of the Boyne: William III defeats James II, ending Stuart hopes.

1696–1725 Reign of Peter I, the Great, of Russia.

1698 Thomas Savery makes first effective steam engine in England.

1700–1721 Great Northern War: Sweden fights other Baltic states.

1702 William III dies; succeeded by Anne, the last of the Stuart monarchs.

1701–1713 War of the Spanish Succession.

1704 Britain captures Gibraltar.

1707 Formal union of England and Scotland.

1709 Battle of Poltava: Charles XII of Sweden beaten by Peter the Great.

1713 Height of slave trade between West Africa and the New World.

1714 Elector George of Hanover becomes King George I of England, ensuring Protestant succession.

1715–1774 Reign of Louis XV of France, great-grandson of Louis XIV.

1715 Jacobite (Stuart) rebellion in Britain fails.

1718 Quadruple Alliance of Britain, the Empire, France, and the Netherlands against Spain.

1721 Robert Walpole, world's first prime minister, becomes First Lord of the Treasury in Britain.

1733–1735 War of the Polish Succession.

1739 War of Jenkins' Ear between Britain and Spain.

1740–1786 Reign of Frederick II, the Great, of Prussia.

1740–1748 War of the Austrian Succession: dispute over Maria Theresa's right to inherit throne of Austria.

1745–1746 Second Jacobite rebellion in Britain fails.

1751 Robert Clive for Britain captures Arcot from French in India.

1755 Lisbon earthquake: 30,000 people die.

1756 Start of Seven Years' War; Britain, Hanover, and Prussia against Austria, France, Russia, and Sweden.

1756 Black Hole of Calcutta; 146 Britons imprisoned in small room – most die.

1759 British capture Quebec from French.

1760–1820 Reign of George III of Britain.

1762 War between Britain and Spain.

1763 Peace of Paris ends Seven Years' War.

1764 James Hargreaves invents the spinning jenny, marking start of Industrial Revolution in England.

1767 British government imposes import taxes on North American colonies.

1769 Richard Arkwright erects spinning mill.

1770 British navigator James Cook discovers New South Wales.

1770 Boston massacre: British troops fire on American mob, killing five people.

1773 Boston Tea Party, protest against tea tax.

1774 Joseph Priestly discovers oxygen.

1775–1783 American Revolutionary War.

1775 Battles of Lexington, Concord and Bunker Hill.

1776 Declaration of Independence.

1777 Battle of Saratoga: a British army surrenders to Americans.

1778–1779 War of the Bavarian Succession between Austria and Prussia.

1778 France declares war on Britain to support American colonies.

1779 Spain joins war against Britain.

1781 British forces surrender at Yorktown.

1783 Peace of Paris: Britain recognizes independence of United States of America.

1785 First balloon crossing of English Channel.

1788 United States adopts its constitution.

1789 George Washington first president of the United States.

1789–1799 French Revolution begins with the fall of the Bastille, a prison.

1790 Washington, D.C. founded.

1792 France proclaimed a republic; Louis XVI and family imprisoned.

1792–1799 War of the First Coalition: Austria, Britain, the Netherlands, Prussia, Spain against France.

1793 Louis XVI of France executed; Reign of Terror (to 1794).

1796–1797 Corsican general Napoleon Bonaparte conquers most of Italy for France.

1798 Napoleon Bonaparte in Egypt: cut off by Horatio Nelson's naval victory in Battle of the Nile.

1799 Coup d'état of Brumaire: Napoleon becomes First Consul of France.

1799–1801 War of the Second Coalition.

1800 British capture Malta.

1801 Britain and Ireland united.

1803 Louisiana Purchase: United States buys Louisiana territory from France.

1803 Robert Emmet leads Irish rebellion against the British.

1804 Napoleon crowned Emperor of France.

1805–1808 War of the Third Coalition: Austria, Britain, Naples, Russia, Sweden against France and Spain.

1805 Battle of Trafalgar: Nelson defeats French and Spanish fleets.

1805 Battle of Austerlitz: Napoleon defeats Austrians and Russians.

1806 Napoleon ends Holy Roman Empire, makes his brothers kings of Naples and Holland.

1807 Britain abolishes slave trading.

A detail from the The Declaration of Independence *by John Trumbull.*

1808–1814 Peninsular War in Spain and Portugal against French invaders.

1809–1825 Wars of Independence in Latin America.

1812 Napoleon invades Russia; forced to retreat, losing most of his army.

1812–1815 War between United States and Britain over searching of neutral shipping.

1813 Napoleon defeated at Battle of Leipzig; French driven from Spain.

1814 Napoleon abdicates; exiled to Elba.

1815 Napoleon tries to regain power; finally defeated at Battle of Waterloo and exiled to St. Helena.

1816 Argentina becomes independent.

1818 Chile becomes independent.

1819 United States gains Florida from Spain.

1821 Mexico and Peru gain independence.

1822 Greece and Brazil declare their independence.

1823 Monroe Doctrine: United States guarantees Western Hemisphere against European interference.

1825 First passenger railroad opens in England (Stockton to Darlington).

1825 Bolivia and Paraguay become independent.

1826 First photograph taken by Nicéphore Nièpce of France.

1830 July Revolution: Charles X of France deposed; Louis Philippe elected king.

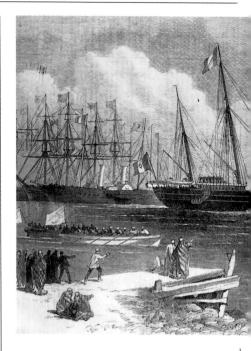

The Suez Canal was opened in 1869, opening up a faster sea route to the Orient.

1830 Belgium and Ecuador become independent.

1833 Slavery abolished in British colonies.

1836 Great Trek: Boer colonists move north from Cape Colony in South Africa. Texas achieves independence from Mexico.

1837–1901 Reign of Queen Victoria of Britain.

1839 Guatemala becomes a republic.

1840 Prepaid adhesive postage stamps introduced in Britain.

1841 New Zealand becomes British colony.

1841 Upper and Lower Canada united.

1842 China yields Hong Kong to Britain.

1845–1846 Great Famine in Ireland: a million people die, a million emigrate.

1848 Gold discovered in California.

1848 Year of Revolutions: in France, Berlin, Budapest, Milan, Naples, Prague, Rome, Venice, and Vienna.

1848 France becomes republic, with Louis Napoleon as president.

1848 Karl Marx and Friedrich Engels publish *Communist Manifesto*.

1849 Britain annexes Punjab.

1851 Australian gold rush begins.

1852 Napoleon III proclaimed Emperor of the French.

The Duke of Wellington (1769–1852) defeated Napoleon at Waterloo in 1815.

1896 Klondyke gold rush begins.

1898 Battle of Omdurman, Sudan: British forces defeat the Mahdi and his dervishes.

1898 Spanish-American War: United States wins Guam, Puerto Rico, and Philippines; Cuba wins independence.

1899–1902 Second Boer War; British victory.

1900 Boxer Rebellion in China.

1901 Australia becomes independent Commonwealth.

1901 First radio signals sent across Atlantic.

1903 Wright Brothers make first heavier-than-air flight.

1904–1905 Russo-Japanese War: Japan wins.

1905 Revolution in Russia: Tsar Nicholas II grants limited reforms.

1907 New Zealand becomes a Dominion.

1909 Robert Peary reaches North Pole.

1910 South Africa becomes a Dominion.

1911 Roald Amundsen reaches the South Pole.

1911–1912 Italo-Turkish War: Italy gains Tripoli and Cyrenaica.

1912 China proclaimed a republic.

1912–1913 First Balkan War.

The 1885 type Benz, recognized as the world's first true car.

1854–1856 Crimean War: Turkey, Britain, France, Sardinia against Russia.

1857–1858 Indian Mutiny; British government takes over rule from East India Company.

1861 Unification of Italy.

1861–1865 American Civil War over slavery; Southern states secede.

1863 Slavery abolished in United States; Battle of Gettysburg.

1865 Confederate General Robert E. Lee surrenders at Appomattox Court House.

1867 Canada proclaimed a Dominion.

1867 United States buys Alaska from Russia.

1867 Luxembourg becomes independent.

1868 Shogunate abolished; Meiji government begins to "westernize" Japan.

1869 Suez Canal opened.

1870–1871 Franco-Prussian War: fall of Napoleon III; France a republic again; Germany united under William of Prussia.

1876 Alexander Graham Bell invents the telephone.

1876 France and Britain take joint control of Egypt.

1877 Romania becomes independent.

1880–1881 First Boer War; Britain defeats Boer setters in South Africa.

1884 Leopold II of Belgium sets up private colony in the Congo.

1887 First automobiles built in Germany.

1913 Second Balkan War.

1914–1918 World War I: begun by assassination of Archduke Ferdinand of Austria at Sarajevo.

1914 Panama Canal completed

1915 Allies fail in Dardanelles campaign against Turkey.

1916 Easter Rebellion in Ireland fails.

1916 Battle of Jutland; defense of Verdun; Battle of the Somme; first use of tanks, by the British.

1917 Revolutions in Russia: Bolsheviks under Lenin seize control; United States enters the war; Battles of Aisne, Cambrai, Passchendaele.

Adolf Hitler's dream of a thousand-year German domination of Europe led to World War II.

1918 War ends after final German offensive fails; Germany becomes republic.

1920 League of Nations meets for first time; Americans refuse to join.

1920 Civil war in Ireland.

1921 Greece makes war on Turkey.

1921 Southern Ireland becomes a Dominion.

1922 Russia becomes the Union of Soviet Socialist Republics.

1922 Fresh civil war in Ireland.

1923 Turkey becomes a republic.

1924 First Labor government in Britain.

1926 General Strike in Britain.

1927 Charles Lindbergh makes first solo flight across Atlantic Ocean.

1929 Wall Street crash: start of world depression.

1933 Adolf Hitler becomes chancellor of Germany: burning of Reichstag.

1934 Hitler becomes Führer of Germany.

1935 Germany regains Saarland.

1935–1936 Italians conquer Ethiopia.

1936–1939 Civil War in Spain; Francisco Franco becomes dictator after Nationalists defeat Republicans.

1936 Germany reoccupies Rhineland.

1938 The Anschluss; Germany annexes Austria.

1938 Munich crisis: France, Britain, and Italy agree that Germany should take Sudetenland from Czechoslovakia.

1939 Germans occupy remainder of Czechoslovakia.

1939 Russo-German treaty.

1939–1945 World War II: Germany invades Poland; Britain and France declare war.

1940 Germans invade Denmark, Norway, Belgium, the Netherlands, and France; Britain and Empire left to carry on fight.

1940 Battle of Britain: German air attack fails.

1941 Germans invade Greece, Yugoslavia, and Russia.

1941 Japanese attack on Pearl Harbor brings United States into war.

1942 Japanese capture Malaya, Singapore, Burma, and Philippines; Battle of El Alamein in Egypt marks turning point in war.

1943 Allies invade North Africa, Sicily, and Italy; German army surrenders at Stalingrad (now Volgograd).

1944 Allies land in Normandy, liberating France and Belgium; major Russian attack begins.

1945 Germany overrun from east and west; Hitler commits suicide; atomic bombs on Japan end war in East.

1946 First session of United Nations General Assembly.

A "Memphis Belle". World War II was largely dominated by air power.

1947 India, Pakistan, and Burma independent.

1948 Israel becomes independent.

1948 Russians blockade West Berlin.

1949 North Atlantic Treaty Organization formed.

1949 Communist rule established in China.

1950–1953 Korean War: United Nations force helps defend South Korea.

1953 New Zealander Edmund Hillary and Sherpa Tenzing Norgay become first men to climb Mount Everest.

1954 The U.S. Supreme Court ruled compulsory segregation in public schools unconstitutional.

1954 French Indochina becomes independent countries of Laos, Cambodia, South Vietnam, and North Vietnam after fierce Communist attacks.

1956 Egypt becomes a republic; Suez Canal nationalized.

1956 Russia crushes Hungarian uprising.

1956 Morocco, Tunisia, Sudan all independent.

1957 European Common Market set up.

1957 Russia launches first spacecraft.

1957 Ghana and Malaysia independent.

1958 Guinea becomes independent.

1959 Fidel Castro establishes Communist rule in Cuba.

1960 Year of Independence for Cameroon, Central African Republic, Chad, Congo (Brazzaville), Congo (now Zaïre), Cyprus, Dahomey, Gabon, Ivory Coast, Madagascar, Mali, Mauritania, Niger, Nigeria, Senegal, Somalia, Togo, Upper Volta (Burkina Faso).

1960 Earthquake destroys Agadir.

1961 First man in space: Yuri Gagarin of the Soviet Union.

1961 Alan B. Shepard became the first American in space.

1961 Kuwait, Sierra Leone, Tanzania become independent.

1962 The Soviet Union removed missiles from Cuba, ending a threat of war with the United states.

1962 Independence of Algeria, Burundi, Jamaica, Rwanda, Trinidad and Tobago, Uganda.

1963 Assassination of U.S. President John F. Kennedy.

1964 Kenya achieves full independence.

1964 Malawi, Malta, and Zambia become independent.

1965 Gambia, Maldive Islands, Singapore become independent; Rhodesia proclaims own independence with White minority rule.

As president, John F. Kennedy (1917–1963) strived to solve America's social problems.

1967 Six-Day War: Israel defeats Arab countries.

1967 South Yemen becomes independent.

1968 Russian troops occupy Czechoslovakia.

1968 Independence of Nauru, Equatorial Guinea.

1969 First man on Moon (Neil Armstrong).

1969 Civil disturbances in Northern Ireland begin to escalate.

1970 Bloodless coup led by Lon Nol topples Cambodia's Prince Sihanouk.

1970 Guyana and Fiji become independent.

1971 East Pakistan rebels and becomes independent as Bangladesh; Qatar, Bahrain also independent.

1973 American forces end military intervention in Vietnam War.

1973 Independence of Bahamas.

1973 The October War: Arab states attack Israel; war halted after five weeks.

1973 Arab oil-producing states raise oil prices; world economic crisis begins.

1974 President Richard M. Nixon resigns because of Watergate scandal.

1974 Portugal's African colonies win independence agreement.

1975 Communists win decisive victories in Indochina: South Vietnam surrenders to North Vietnam.

1975 Independence of Papua New Guinea, São Tomé and Príncipe, and Angola.

1975 Reopening of Suez Canal to shipping

after years of closure.

1975 Death of Spanish dictator Francisco Franco; Prince Juan Carlos crowned King of Spain.

1976 North and South Vietnam reunified.

1976 Independence for the Seychelles within the British Commonwealth.

1976 Two earthquakes destroy mining town of Tangshan in China; more than 700,000 people die.

1976 Death of China's Chairman Mao Zedong.

1976 The United States celebrated its bicentennial.

1977 UN report tells of massacres and murders in Uganda under General Amin's rule (80,000–90,000 killed 1971–72).

1977 President Sadat of Egypt and Prime Minister Begin of Israel meet in attempt to gain peace for Middle East.

1979 Cambodia's capital, Phnom Penh, captured by Vietnamese and rebels.

1979 Kampala captured by Tanzanian troops and Ugandan exiles; General Amin forced to flee for his life.

1979 Shah of Iran deposed; exiled Muslim leader, the Ayatollah Khomeini, returns to Iran which is declared an Islamic Republic.

1979 Margaret Thatcher becomes Britain's first woman prime minister after Conservative election victory.

1979 Russian forces move into Afghanistan.

1980 Rhodesia becomes independent as Zimbabwe with Black majority rule.

1980 War begins between Iran and Iraq.

1981 Ronald Reagan becomes 40th President of the United States.

1981 American hostages in Iran freed.

1981 President Sadat of Egypt assassinated.

1981 Assassination attempts on President Reagan and Pope John Paul fail.

1982 Argentine annexation of Falkland Islands and South Georgia. British task force reoccupies them.

1983 Famine hits Ethiopia.

1983 Yuri Vladimirovich Andropov is elected president of the USSR.

1984 Yuri Andropov dies; is succeeded as Soviet leader by Konstantin Chernenko.

1984 Canadian PM Pierre Trudeau resigns.

1984 Indian PM Indira Gandhi assassinated.

1984 Chemical leak kills 2000 and injures 200,000 at Indian town of Bhopal.

1985 Konstantin Chernenko dies: succeeded as Soviet leader by Mikhail Gorbachev.

1985 British soccer fans riot in Brussels: England banned from European football.

1985 "Live Aid" concert raises $70 million for Ethiopia's starving people.

1986 Space shuttle *Challenger* explodes on launch, killing its crew of seven.

1986 Philippines President Marcos is expelled; succeeded by Mrs. Corazon Aquino.

1986 Nuclear reactor at Chernobyl, Ukraine, blazes; fall-out affects much of Europe.

1987 Ferry capsizes at Zeebrugge; 188 die.

1987 Worst storm for 200 years hits England, causes severe damage.

1987 The United States celebrated the bicentennial of the signing of the U.S. Constitution.

1987 World stock markets crash.

1988 Ceasefire halts Iran–Iraq War.

1988 Earthquake kills 45,000 people in Soviet Armenia, injures 20,000.

1988 Benazir Bhutto becomes PM of Pakistan; overthrown 1990.

1989 Emperor Hirohito of Japan dies.

1989 Kampuchea changes its name back to Cambodia.

1989 Chinese troops massacre student protesters in Beijing.

1989 Communist rule ends in Poland, Hungary, Czechoslovakia, Bulgaria, and East Germany; Berlin Wall goes.

1989 In a coup, President Ceausescu of Romania is overthrown and shot.

1990 African National Congress leader Nelson Mandela is freed from prison after 27 years.

1990 U.S. troops overthrow President Manuel Noriega of Panama.

1990 Soviet republics led by Lithuania, Russia, and Azerbaijan declare they want independence from the USSR.

1990 Romania declares Communism illegal.

1990 East and West Germany reunite.

1990 South Africa: ban on ANC and other political organizations is lifted.

1990 President Saddam Hussain of Iraq invades and annexes Kuwait; UN imposes sanctions and sends force to guard Saudi Arabia.

1990 President Gorbachev is given powers to westernize the ailing Soviet economy.

1991 UN force drives Iraqis out of Kuwait.

1991 Serbs and Croats fight in Yugoslavia. Soviet Union breaks up into independent states.

SEVEN WONDERS OF THE WORLD

Pyramids of Egypt Oldest and only surviving "wonder." Built in the 2000s B.C. as royal tombs, about 80 are still standing. The largest, the Great Pyramid of Cheops, at el-Gizeh, was 481 ft. (147 m) high.

Hanging Gardens of Babylon Terraced gardens adjoining Nebuchadnezzar's palace said to rise from 75–300 ft.(23–91 m). Supposedly built by the king about 600 B.C. to please his wife, a princess from the mountains, but they are also associated with the Assyrian Queen Semiramis.

Statue of Zeus at Olympia Carved by Phidias, the 40 ft. (12 m) statue marked the site of the original Olympic Games in the 400s B.C.. It was constructed of ivory and gold, and showed Zeus (Jupiter) on his throne.

Temple of Artemis (Diana) at Ephesus Constructed of Parian marble and more than 400 ft. (122 m) long with over 100 columns 60 ft. (18 m) high, it was begun about 350 B.C. and took some 120 years to build. Destroyed by the Goths in A.D 262.

Mausoleum at Halicarnassus Erected by queen Artemisia in memory of her husband King Mausolus of Caria (in Asia Minor), who died 353 B.C.. It stood 140 ft. (43 m) high. All that remains are a few pieces in the British Museum and the word "mausoleum" in the English language.

Colossus of Rhodes Gigantic bronze statue of sun-god Helios (or Apollo); stood about 117 ft. (36 m) high, dominating the harbor entrance at Rhodes. The sculptor Chares supposedly labored for 12 years before he completed it in 280 B.C.. It was destroyed by an earthquake in 224 B.C..

Pharos of Alexandria Marble lighthouse and watchtower built about 270 B.C. on the island of Pharos in Alexandria's harbor.

Statue of Zeus

Pharos of Alexandria

Pyramids of Egypt

Hanging gardens of Babylon

Mausoleum at Halicarnassus

Temple of Artemis

Colossus of Rhodes

Human Body

The human body is a miracle of coordination. The heart beats 70 times a minute pumping blood through the veins and arteries, taking life-giving oxygen to the brain. The body fights off infection and repairs itself: wounds can heal and broken bones knit together. Three billion of the body's cells die every minute and are replaced; only the brain cells cannot be renewed, but these last 100 years. The brain sends messages to our 639 muscles; these respond, moving our 206 bones to command. Our senses keep us in touch with the world.

The body is complicated and finely balanced. It is made up of many different parts; each has its own job and the healthy body depends on their all working together.

Australopithecus
4–1 million
years ago

Homo habilis
2–1.5 million
years ago

DNA double helix

HEREDITY

Heredity concerns the inheritance of characteristics from our parents' genes. The nucleus of all human cells (except eggs and sperm) contains 46 threadlike structures called **chromosomes**. These contain a chemical known as **DNA** (deoxyribonucleic acid), of which each molecule has a structure like a twisted ladder called a double helix (see right). The two parts of the "rungs" of this ladder are arranged in lots of different combinations which form coded instructions called **genes**.

We need to look after our body. We need to supply it with food, sleep, and exercise. However, much of the regular maintenance is done by the body itself.

People live in environments as different as the frozen wastes of the Arctic and the steaming jungles of South America. The human body can adjust to cope with most of the climatic conditions on Earth, keeping the body temperature constant and all the systems working.

The body is also very good at repairing accidental damage. If cut, it does its best to stop the bleeding, and for all small cuts the normal body can do so without help. The skin heals up, leaving perhaps a small scar. Broken bones knit together to form strong new ones. The body fights off infection, with the help of its immune system.

The development of the human species has taken millions of years. Our earliest human-like ancestors lived in Africa some 4 million years ago.

Homo erectus
1.5–0.1 million
years ago

Neanderthal man
100,000–35,000
years ago

Modern man
Some 100,000
years ago

Often, the work of doctors and surgeons is to give the body the best possible conditions to cure itself. Only when an injury is severe or a particularly virulent set of germs has invaded, are stronger methods needed, such as sewing up wounds, removing diseased tissue, or killing micro-organisms.

Occasionally, part of the body breaks down completely. Today, we are able to replace some organs by the process of transplant surgery; for example we can give people new hearts and lungs, kidneys or livers.

The body of an athlete is like a finely tuned engine. Training helps to develop body strengths and skills to a level far above the average.

Groups of organs working together to perform a particular task are called systems. These are the body's seven systems and their functions.

The skeletal-muscular system provides a protective framework for the body and the means for moving it about. Muscles, which are responsible for our movement, are attached to our bones.

The digestive system takes in food, processes it to keep the body running, and gets rid of waste material. It consists of a long tube that begins at the mouth and ends at the anus.

The urinary system balances the body's liquid intake. It plays a major part in clearing the body of waste products.

The respiratory system takes in oxygen every time you breathe in. Oxygen is needed by every part of the body.

When you breathe out, the gas carbon dioxide (a waste product) is cleared out of your body. The respiratory system also gets rid of some moisture.

The heart and circulatory system takes the oxygen from the respiratory system and sends it all around the body in the blood. The blood picks up carbon dioxide and takes it back to the heart, which transfers it to the lungs for disposal.

The nervous system is the body's control system. The brain is the control center, and nerves carry messages to and from the brain, all over the body. The messages travel along the nerve fibers in the form of electrical impulses. Some of the information received by the brain is stored as memory for future use.

The reproductive system is the means by which babies are produced to carry on the human race. As in other animals, a sperm cell from a male is united with an egg cell in a female to start the reproductive process.

Various organs of the body take part in one or more of these systems. The glands make chemical substances that the body needs in order to keep running. The sense organs – eyes, ears, nose, taste buds, and the sense of feeling in the skin – supply the brain with information about the world around the body.

There are still many things about the body that we do not fully understand. One of the most wonderful is the mechanism that controls how we grow and develop as children – and what makes us stop growing when we have reached full size.

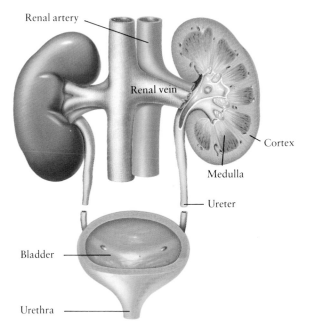

The urinary system. The two kidneys (one of which has been cut away to show its structure) act as filters removing waste products and excess water from the blood. Urine produced in this way drips down the ureters into the bladder.

119

THE SKELETON

The skeleton is the main framework that supports your body. It is built up of bones. All bones are made of the same substances, mostly calcium. Bones are hard on the outside, but have a hollow center, filled with a soft substance called bone marrow. This is where red and white cells of the blood are made.

There are several different kinds of bones in the skeleton. The arms and legs have long bones; ankles, wrists, hands, and feet have short bones; and the shoulder blades and the skull are made up of flat bones. Broken bones knit together again if they are set (aligned) correctly and held in place by a splint or plaster while the body repairs the break.

The bones are linked together by joints, which allow the skeleton to be flexible. Some are hinge joints, such as those at the knee; some are pivot joints, which allow the bones to rotate against one another – the elbow has pivot and hinge joints. Some are ball and socket joints, such as those at the hips and shoulders. Ball and socket joints allow movement in any direction.

The main structure of the skeleton is built around the spine or backbone, which consists of 26 separate bones called vertebrae, with soft disks of cartilage between them as padding. The joints of the spine bend less than many other joints, such as those of the arms and legs.

Below: The spine or backbone is made up of bones called vertebrae, protecting the nerves of the spinal cord.

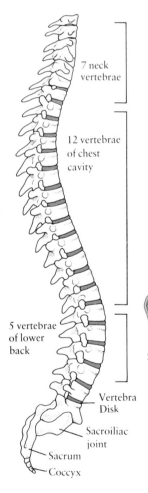

7 neck vertebrae

12 vertebrae of chest cavity

5 vertebrae of lower back

Vertebra Disk

Sacroiliac joint

Sacrum

Coccyx

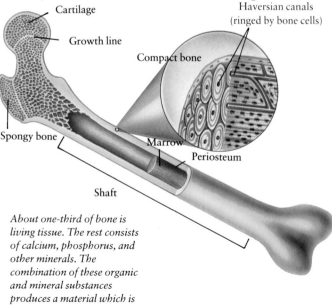

Cartilage

Growth line

Compact bone

Haversian canals (ringed by bone cells)

Spongy bone

Marrow

Periosteum

Shaft

About one-third of bone is living tissue. The rest consists of calcium, phosphorus, and other minerals. The combination of these organic and mineral substances produces a material which is hard and tough, yet elastic.

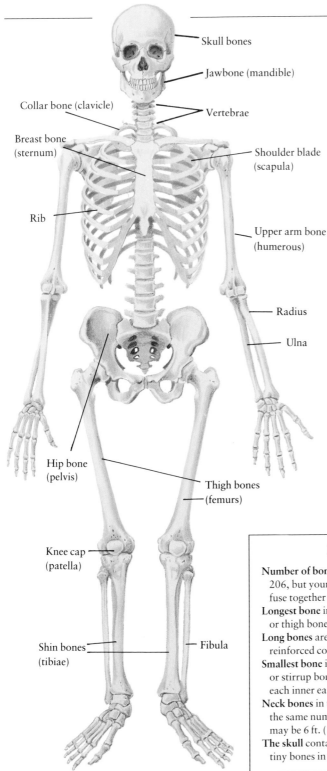

Skull bones

Jawbone (mandible)

Collar bone (clavicle)

Vertebrae

Breast bone
(sternum)

Shoulder blade
(scapula)

Rib

Upper arm bone
(humerous)

Radius

Ulna

Hip bone
(pelvis)

Thigh bones
(femurs)

Knee cap
(patella)

Shin bones
(tibiae)

Fibula

Left: *The skeleton is built of more than 200 rigid but living bones. It supports and protects the body yet it allows great freedom of movement. Without it, people would be shapeless blobs, unable to move.*

Below: *X rays are invisible waves that are used by doctors to examine the state of a patient's bones. The rays pass through the muscles, so a clear picture of the bone structure can be seen. The photograph below is an x ray of an adult's hand. It reveals the pattern of small bones that make the hand such a skillful part of the body.*

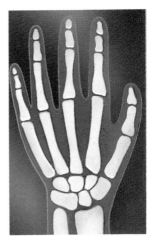

BONE FACTS

Number of bones in the adult human body is 206, but young children have more: the bones fuse together as children grow.

Longest bone in the human body is the femur, or thigh bone. It is also the strongest.

Long bones are much stronger and lighter than reinforced concrete.

Smallest bone in the human body is the stapes or stirrup bone, one of three tiny bones in each inner ear.

Neck bones in the human body total seven – the same number as in a giraffe, whose neck may be 6 ft. (1.8 m) long, or more.

The skull contains 22 bones, excluding the six tiny bones in the ears.

MUSCLES

Joints allow your bones to move, but the actual movements are produced by the muscles. Muscles are attached to your bones by strong bands of tissue called tendons. When muscles contract, they pull your bones. They can only pull, they cannot push, so most muscles come in pairs and work together to pull in turn. The brain sends them the instructions to contract or relax.

Muscle cells can shorten by up to one third of their length. When they contract they always shorten as much as they can. If all the cells in a muscle shorten at the same time the result is a jerky movement, as occurs when you snatch at something. But usually muscle cells contract in sequence, producing a smooth movement of the whole muscle.

There are three types of muscle in the human body. Most

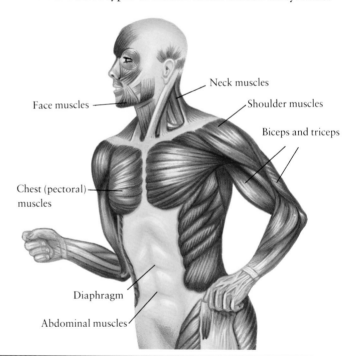

Neck muscles

Face muscles

Shoulder muscles

Biceps and triceps

Chest (pectoral) muscles

Beneath the skin many muscles are partially contracted and ready for movement. In addition to the muscles we can control, there are 30 more that work automatically. These are the muscles of the heart, lungs, and digestive system.

Diaphragm

Abdominal muscles

MUSCLE FACTS

Number of muscles in the human body totals 639.

Largest muscle is the gluteus maximus, found in the buttock. It extends the thigh or the trunk. Even when you are standing still, some muscles must contract to keep you upright.

Smallest muscle is the stapedius, a tiny muscle in the ear which controls movement of the stapes (stirrup bone).

Forty percent of your body weight consists of muscles.

Walking requires the use of 200 muscles.

muscles are long and thin, and are made up of many cells arranged in fibers. The kind of muscles that move your arms and legs are called skeletal or striped muscles, because they look striped under a microscope. These are the voluntary muscles under the direct control of the brain, such as those you use when walking.

Other muscles, such as the diaphragm, are flat sheets of tissue. Smooth muscles appear unstriped. These are the involuntary muscles, which work without direct control. They power all sorts of body functions, such as normal breathing and digestion, which must go on all the time whether you are awake or asleep. The third kind of muscle, found only in the heart, is a strong and specialized type called cardiac muscle.

Smooth muscles are made of short, unstriped cells with one nucleus in each cell. Cardiac or heart muscles have shorter, less striped cells, which contain only one nucleus. Striped or skeletal muscles have long striped cells with several nuclei in each cell.

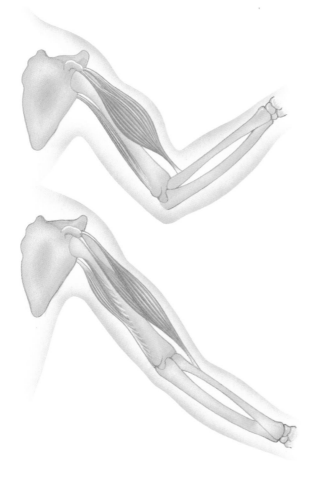

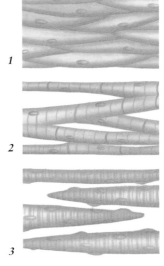

Muscles are made up of bundles of fibers. As the fibers contract, the muscles become shorter and thicker. The muscle fibers are made up of muscle cells. The muscles of the arm work in pairs. As one contracts the other relaxes, straightening and bending the arm.

Valves in the heart and veins control blood flow. Blood flowing forward forces valve flaps open.

Blood attempting to flow backward forces flaps to close.

Aorta

Vena cava

Artery

Lungs, Blood, and Heart

One substance that is essential for life is the gas oxygen, which forms about 21 percent of the air we breathe. Keeping the body supplied with oxygen is the work of the lungs and heart, with the help of the blood. Oxygen is drawn in by the lungs and transferred there to the blood. Blood is pumped around the body by the heart, carrying the oxygen to every living cell in the body.

When a person breathes in, the air is drawn through the nose and mouth. It passes down the trachea (windpipe), which branches into two tubes called bronchi. One bronchus leads to the left lung, the other to the right lung. In the lungs the bronchi branch into a mass of tiny twig-like bronchioles. The smallest bronchioles end in a bunch of tiny alveoli (air sacs). These absorb the oxygen from the air and pass it into the bloodstream.

The heart is a very efficient pump containing four chambers, the left and right atria at the top and the left and right ventricles below. Freshly oxygenated blood coming from the lungs flows into the left atrium. It is pumped through a one-way valve into the left ventricle, and then around the body.

Blood returning from the body has lost its oxygen, but contains a waste product, carbon dioxide gas. This used blood comes into the right atrium, and is pumped through a valve into the right ventricle, and thence to the lungs to have the carbon dioxide removed and more oxygen added.

The blood is carried around the body in a series of tubes called blood vessels. Fresh blood from the heart flows through blood vessels called arteries. As with any pipe system, the arteries start large, and branch into smaller and smaller vessels, and finally into thin blood vessels called capillaries. The capillaries have thin walls which allow oxygen and food substances in the blood to pass into the body cells, and waste products to be returned. Finally the blood flows back to the heart through a return system of veins.

Arteriole

Vein

Venule

The aorta is the main artery of the body. It carries fresh oxygentated blood from the heart. Its branches lead to all parts of the body.

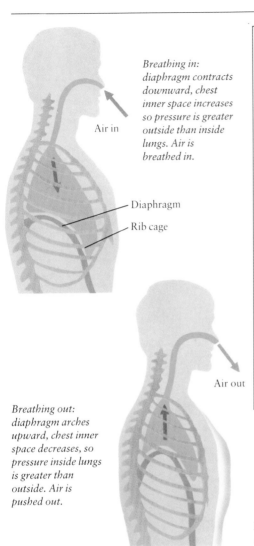

Breathing in: diaphragm contracts downward, chest inner space increases so pressure is greater outside than inside lungs. Air is breathed in.

Air in

Diaphragm

Rib cage

Air out

Breathing out: diaphragm arches upward, chest inner space decreases, so pressure inside lungs is greater than outside. Air is pushed out.

LUNG FACTS

The alveoli (air sacs) in the lungs total more than 300 million.

Walls of the air sacs cover between 600–1,000 sq. ft. (56 and 93 sq. m).

Capacity of an adult's lungs is about 5 pints (3 liters) of air.

Air is expelled and breathed in about 15 times a minute, about 1 pint (less than 0.5 liter) at a time.

The diaphragm can move as much as 2 in. (5 cm) when breathing deeply.

BLOOD FACTS

Volume of blood in an average-sized adult is about 1 gallon (5 liters). Smaller people have less, larger people more.

Total number of red cells in the blood of an average man is 25 trillion.

Blood groups There are four basic blood groups, A, AB, B, and O. World wide, Group O is the most common, but other groups are more common in various countries.

Total length of the blood vessels in an average-sized adult is about 100,000 miles (160,000 km).

HEART FACTS

The heart beats about 37 million times a year, or 70 times a minute.

The heart rests between beats; in a lifetime of 70 years, the total resting time is about 40 years.

Total weight of blood pumped every day by the heart is about 13 tons, or 3,000 gallons (13,640 liters)

Weight of the heart is about 11 oz. (310 g) for a man, 9 oz. (260 g) for a woman.

Largest artery is the aorta, which leaves the left ventricle of the heart. It is 1 in. (2.5 cm) across.

The Heart

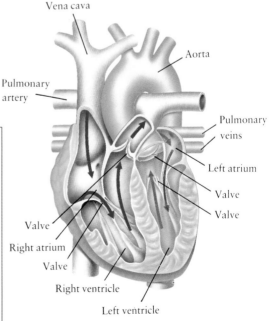

Vena cava

Aorta

Pulmonary artery

Pulmonary veins

Left atrium

Valve

Valve

Valve

Right atrium

Valve

Right ventricle

Left ventricle

125

Impulses from brain

Nucleus

Dendrites

Axon

Myelin sheath
(insulates axon)

Axon endings

A motor nerve (greatly enlarged). Motor nerves conduct messages in the form of electrical impulses, which travel from the brain to the muscles.

THE BRAIN AND THE SENSES

The brain, nerves, and senses are the great control and communications system of the body. The brain is located in the skull. Messages to it come from the five senses – sight, hearing, smell, taste, and feeling. They tell the brain what is happening outside the body. The brain processes this information and issues instructions to the rest of the body in response.

Nerves are long fibers made up of cells, or bundles of fibers. The brain is attached to the spinal cord, and the two together are known as the central nervous system. The rest of the nerves, which extend all over the body, form the peripheral (outer) nervous system. Sensory nerves carry messages from the sense organs to the brain, while motor nerves carry messages from the brain to the muscles.

As you read this page, your brain is combining the letters into words and sentences. Some of this information will be stored as memories. Your brain is also sending messages to control your breathing rate, digestion of your food, and many other body functions. Because of your nervous system, you know where you are and what you are doing.

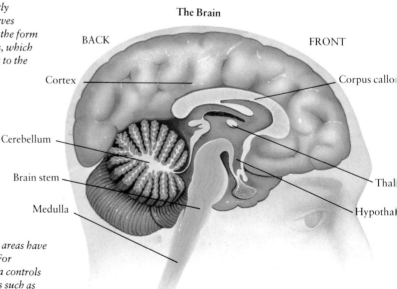

The Brain

BACK   FRONT

Cortex

Corpus callo[

Cerebellum

Brain stem

Medulla

Thal[

Hypotha[

The brain's different areas have different functions. For example, the medulla controls involuntary activities such as breathing. The largest area, the cortex, controls conscious feelings and voluntary movements and is responsible for intelligence and learning.

NERVOUS SYSTEM FACTS

Weight of an average adult brain is about 3 lb. (1.4 kg)

Total number of nerve cells in the brain is about 12 billion. Once growing is complete, thousands of cells are lost every day and not replaced.

Nerve impulses travel at slightly over 200 mph (320 km/h).

The spinal cord is about 17 in. (430 mm) long and about ¾ in. (20 mm) thick. It weighs about 1½ oz. (43 g), and contains 31 pairs of spinal nerves which control the body's muscles.

SENSES FACTS

Color vision is so sensitive that some people can distinguish as many as 300,000 different shades.

The human ear can distinguish more than 1500 different musical tones.

The spiral canal of the inner ear is about the size of a pea, but if uncoiled it would be about 38 mm (1½ in) long.

Taste buds on the tongue have specialized roles. Those on the tip detect sweet and salt flavours; those at the sides sour flavours; and those towards the back bitter flavours.

Our sense of smell helps us to taste things. Nerve fibers high in the nose pick up smells.

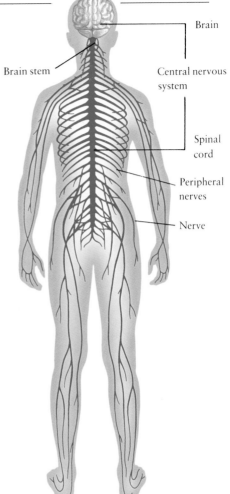

- Brain
- Central nervous system
- Brain stem
- Spinal cord
- Peripheral nerves
- Nerve

The Cortex

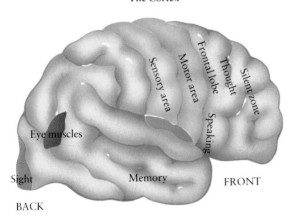

Sensory area
Motor area
Frontal lobe
Thought
Silent zone
Speaking
Eye muscles
Sight
Memory
FRONT
BACK

Above: *The brain sends nerve impulses through the nerves within the spinal cord.*

The cortex is the outer layer of a large, folded area called the cerebrum. The different functions of the cerebrum are shown above. The left side of the cortex controls the right side of the body. The right side controls the left. Sight, hearing, smell and taste are controlled from sensory areas. Motor areas send messages to other parts of the body.

127

Reproduction

A baby begins its life when a sperm cell from its father meets an ovum – an egg cell – from its mother inside the mother's body. When the ovum is fertilized by the sperm, the two cells unite to form one cell, which then divides until a ball of 64 cells attaches itself to the lining of the uterus. The baby develops very quickly and has all its organs after about 12 weeks.

The baby takes about nine months to become fully formed and ready to be born. At birth powerful muscles in the uterus (womb) contract and force the baby out through the mother's vagina.

It is possible to take an ultrasound picture of a baby in the womb. A scan may be given to check the size, health, and position of the baby, and to see if the mother is carrying twins. The scan uses waves to pick up the outline of the baby. It is a safer method than an x ray.

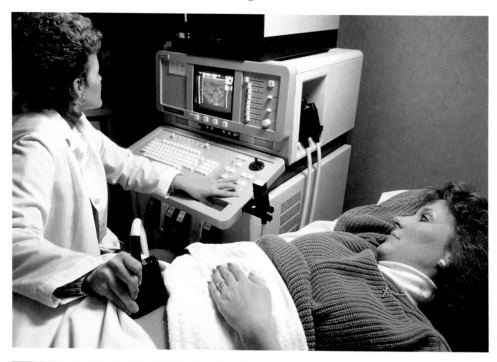

DID YOU KNOW?

The **uterus** is only about the size and shape of a pear, but during pregnancy it can stretch to about 12 in. (30 cm) in length.

The **epididymis** is nearly 20 ft. (6 m) long if uncoiled.

A **baby girl** is born with several thousand immature ova in her ovaries. Only a few hundred of these cells mature and are released during her lifetime.

The **testes** are outside the body in the scrotum because a cooler temperature helps the production of sperm.

An **ovum** from the mother and a **sperm** from the father each has 23 DNA-coded chromosomes in its nucleus.

A **mature sperm** is about $\frac{1}{500}$ in. ($\frac{1}{20}$ mm) long. Out of hundreds of millions of sperm released together, only one fertilizes the ovum.

REPRODUCTION GLOSSARY

afterbirth The discarded placenta.
amnion Protective "bag" filled with fluid in which the fetus develops.
cervix Opening at the bottom of the uterus.
copulation Sexual intercourse, after which a man's sperm may fertilize a woman's ovum.
embryo A baby in its first eight weeks of development.
epididymis Coiled tube in which sperm are stored.
fallopian tubes Pair of tubes leading from the ovary to the uterus.
fertilization Fusion of sperm and ovum.
fetus A developing baby after the first eight weeks.
labor The period during which the mother experiences contractions.
menstruation Monthly discharge of unfertilized egg and blood from the vagina.
ovaries Pair of organs in which a woman's egg cells are stored.
ovum (plural ova) The female egg cell.
penis Male external organ for passing water and copulation.
placenta Tissue that forms in the uterus to link the mother's blood supply to her baby.
pregnancy Condition in which a woman is carrying a baby.
scrotum The pouch of skin outside the body containing a man's testes.

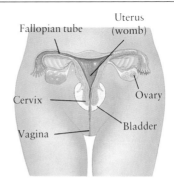

The reproductive organs of a woman. From puberty, a mature egg is released from the ovary every 28 days.

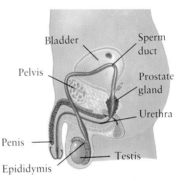

The reproductive organs of a man. Sperm are produced in the testes and mature in the epididymus. They travel to the penis in a fluid that is made in the seminal vesicles and prostate gland.

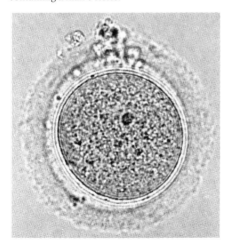

An ovum is about 0.008 inch (0.1–0.2 mm) in diameter. In just nine months, one fertilized ovum will divide to form the two million cells that make up the tissues, organs, and fluids of the new-born baby's body.

semen The mixture of sperm and special fluids produced by a man.
sperm The male reproductive cells.
testes (singular testis) Male organs in which sperm is produced.
twins Two children conceived at the same time; identical twins result from the splitting of an embryo at a very early stage; non-identical twins result from the fertilization of two ova.
umbilical cord Tube linking fetus to mother through the placenta.
urethra Tube inside the penis through which semen leaves a man's body.
uterus Hollow female organ where fertilization and development take place.
vagina in a woman, the canal leading from the cervix to the exterior of the body.
womb The uterus.

129

THE DIGESTIVE SYSTEM

The digestive system is the body's fuel processing plant. The food and drink you consume is turned partly into materials to rebuild and replace the body's cells, and partly into energy.

The body produces chemical substances called enzymes, which digest (break down) the food so it can be absorbed. Digestion begins in the mouth, where saliva contains the first of the many enzymes. In the stomach more chemicals are poured on the food to break it down still further. From the stomach the partly digested food goes through the long tube called the small intestine, where most digestion is done. Liquids are processed by the kidneys, which filter out any substances the body still needs.

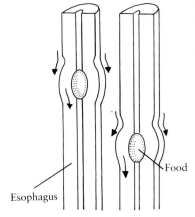

Esophagus

Food

Above: *The esophagus takes food from the mouth to the stomach.*
Right: *The stomach squeezes and moves food along, as gastric juices break down the food into a kind of soup. In the small intestine, bile and other juices mix with the soup. Fats, sugars, proteins, and vitamins move into the bloodstream. Finally water and waste move into the large intestine. Solid waste is evacuated by way of the rectum.*

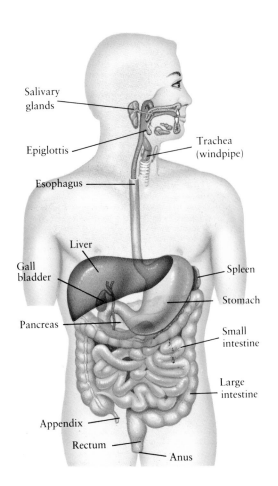

Salivary glands

Epiglottis

Trachea (windpipe)

Esophagus

Liver

Gall bladder

Spleen

Stomach

Pancreas

Small intestine

Large intestine

Appendix

Rectum

Anus

DIGESTION FACTS

The gullet, or esophagus, is a tube about 10 in. (250 mm) long and ½–1 in. (12.5–25 mm) in diameter. It takes food from the mouth to the stomach.

The stomach contains powerful hydrochloric acid, which breaks down food and kills germs; it is protected against the effects of this acid by a lining of mucus (a slimy substance which coats the walls).

The small intestine is about 20 ft. (6 m) long. It is about 1½ in. (35 mm) in diameter. Here food is digested and absorbed. Remaining material passes into the large intestine.

The large intestine is about 5 ft. (1.5 m) long and 2 in. (50 mm) in diameter. Much of the water from the undigested material is absorbed at this point.

The appendix is a thin pouch about 3½ in. (90 mm) long. It seems to have no function in the human digestive system, though it has an important role in grass-eating animals.

FOOD FACTS

Cholesterol, a fatty substance in eggs and animal products, may increase the risk of a heart attack.

Insufficient iron in the diet can lead to anemia, a blood deficiency. Iron is found in bread, meat, fruit, and vegetables.

Too much salt in the diet can lead to high blood pressure.

Scurvy, a disease producing swollen gums and inflamed skin spots, can result from not having enough Vitamin C (found in fruit and vegetables).

Certain foods should be eaten every day for a healthy diet and lifestyle:

Protein helps the body to build and repair itself. All protein contains *amino acids*, substances found in all living cells. Foods high in protein include meat, milk, fish, beans, and nuts. One should aim for two servings of protein a day.

Fats – eaten sensibly provide energy; they are found in butter, oil, and milk. Fat is stored in the body as a food reserve which the body can draw on when its daily food supply is not providing enough energy.

Carbohydrates also provide energy and are found in sugars, bread, and potatoes.

Fiber is found in wholewheat bread and raw vegetables – it helps digestion by providing the intestines with roughage.

HUMAN BODY GLOSSARY

abscess A painful, swollen area inside the body, caused by bacteria and filled with pus. A gumboil is a type of abscess caused by an infected tooth.

acne Spots, blackheads, or whiteheads caused by inflammation of the oil glands in the skin. Four out of five teenagers suffer from it.

Adam's apple The piece of cartilage which sticks out over the front of the larynx. It is more prominent in men than in women.

adenoids Small glands made of lymph tissue at the back of the nasal passages. They help to protect the lungs from infection.

adolescence Development from a child to an adult.

adrenaline A hormone which stimulates the heart and increases muscular strength and endurance.

allergy A reaction, such as a running nose, rash, or wheezing, caused when a person is sensitive to certain substances. Hay fever is an allergy to pollen.

amino acids The chemical substances which make up proteins. When protein in food is digested (broken down), the amino acids are transported around the body and assembled into new proteins in the cells.

antibiotics Drugs which can kill bacteria by preventing them from growing or reproducing.

antibodies Substances produced by the body's immune system. They destroy harmful bacteria and viruses.

antiseptics Substances which kill certain microorganisms or slow down their growth.

arteries Any blood vessels which carry blood away from the heart to the rest of the body.

bacteria Microscopic one-celled organisms found everywhere – in water, in soil, and on and in our bodies. Most are harmless; some are essential, such as those in the intestines; a few cause disease.

benign Word used to describe a tumor or growth which is harmless and not likely to become worse.

bile Greenish liquid produced by the liver. It is stored in a sac called the gall bladder and helps to digest fat in the small intestine.

blood vessel Any of the many tubes – arteries, veins and capillaries – that carry blood around the body.

bronchus One of the branches of the windpipe, leading to the lungs.

capillaries The smallest type of blood vessels.

cardiac Referring to the heart.

cartilage Soft, elastic tissue, often called gristle.
cells The basic living units of the body, sometimes called the "building blocks" of life. Every part of the body is made up of cells – one trillion of them in an average man.

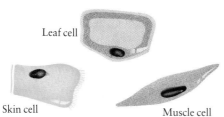

Leaf cell

Skin cell

Muscle cell

Cells in an animal's body lack the cellulose wall of a plant cell

central nervous system The brain and spinal cord.
chromosome One of 46 structures found in the nucleus of every human cell. Chromosomes carry the genes which determine inherited characteristics, such as sex, hair color, and height.
colon Lower part of the large intestine.
coronary Referring to the blood vessels that supply the heart. Coronary arteries over the surface of the heart provide oxygen for its cells.
diaphragm Flat muscle which separates the chest from the abdomen.
DNA (Deoxyribonucleic Acid) Complicated chemical that makes up genes and chromosomes.
enzymes Chemical substances that speed up chemical reactions within the body and control processes such as digestion.
epiglottis Small flap at the back of the tongue which blocks the windpipe when you swallow and so prevents food "going down the wrong way."
esophagus Gullet or food pipe leading from the throat to the stomach.
follicle Small pocket in the skin from which a single hair grows.
gall bladder Small sac, about 3–4 in. (80–100 mm) long, which stores bile.
genes Combinations of DNA which make up the chromosomes in each cell.
glands Organs in the body, such as the salivary glands, the kidneys, and liver, which produce or work on chemical substances.
hormones Sometimes called the body's chemical messengers; produced in certain glands and released into the blood. They control many body processes, such as growth or the amount of sugar in the blood.

immune system The body's own defenses against infection.
intestines The long tube, beginning at the stomach and ending at the anus, in which food is digested.
keratin The hard substance found in hair, nails, and skin.
kidneys Two organs that filter waste from the blood and produce urine, which collects in the bladder. They lie on either side of the spine.
larynx The voice box, located at the top of the trachea and containing the vocal cords.
ligaments Tough elastic bands of tissue which hold bones together at a joint.
liver the body's largest gland; it stores iron and some glucose, processes amino acids and produces bile.
lymph Clear liquid which contains white blood cells. It flows through a set of vessels (tubes) called the "lymphatic system."
marrow Soft, jellylike substance found in the center of bones; blood cells are made in some bone marrow.
membrane Thin layer of cells which lines or covers various parts of the body.
microorganisms Tiny living things such as bacteria and viruses; often called germs.
organ Group of tissues which work together, for example the heart or the liver.

The lymphatic system

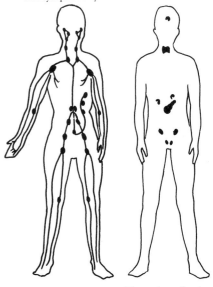

The main endocrine glands of the body

pancreas Gland which produces the hormone insulin, which controls the level of glucose in the blood.

plasma Liquid part of blood.

proteins Body-building chemicals, made of amino acids.

pulse Rhythmic throbbing which can be felt in the arteries as your heart beats.

pus Whitish-yellow liquid produced in certain infections.

reflex actions Actions that are automatic and cannot be controlled by thinking about them.

renal Referring to the kidneys.

respiration Breathing; also the use of oxygen in the cells to release energy from glucose, and the release of carbon dioxide.

saliva Liquid released by three pairs of glands in the mouth; it starts the process of digestion.

sebaceous gland Oil-producing gland in the skin.

sinuses Four sets of cavities in the skull, where the air you breathe in is warmed.

spinal cord Thick cord of nerves which begins at the base of the brain and extends to the bottom of the back.

spleen An organ that is part of the lymphatic system and helps to fight infection.

tendons Very strong bands of tissue which connect muscles to bones.

thymus Gland in the lower neck, which helps in the immune process.

thyroid Gland in the neck that produces a hormone, thyroxine, which controls growth rate and the speed of chemical processes.

tissues Groups of similar cells which form various parts of the body, such as nerves or muscles.

trachea Windpipe, leading from the larynx to the lungs.

tumor Swelling caused by abnormal growth of cells. It may be benign or cancerous.

ulcer Open sore on the skin, or on a membrane inside the body.

ureters Tubes which carry urine from the kidneys to the bladder.

urethra Tube which leads from the bladder to the outside of the body.

veins Blood vessels that carry used blood back to the heart.

viruses Micro-organisms that cause disease if they invade the body.

vitamins Group of about 15 substances found in food. They are needed for good health.

vocal cords Two ligaments stretched across the larynx. They vibrate as air passes over them, enabling speech.

AIDS

AIDS stands for Acquired Immune Deficiency Syndrome. It is a serious disorder brought about by a virus called Human Immunodeficiency Virus. It has this name because it attacks the white blood cells which form part of the body's immune system. This system guards the body against disease.

Cause is one of two viruses in the group called retroviruses.

Symptoms include diarrhea, fever, tiredness, night sweats, loss of appetite and weight, and enlarged lymph glands.

Transmission is by intimate sexual contact, or by exposure to infected blood (for example, by sharing hypodermic needles with an infected person). An infected woman who is pregnant can pass the virus to the fetus.

Treatment: no cure has yet been found.

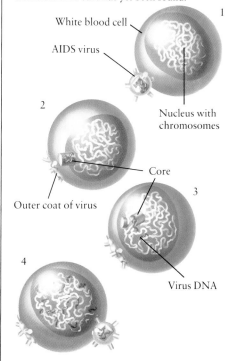

White blood cell

AIDS virus

Nucleus with chromosomes

Core

Outer coat of virus

Virus DNA

The AIDS virus prevents the white blood cells, the body's natural defense mechanism, from working. 1. The virus attaches itself to and 2. moves into a white blood cell. Once inside 3., the core of the virus breaks open and releases DNA to match that of the white blood cell. The blood cell makes copies of the virus and dies, reducing the body's defense.

The English naturalist, Charles Darwin (1809–82), put forward the theory that all living things have evolved (developed) over millions of years from primitive forms of life.

Below: *Darwin noticed differences in the finches that lived on several islands in the Pacific, and this led him to his theory of evolution which he called "natural selection".*

Animals

The last dinosaur died 65 million years ago, the dodo is dead, and other animals are in danger of extinction, yet there are still well over a million known species left, from the speedy cheetah to the tardy snail, and the egg-laying platypus to the remarkably skilled termite.

Animals dominate the Earth today. They have done so for only about 500 million years, a fraction of the Earth's 4.6 billion-year existence. The number of species (kinds) may well be as many as two million, and nobody can calculate how many different individuals there are.

Animal life became possible when the Earth built up a sufficient stock of oxygen, which all animals must breathe in order to live. Some, such as fish, extract oxygen from the waters of the oceans and rivers. Others draw it from the atmosphere. Animals also depend on plants for their food, either directly, as cows do, or indirectly, as flesh-eating animals such as lions and wolves do.

The easiest way to divide the many species of animals is into the vertebrates – those with backbones – and the invertebrates – those without.

The vertebrates are the "higher" animals, those with the most developed brains. They are, in ascending order of development, fishes, amphibians, reptiles, birds, and mammals. They include all the large animals which appear to rule the world. But they are not necessarily the most successful.

The invertebrates – all the rest – are much simpler creatures. Some, such as amoebas and sponges, are very simple indeed. Others, in particular the insects, are more complex and successful in finding food and habitats. There are more kinds of insects than of any other land-based creature. They make their homes almost everywhere on land, and if something can be eaten, an insect has evolved that can eat it. Most insects themselves are in danger of being eaten by some other creature.

Large numbers of animals live in the seas, which cover almost three-fourths of the Earth's surface. There are fish, and countless millions of invertebrates such as krill, squid, jellyfish, and other small creatures. All these animals take their oxygen from water. There are also a few mammals – whales, seals, and their relatives – which have moved from land to live in water. However, they still breathe air, so they have to surface regularly.

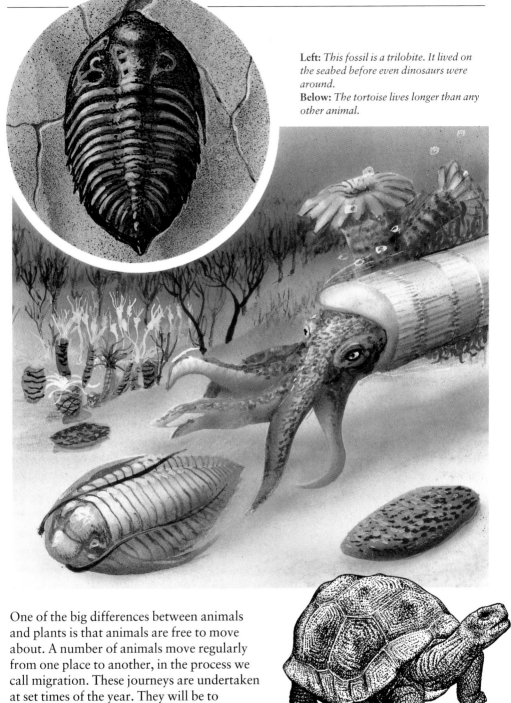

Left: *This fossil is a trilobite. It lived on the seabed before even dinosaurs were around.*
Below: *The tortoise lives longer than any other animal.*

One of the big differences between animals and plants is that animals are free to move about. A number of animals move regularly from one place to another, in the process we call migration. These journeys are undertaken at set times of the year. They will be to breeding or feeding grounds. For example, many of the great whales will travel from the Arctic or Antarctic to give birth in the warmer waters of the tropics.

135

The most obvious migration is that of birds. Many species spend the winter months in the warmer parts of the world, nearer the Equator, and fly north or south to temperate climates to lay their eggs and rear their young. Some insects migrate, notably the monarch butterflies of North America, which fly south to hibernate.

Some mammals also migrate. For example, in East Africa grazing animals – antelopes, zebras, giraffes and others – move in a huge circle to graze on fresh vegetation.

Fish also migrate. Young salmon swim down river to the sea. When full grown, they return to the river where they hatched, struggling up river to reach the breeding ground.

ANIMAL SPEED RECORDS*

	mph	km/h
Peregrine falcon	180	290
Spine-tailed swift	106	170
Sailfish	68	109
Cheetah	65	105
Pronghorn antelope	60	97
Racing pigeon	60	97
Lion	50	80
Gazelle	50	80
Hare	45	72
Zebra	40	64
Racehorse	40	64
Shark	40	64
Greyhound	39	63
Rabbit	35	56
Giraffe	32	51
Grizzly bear	30	48
Cat	30	48
Elephant	25	40
Bee	11	18
Pig	11	18
Chicken	9	14
Spider	1.17	1.88
Tortoise	0.5	0.8
Snail	0.03	0.05

* Maximum speeds over a short distance

Above: *The swifts include the world's fastest flyer in level flight. Swifts may spend weeks in the air, catching insects and even sleeping on the wing. Their small feet render them virtually helpless on level ground.*

Right: *An Arctic tern on its nest. On the long journey north or south, Arctic terns eat small fish, mollusks, crustaceans, and also insects.*

THE ANIMAL KINGDOM

Arthropoda: the largest animal phylum; includes arachnids, crustaceans, insects, and others.

Mollusca: the second-largest phylum; soft-bodied animals, most have a shell to protect them; includes snails, bivalves and octopuses.

Annelida: limbless animals; soft bodies, divided into segments; includes earthworms and their relatives.

Coelenterata: soft-bodied animals, most of which live in the sea; includes jellyfish, sea anemones, corals.

Protozoa: microscopic, single-celled animals; there are more than 30,000 kinds of protozoa.

Mammalia: mammals; warm-blooded animals with hair. Offspring are fed on milk from the mother.

Aves: birds; separated from all other animals by their feathers; all hatch from eggs and have wings.

Reptila: reptiles; scaly, cold-blooded animals; include lizards, snakes, crocodiles and tortoises.

Amphibia: cold-blooded animals which can breathe in water and on land; include frogs, toads, and newts.

Chordata: fish; all live in water, and swim with fins; almost all breathe through gills.

Aves

Arachnids

Crustaceans

Mammalia

Snails

Octopuses

Bivalves

Insects

Amphibia

Reptilia

Annelida

Coelenterata

Fishes

Echinoderms

Sponges

Protozoa

The main groups in the animal kingdom. Animals with one or more of the same body characteristics are separated into major groups called phyla. Animals with backbones (vertebrates) *plus a few other creatures belong to the phylum* Chordata. *All the other phyla contain more than 950,000 species of animals without backbones, called invertebrates.*

MIGRATION

Longest bird migration is by the Arctic tern (*Sterna paradisaea*), which leads a life of perpetual summer. It leaves the Arctic as summer ends and flies 11,000 miles (18,000 kilometers) to Antarctica. At the end of the Antarctic summer it flies back to its breeding ground – so making a round trip of 22,000 miles (36,000 kilometers).

Longest mammal migration is by the Alaska seal (*Callorhinus ursinus*), which does a round trip of 6,000 miles (9,600 kilometers).
Most traveled butterfly is the monarch butterfly (*Danaus plexippus*) of North America, which migrates 1,800 miles (3,000 kilometers) from Hudson Bay to Florida and back, stopping to lay its eggs on the way.

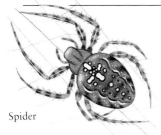

Spider

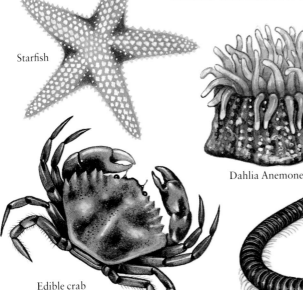

Millipede
and pill

Starfish

Dahlia Anemone

Edible crab

Centipede

ANIMALS WITHOUT BACKBONES

Animals without backbones are called *invertebrates*. Most of them do not have any form of internal skeleton, though some, such as the cuttlefish, have internal shells. Many have *exoskeletons* (external skeletons). Invertebrates range from sponges to insects, snails, and worms. Many of them live in water.

There are more than 20 *phyla* (groups) of invertebrates. Several of them are particularly important. The coelenterates include jellyfish, sea anemones, and corals. Mollusks mostly have shells. They include winkles, oysters, limpets, snails, octopuses, and squids.

Annelids are worms of various kinds, including the familiar earthworms. Arthropods (the name means "joint-footed") are very diverse indeed. They include insects, spiders, centipedes, millipedes, and crustaceans such as crabs, lobsters, and woodlice. Echinoderms are starlike animals with five limbs. They include starfish and sea urchins.

The chordates are a very mixed bunch. They have some kind of internal rod to support the body, although some lose it when they are adults. There are about 1,300 species which rank as invertebrates, including sea squirts and salps. The most important chordates are the vertebrates, or animals with true backbones.

The invertebrates make up over 95% of the million-plus existing animal species. The animals shown here, and the Portugese Man-o'-War shown on the opposite page, are all invertebrates.

138

INVERTEBRATE CLASSIFICATION

Phylum	Common name, if any	Number of species
Mesozoa	None	About 50
Porifera	Sponges	About 5,000
Coelenterata	Jellyfish and relatives	About 9,500
Ctenophora	Comb jellies	About 100
Platyhelminthes	Flatworms	About 15,000
Nemertea	Ribbonworms	750
Nematoda	Roundworms	10,000
Rotifera	Rotifers	2,000
Gastrotricha	Hairy backs	175
Kinorhyncha	None	100
Acanthocephala	Thorny-headed worms	300
Bryozoa	Moss animals	4,000
Brachiopoda	Lamp shells	260
Annelida	Earthworms and relatives	About 7,000
Arthropoda	Spiders, insects, crustaceans	About 1,150,000
Sipunculoidea	Peanut worms	250
Echiuroidea	Echiurid worms	60
Pentastomida	Tongue worms	70
Tardigrada	Water bears	180
Mollusca	Mollusks	More than 65,000
Chaetognatha	Arrow worms	65
Pogonophora	Beard worms	About 80
Echinodermata	Starfish and relatives	About 5,500
Hemichordata	Acorn worms and relatives	90
Chordata	Chordates	About 2,000 plus back-boned animals

Note: This list includes only the major phyla of invertebrates.

INVERTEBRATE RECORDS

Largest spiders are some of the bird-eating spiders (family Theraphosidae) of South America – bodies more than 3 in. (75 mm) long; leg span more than 10 in. (250 mm).

Largest centipede is the giant scolpender (*Scolpendra giganta*) of Central America – up to 12 in. (300 mm) long by 1 in. (25 mm).

Centipedes with most legs are those in the order Geophilomorpha. Adults may have up to 177 pairs of legs, or 354 legs altogether.

Millipedes have fewer than 1,000 legs, despite their name. Several species are known to have more than 700 legs. There are over 8,000 species throughout the world.

Wood Ant

INSECTS

Of all forms of life, the most varied are the insects. More than 1,000,000 species are known, and more are being discovered and classified every year. There are more species of insects than all of the rest of the animal kingdom put together. The number of individual insects is beyond calculation.

An adult insect has six legs, and a body in three sections with a hard outer casing. Most adult insects have wings. They have what are called compound eyes, which may have as many as 30,000 tiny lenses called facets. Each facet conveys a very small part of the whole picture to the insect's brain.

House fly   Common wasp   White-tailed bumblebee

Top: *Wood ants make their nests in wooded areas, covering the mounds with leaves and twigs.*
Above: *The housefly is a pest that carries disease.*
Right: *The wasp uses its sting to defend itself.*
Far right: *The white-tailed bumblebee often nests in old mouse holes.*

Insects have senses of smell and taste, and many kinds can hear, too. They have cold blood which may be colorless, green, or yellow.

Insects are grouped into 33 orders, each containing many families, genera, and species. Some orders of insects are little known, and have no common name.

Apterygote insects are the simplest kinds. They have no wings, and the young are similar in appearance to the adults, except in size. They include the familiar silverfish, which is often found in houses.

Exopterygote insects mostly have wings. They pass through three stages of development – egg, nymph, and adult. They include dragonflies, mayflies, and stoneflies, which pass their pre-adult life in water; grasshoppers; stick insects; cockroaches; termites; earwigs; lice; and the true bugs, including cicadas and aphids.

Endopterygote insects are often winged. They go through four stages of development: egg, larva, pupa, and adult. They include beetles, the most numerous of them all; butterflies and moths; true flies; bees, wasps, and ants which, with termites, are called the "social insects;" and caddis flies, whose larvae live in water.

INSECT RECORDS

Heaviest insects are several forms of beetles (order Coleoptera). They include the goliath beetles (genus *Goliathus*), the rhinoceros beetle (*Dynastes hercules*), and the longhorn beetle (*Titanus giganteus*), which have all been found at weights of around 3½ oz. (100 g).

Longest insects are varieties of stick insects (genera *Palophus* and *Pharnacia*), known to grow more than 12 in. (300 mm) long.

Smallest insects are the feather-winged beetles (family Ptiliidae), which are less than 1/100 in. (0.2 mm) long.

Most remarkable builders are various species of termites (order Isoptera). They build nests of soil that may be as much as 23 ft.(7 m) tall, with deep cellars as well. Many species build their nests with "air conditioning," while the compass termites of Australia (*Amitermes meridionalis*) build wedge-shaped mounds with the two short sides facing north-south, so the midday heat strikes as small a surface as possible.

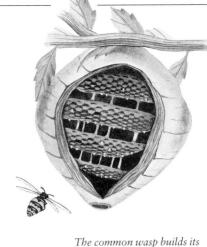

The common wasp builds its nest with paper, which it makes by chewing wood.

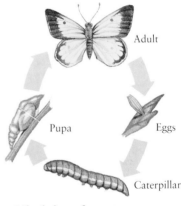

Adult

Pupa

Eggs

Caterpillar

Life of a butterfly

Caddis fly

The caddis fly is usually seen only at night. Its wings are clothed with hairs.
The great diving beetle is found mainly in ponds and streams.

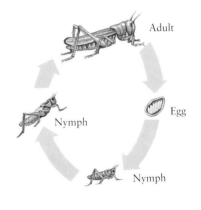

Adult

Nymph

Egg

Nymph

Lifecycle of a grasshopper

Great diving beetle

ANIMALS WITH BACKBONES

FISH

Fish form the largest group of vertebrates. There are altogether about 21,000 species. They fall into three groups: jawless fish, fish with skeletons of cartilage (gristle), and bony fish.

There are two main kinds of jawless fish – hagfish and lampreys. Instead of jaws they have circular mouths with rasping teeth. The cartilaginous fish, of which there are about 575 species, include chimaeras (better known as ratfishes or elephantfishes), sharks, and rays.

The bony fish are the most numerous. They include well-known species such as eels, herring, and salmon, as well as a large variety of lesser-known species.

Left: *The sea horse, despite its name, is a fish. It swims upright, propelled by its dorsal fin.*
Right: *Sting rays have whiplike tails armed with poisoned spines.*

Right: *The South American piranha is a small but ferocious feeder. Like the Glass Tetra, Schreitmuller's Metynnis, and the Bucktoothed Tetra (below), it is a member of the fish family* Characidae. *All members of this family have teeth and are meat-eaters.*

Bucktoothed

FISH RECORDS

Longest bony fish is probably the giant oarfish (*Regalecus glesne*), a rarely seen deepwater fish. Specimens have been known to reach a length of 30 ft. (9 m), and may be the origin of legends about sea serpents.

Heaviest bony fish is the ocean sunfish (*Mola mola*), which can weigh up to 2 tons. Found in all temperate and tropical oceans.

Smallest fish and also the smallest vertebrate is the dwarf goby (*Pandaka pygmaea*), found in fresh water in the Philippines and the Marshall Islands. The maximum size for these fish is ½ in. (12.5 mm).

Largest shark (and largest fish) is the whale shark (*Rhincodon typus*), which can reach a length of 50–60 ft. (15–18 m), and weigh 15 tons or more.

Largest rays are the devil rays in the family Mobulidae, which measure up to 20 ft. (6 m) across. They "fly" through the water by flapping their pectoral fins like wings. Some can even leap quite high into the air.

FISH CLASSIFICATION

Order	Common name	No. of species
CLASS AGNATHA – *jawless fish*		
Cyclostomata	Lampreys and hagfish	45
CLASS CHONDRICHTHYES – *fish with a cartilage skeleton*		
Lamniformes	Sharks	200
Rajiformes	Rays and skates	350
Chimaeriformes	Chimaeras	25
CLASS SARCOPTERYGII – *fish with fleshy fins*		
Crossopterygii	Coelacanth	1
Dipnoi	Lungfish	5

Order	Common name	No. of species
CLASS ACTINOPTERYGII – *fish with ray fins*		
Polypteriformes	Bichirs	12
Acipenseriformes	Sturgeons	22
Amiformes	Bowfin	1
Semionotiformes	Garpikes	7
Elopiformes	Tarpons	12
Anguilliformes	Eels	500
Notacanthiformes	Spiny eels	20
Clupeiformes	Herring and relatives	400
Osteoglossi-formes	Bony tongues	16
Mormyriformes	Mormyrids	150
Salmoniformes	Salmon, trout	1,000
Myctophiformes	Lantern fish	300
Ctenothrissi-formes	Macristid fish	1
Gonorhynchiformes	Milk fish	15
Cypriniformes	Carp and relatives	3,500
Siluriformes	Catfish	2,500
Percopsiformes	Pirate perch	10
Batrachoidi-formes	Toadfish	45
Gobiesociformes	Clingfish	100
Lophiiformes	Angler fish	200
Gadiformes	Cod and relatives	800
Beryciformes	Whalefish, squirrelfish	150
Atheriniformes	Flying fish, killifish	600
Zeiformes	John Dory	60
Lampridiformes	Ribbonfish	50
Gasterostei-formes	Seahorses and relatives	150
Channiformes	Snakeheads	5
Synbranchi-formes	Swamp eels and cuchias	7
Scorpaeniformes	Gurnards and relatives	700
Dactylopteri-formes	Flying gurnards	6
Pegasiformes	Sea moths, dragonfish	4
Tetraodonti-formes	Triggerfish, puffer fish	320
Pleuronecti-formes	Flatfish	500
Perciformes	Perch and relatives	6,500

Schreitmuller's Metynnis

Glass Tetra

South American piranha

Above: *The plains spadefoot toad of North America has a wedge-shaped "spade" on its hind feet.*
Below: *The Hermann's tortoise has a particularly solid shell.*
Below, center: *The slow worm is not a worm, but a lizard without legs.*
Below right: *The coral snake is related to the cobra. It is brightly colored and highly poisonous.*

AMPHIBIANS AND REPTILES

Amphibians – animals with backbones that can live both in water and air – are the last survivors of the first true land vertebrates that ever existed. They have cold blood – that is, they take their body temperatures from their surroundings.

There are three orders of amphibians, with a total of over 3,000 species. They are caecilians (simple wormlike creatures); newts and salamanders; and toads and frogs. Most amphibians lay their eggs in water. The eggs hatch into a larval form called a tadpole.

Reptiles are cold-blooded, air-breathing animals with backbones. There are 6,000 species alive today.

Reptiles vary in size from 2 in. (50 millimeters) long to more than 30 ft. (9 meters). They usually have scaly skins and most of them lay eggs. A few give birth to live young. They have lungs, like mammals, and most of them are carnivores.

There are four living orders of reptiles: alligators and crocodiles; tuataras (of which only one species exists); tortoises, terrapins, and turtles; and lizards and snakes.

SNAKE NOTES

Skin is changed several times a year by a process known as sloughing. The snake slips out of its old skin, revealing the new one beneath.

Breathing for most snakes is done on one lung only. The left lung is either greatly reduced in size or missing altogether.

Pit vipers have sense organs that can detect heat. These organs help them detect their prey.

Gastric juices in a snake can digest bones and teeth – but not hair and fur.

Burrowing snakes burrow into the ground. They feed largely on ants and termites.

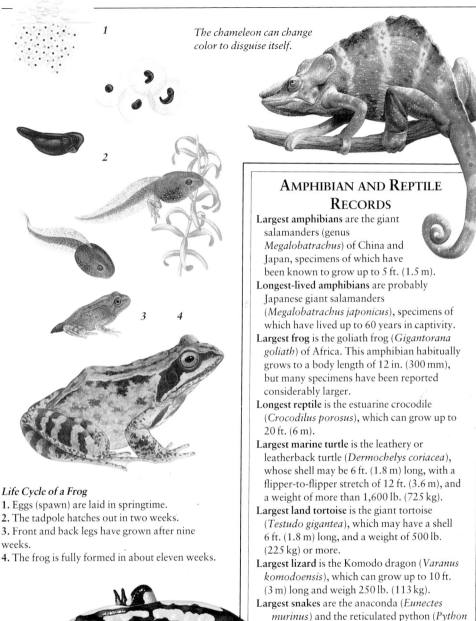

1

The chameleon can change color to disguise itself.

2

3   4

Life Cycle of a Frog
1. Eggs (spawn) are laid in springtime.
2. The tadpole hatches out in two weeks.
3. Front and back legs have grown after nine weeks.
4. The frog is fully formed in about eleven weeks.

The fire salamander gives off unpleasant skin secretions.

AMPHIBIAN AND REPTILE RECORDS

Largest amphibians are the giant salamanders (genus *Megalobatrachus*) of China and Japan, specimens of which have been known to grow up to 5 ft. (1.5 m).

Longest-lived amphibians are probably Japanese giant salamanders (*Megalobatrachus japonicus*), specimens of which have lived up to 60 years in captivity.

Largest frog is the goliath frog (*Gigantorana goliath*) of Africa. This amphibian habitually grows to a body length of 12 in. (300 mm), but many specimens have been reported considerably larger.

Longest reptile is the estuarine crocodile (*Crocodilus porosus*), which can grow up to 20 ft. (6 m).

Largest marine turtle is the leathery or leatherback turtle (*Dermochelys coriacea*), whose shell may be 6 ft. (1.8 m) long, with a flipper-to-flipper stretch of 12 ft. (3.6 m), and a weight of more than 1,600 lb. (725 kg).

Largest land tortoise is the giant tortoise (*Testudo gigantea*), which may have a shell 6 ft. (1.8 m) long, and a weight of 500 lb. (225 kg) or more.

Largest lizard is the Komodo dragon (*Varanus komodoensis*), which can grow up to 10 ft. (3 m) long and weigh 250 lb. (113 kg).

Largest snakes are the anaconda (*Eunectes murinus*) and the reticulated python (*Python reticulatus*), both of which are reported to grow up to 30 ft. (9 m) long.

BIRDS

Birds are animals with feathers, wings and beaks. Nearly all of them can fly. They are warm-blooded – they make their heat from the food they eat and they lay eggs.

There are about 8,600 species of birds, and they are grouped into 27 orders. Birds can be classified in many different ways. Water-birds spend their lives on or near water. They include wildfowl – ducks, geese, and swans – waders, gulls, albatrosses, and penguins.

Perching birds are land-based birds that spend their lives in trees or other high places when they are not flying. Game birds include chicken, guinea fowl, partridges, and turkeys. Birds of prey hunt other birds and small mammals. They

There are over 300 species of hummingbird. They are small birds and are expert flyers. They can hover, move up, down, sideways, and even backward – their wings beating at up to 100 times a second.

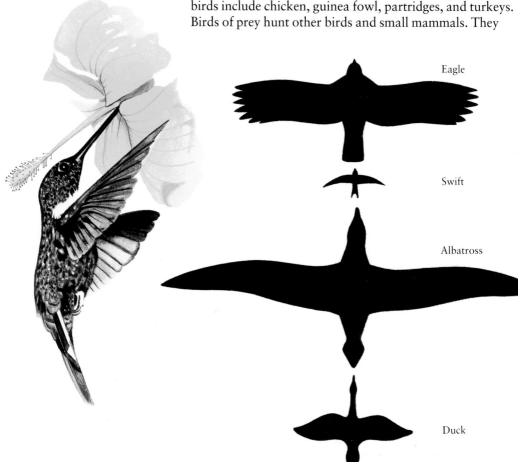

Eagle

Swift

Albatross

Duck

The broad wings of an eagle allow it to soar high up in the sky.
The narrow, pointed wings of a swift enable it to fly and turn quickly to catch insects in flight.

Albatrosses can glide for days with the help of their long wings.
The short, wide, and powerful wings of a duck give it plenty of lift, so it can leave the water quickly if disturbed.

include eagles, hawks, and vultures. Owls, which are mostly night-flying, also hunt game.

Birds are directly descended from reptiles. They have some links with their ancestors: many birds have scales on their legs, like those of reptiles, while their feathers are made of the same substance – keratin – as scales.

Feathers grow unevenly on a bird's body. Some parts are well covered, others are lightly protected. Flight feathers grow on the wings, contour feathers cover the body, and downy feathers are found on the breast. A bird may have between 1,300 and 12,000 feathers. Their most important job is to do with flight. Strong, long, tail and wing feathers provide the life. Body feathers give the bird a streamlined shape to allow it to move through the air easily. Some species of bird have brilliantly colored feathers which are important signals in the bird's social life. Other birds have dull feathers which help them to hide from predators.

Birds have a light skeleton to make flight easier. The bones of the body are hollow with struts inside to strengthen them. All flying birds have a large breastbone to which the strong wing muscles are attached.

Above: *Just before the female hornbill of Africa and Asia lays her eggs, the male seals her inside the nest by plastering up the entrance with mud.*

BIRD RECORDS

Largest bird is the male African ostrich (*Struthio camelus*), which grows to a height of about 8 ft. (2.5 m). Specimens have been found weighing as much as 340 lb. (155 kg).

Heaviest flying birds are the Kori bustard (*Choriotis kori*) of Africa, and the mute swan (*Cygnus olor*) of Europe, which may weigh as much as 40 lb. (18 kg).

Smallest bird is the bee hummingbird (*Calyptae helenae*) of Cuba. It is about 2¼ in. (60 mm) long and weighs only about 0.07 oz. (2 g). Its nest would fit into half a walnut shell.

Greatest wingspan belongs to the male wandering albatross (*Diomedea exulans*) which has an average wingspan of 10 ft. (3 m). It can stay in the air for days.

Fastest fliers include the peregrine falcon, duck hawks, and golden eagles, which dive at speeds estimated at up to 180 mph (290 km/h). Some spine-tailed swifts have been known to fly at speeds of up to 106 mph (170 km/h).

Fastest runner is the ostrich, which can maintain a speed of 34 mph (55 km/h), with bursts up to 50 mph (80 km/h).

The sparrow is found worldwide, usually close to human settlement.

There are 87 species of kingfisher found all over the world. They have a long, slender beak and most of them are fisheaters. The kookaburra of Australia is one exception.

Right: *The European cuckoo lays her eggs in the nests of other birds. When a young cuckoo hatches, it gets rid of any eggs or young birds in the nest. The foster parents do not realize that it is not one of their own hatchlings.*

Below: *The pelican uses the pouch beneath its large bill when catching fish.*
Below right: *A gentoo penguin. Penguins are flightless, but excellent swimmers.*

BIRD CLASSIFICATION

Order	Common name	No. of species	Order	Common name	No. of species
Passeriformes	Perching birds; passerines	5,100	Gruiformes	Cranes and relatives	197
Piciformes	Woodpeckers and relatives	400	Galliformes	Game birds	250
Coraciiformes	Kingfishers and relatives	190	Falconiformes	Birds of prey	271
Coliformes	Mousebirds	6	Anseriformes	Ducks and relatives	148
Trogoniformes	Trogons	36	Ciconiiformes	Storks and relatives	115
Apodiformes	Swifts and hummingbirds	400	Pelecaniformes	Pelicans and relatives	59
Caprimulgiformes	Nightjars and relatives	94	Procellariiformes	Albatrosses and relatives	91
Strigiformes	Owls	130	Sphenisciformes	Penguins	18
Cuculiformes	Cuckoos and relatives	147	Gaviiformes	Divers	5
Psittaciformes	Parrot family	315	Podicipediformes	Grebes	21
Columbiformes	Pigeons and relatives	300	Tinamiformes	Tinamous	50
			Casuariiformes	Emu and cassowaries	4
Charadriiformes	Gulls and relatives (mainly waders)	300	Rheiiformes	Rheas	2
			Struthioniformes	Ostrich	1
			Dinornithiormes	Kiwis	1

The owl is a nocturnal hunter, with superb hearing and night vision. Owls range in size from slightly bigger than a sparrow to almost as big as an eagle.

Barb

Barbule

Shaft

Contour feathers, like the one shown here, cover the outer body of the bird and give it a smooth shape.

149

Mammals

Mammals are animals whose females feed their young on milk from their *mammary glands* (breasts). Most mammals retain their young inside their bodies for a period of development. A few, called the monotremes – platypuses and echidnas – lay eggs. Some, known as the marsupials, such as kangaroos and wombats, give birth to young that are only partly developed and have to crawl into a pouch on the mother's belly to carry on growing.

Even among the other mammals, the young vary in how developed they are when they are born. Some newly-born animals, such as antelopes and horses, can get to their feet and walk within an hour or so of being born. Others, such as puppies and kittens, can do nothing for themselves for some days.

Elephants grow slowly and are among the longest-lived of animals. They are classed in an order of their own and are highly intelligent, vegetarian, and extremely social.

The basic mammal type is an animal with four legs, breathing air, possessing hair, and having warm blood. But there are exceptions in the groups of sea mammals. Seals have four flippers instead of legs, while whales (with their relatives, dolphins and porpoises) and sea-cows have just one pair of flippers.

DOGS

All the members of the dog family, Canidae, belong to the carnivores, the flesh-eaters. They tend to hunt in packs. The domestic dog, *Canis familiaris*, is the best known member of the family. There are more than 100 breeds of domestic dogs. They are probably all originally descended from the wolf.

CLASSIFICATION OF MAMMALS

There are about 4,000 species of mammals, grouped into 19 orders and about 120 families.

Order	Animals	No. of species
Monotremata	Egg-laying mammals – the platypus and echidnas	6
Marsupialia	Pouched mammals, including kangaroos, opossums, koalas	238
Insectivora	Insect-eating animals including hedgehogs, moles, and shrews	293
Chiroptera	Bats, the only mammals that can really fly	690
Primates	Lemurs, monkeys, apes, humans	171
Edentata	Anteaters, armadillos, sloths	30
Pholidota	Pangolins (scaly anteaters)	7
Dermoptera	Flying lemurs	2
Rodentia	Rodents, gnawing animals, including beavers, capybara, hamsters, mice, porcupines, rats, squirrels	1,792
Lagomorpha	Hares, pikas, rabbits	64
Cetacea	Whales, dolphins, porpoises	82
Carnivora	Flesh-eating animals such as bears, cats, dogs, pandas, raccoons	245
Pinnepedia	Seals, sea lions, walrus	32
Artiodactyla	Hoofed mammals with an even number of toes, including antelopes, camels, cattle, deer, giraffe, hippopotamuses, pigs	377
Perissodactyla	Hoofed mammals with an odd number of toes – rhinoceroses, horses, and zebras, tapirs	15
Sirenia	Water mammals – dugong, manatees	4
Tubulidentata	The aardvark	1
Hyracoidea	Hyraxes	6
Proboscidea	Elephants	2

Wild rabbit. Hares and rabbits belong to the order Lagomorpha.

Curiosity

Happiness

Fear

Excitement

Wild dogs are found in India, Siberia, southeastern Asia, southern and eastern Africa, Brazil, and the Guianas. The Australian dingo is a semi-wild dog that may have been domesticated a long time ago. Other members of the dog family include the North American coyote, fennecs, foxes, jackals, and wolves.

THE CAT FAMILY

Cats are the most purely carnivorous carnivores. They have teeth for stabbing and slicing, but not for chewing. Their lithe bodies are built for speed, and their sharp claws are further formidable weapons. The lion of Africa is only a larger version of the small domestic cat. All cats belong to one family, Felidae.

Chimpanzees are highly developed social animals. Each individual has a personality, and a chimp's facial expression reveals its emotions. Four typical expressions are shown here.

BEARS

Bears may look friendly and cuddly; in fact they are among the most ferocious of animals. Although they do not usually attack people, they can be dangerous if provoked.

Brown bears live in Europe and Asia. Their close relatives are the large grizzly bears (*Ursus horribilis*) and Kodiak bears (*Ursus middendorffi*) of North America. Polar bears (*Thalarctos maritimus*) live around the coasts of the Arctic Ocean.

The koala is a member of the marsupial group of mammals. It is found only in east Australia.

HYENAS

Hyenas (family Hyaenidae) have a bad reputation as cowardly, ugly animals. This is partly because they eat the leftovers of bigger predators such as lions. But, like all scavengers, hyenas perform a useful function, helping to clear up meat that would otherwise turn rotten. There are three species. The spotted hyena makes a strange laughing cry.

CUD-CHEWING ANIMALS

Most of the hoofed animals with even numbers of toes belong to the group known as the ruminants, or cud-chewers. They bolt the grass they eat, and later bring it back to the mouth for chewing. They include antelopes, cattle, deer, giraffes, goats, sheep, and yaks.

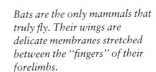

Bats are the only mammals that truly fly. Their wings are delicate membranes stretched between the "fingers" of their forelimbs.

THE POUCHED MAMMALS

Marsupials are mammals whose females have a *marsupium*, a pouch in which to carry their young while they finish developing. They are found only in Australia, New Guinea, and South America, with a few – the Virginia opossums – in North America. They include bandicoots, kangaroos and wallabies, koalas, numbats, and wombats.

The females do not lay eggs but the young are born very early in their development. They crawl through their mother's fur into the pouch where they attach themselves to a teat. They stay there for several weeks until they are developed enough to explore outside the pouch.

BATS

Bats (order Chiroptera) are the only mammals that have mastered the art of powered flight, though several other animals, such as flying squirrels and flying phalangers, can glide. Bats' hands have greatly lengthened fingers, connected with thin membranes of skin to form wings. There are two main kinds of bats. Fruit bats are the largest bats; they fly by day. Insect-eating bats are mostly small and feed at night, catching insects on the wing. They use a form of sonar to detect and catch their prey.

INSECT-EATERS

Insectivores are mostly small animals and include such familiar types as shrews and hedgehogs. Hedgehogs (family Erinaceidae), are animals with a forest of prickly spines all over their backs and sides. True shrews (family Soricidae) are small animals that work and rest on a three-hour shift pattern, day and night. Moles (family Talpidae) are insectivores but eat mostly earthworms.

DINOSAURS

Coelophysis, an early dinosaur from North America, had long legs and a very long neck and tail. It was a meat-eater, and might even have been a cannibal.

In the long course of evolution, many more species of animals have come and gone than are alive today. The most fascinating were the dinosaurs, the huge reptiles that dominated the Earth for about 135 million years, until they all died out about 65 million years ago. A few dinosaurs were quite small.

A GLOSSARY OF DINOSAURS

Allosaurus Huge meat-eating dinosaur over 30 ft. (9 m) long which ran on powerful hind legs.

Ankylosaurus One of the most heavily armored dinosaurs, with bony plates and spikes.

Brachiosaurus Dinosaur which resembled Brontosaurus but was even larger. It was the biggest land animal ever to live on Earth.

Brontosaurus Huge plant-eating dinosaur.

Camptosaurus Ornithopod about 20 ft.(6 m) long which fed mainly on juicy leaves of trees.

Diplodocus The longest of the dinosaurs. It measured 100 ft.(30 m) from head to tail.

Hadrosaurs A group of dinosaurs with broad, toothless beaks which have earned them the name "Duckbills."

Iguanodon A plant-eating ornithopod about 30 ft. (9 m) long which ran on its hind legs.

Ornithischians formed one of the two great groups of dinosaurs. All were plant-eaters.

Ornithomimus was the shape and size of an ostrich. It was a nimble reptile that probably stole eggs from the nests of other reptiles.

Ornithopods A group of plant-eating dinosaurs which walked mainly on their hind legs.

Saurischians formed one of the two great groups of dinosaurs. They included the gigantic sauropods, such as Brachiosaurus, and the fearsome flesh-eaters, such as Tyrannosaurus.

Sauropods A group of gigantic plant-eating dinosaurs with huge bodies, long necks, and tiny heads, such as Brontosaurus and Diplodocus.

Stegosaurus Armored dinosaur about 23 ft. (7 m) long. It had bony plates on its back and spikes on its tail.

Triceratops Armored dinosaur with three long horns on its head and a bony frill around its neck. It was a plant-eater and reached about 30 ft. (9 m) in length.

Tyrannosaurus Largest of the fearsome flesh-eating dinosaurs. It stood 20 ft. (6 m) high on its powerful hind legs.

A DICTIONARY OF ANIMAL LIFE

adaptation Any characteristic that a species of plant or animal has developed which helps it to survive in its environment. The thick coats, small ears and short tails of Arctic mammals are adaptations to cold living conditions.

ecology Study of all the plants and animals in any particular habitat, and the relationships between them.

family An order of animals is divided into groups called families. The members of a family are all closely related and usually quite alike. All cats, for example, belong to one family in the order Carnivora.

genus Many families of animals are divided into a number of genera. The cat family, for example, contains several genera, but most of the small cats, including the domestic cat, belong to the genus *Felis*. Each genus is made up of very similar animals.

habitat A creature's natural environment. Four very different habitats are seashores, hot, sandy deserts, coniferous forests, and grasslands.

hibernation Animals' winter sleep. When an animal hibernates, its body temperature falls, slowing down all the chemical changes that go on in the body, and making the animal sleepy and inactive. This happens as an automatic response to the weather getting cold.

kingdom Major division of living things. Most biologists recognize three kingdoms: Protista, single-celled organisms; Metaphyta or Plantae, plants; and Metazoa or Animalia, animals. Some zoologists add two more: Monera, bacteria; and Mycota, fungi.

larva Stage that many animals pass through between hatching from an egg and becoming adult. The larva is very different from the adult, as a tadpole is from a frog, or a caterpillar from a butterfly.

metamorphosis Drastic change that many animals undergo between the stages of being a larva and being an adult, as when a tadpole becomes a frog or a caterpillar becomes a butterfly.

mimicry Device by which many harmless and otherwise defenseless animals are shaped and colored very much like poisonous or dangerous ones. This makes it more likely that predators will be confused and will therefore not attack them.

mutualism An association between two different kinds of living creature that brings advantages to both. Mutualism is another word for *symbiosis*.

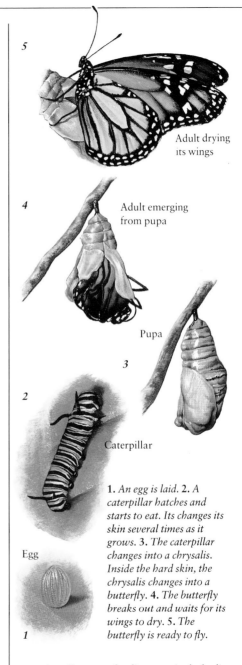

5 Adult drying its wings

4 Adult emerging from pupa

Pupa

3

2

Caterpillar

Egg

1

1. An egg is laid. 2. A caterpillar hatches and starts to eat. Its changes its skin several times as it grows. 3. The caterpillar changes into a chrysalis. Inside the hard skin, the chrysalis changes into a butterfly. 4. The butterfly breaks out and waits for its wings to dry. 5. The butterfly is ready to fly.

parasites Creatures that live on or in the bodies of other creatures (called their "hosts"). A parasite obtains food from its host but gives nothing in return. Parasites are not always dangerous to their hosts but are often a nuisance to them. It is not in the parasite's interest to kill its host, for by doing so it would lose its home and its food supply.

155

phylum Biologists divide the Animal Kingdom into major groups called phyla. All the animals in the same phylum have important features in common. Among the phyla of the Animal Kingdom are coelenterates, rotifers, mollusks, arthropods, echinoderms, and chordates.

predators Animals that live by preying on other animals. Many birds are predators of caterpillars; sharks are predators of fish.

scavengers Animals that feed on dead plants, dead animals, or animal droppings. By doing so they help to keep a habitat clean. Vultures are useful and important scavengers.

social insects Insects that live in communities, with different individuals doing different jobs to help the rest.

species The species is the smallest grouping that is used in the classification of living organisms. Male and female animals of the same species can breed with one another, whereas members of different species are not normally able to breed successfully. Every genus contains one or more species.

territory Specific area that an animal has marked out as its own home and that it is prepared to defend against other animals of its own kind. A robin may chase other robins away from its nest, but pay little attention to sparrows.

The dodo of Mauritius became extinct in the late 17th century.

ANIMALS IN DANGER

Animal	Where last seen	Estimated numbers
Asiatic Buffalo	India, Nepal	2,200
Blue Whale	World oceans	7,500
Bontebok (antelope)	South Africa	800
Crested Ibis (wading bird)	Japan	Under 12
European Bison	Poland	Over 1,000*
Everglades Kite	Florida	100
Florida Panther	Florida	Under 300
Giant Panda	China	200
Imperial Eagle	Spain	100
Indian Rhinoceros	India, Nepal	Under 600
Java Rhinoceros	Indonesia	Under 100
Kakapo (parrot)	New Zealand	Under 100
Key Deer	North America	600
Mediterranean Monk Seal	Mediterranean Sea	500
Orangutan	Borneo, Sumatra	5,000
Père David's Deer	China	600*
Polar Bear	Arctic	8,000
Przewalski's Horse	Central Asia	40–60*
Siberian Tiger	Russia, China, Korea	Under 200
Southern Bald Eagle	North America	600
Whooping Cranes	North America	About 50

Saved from extinction by zoos.

ANIMALS RECENTLY EXTINCT

Animal	Where last seen	When last seen
Great Auk	N. Atlantic coasts	1840s
Aurochs (wild ox)	Europe	1627
Dodo	Mauritius	1681
Elephant Bird	Madagascar	c.1600
Heath Hen	Martha's Vineyard, Mass.	1932
Moa (flightless bird)	New Zealand	1600s
Carolina Parakeet	United States	1904
Passenger Pigeon	North America	1914
Quagga (zebra)	South Africa	1883
Schomburgk's Deer	Thailand	1932

Plants

The plant kingdom extends all over the Earth, in steaming jungles, lush pastures, and the surface waters of the oceans; there are plants that survive in parched deserts and on bleak mountain tops. Plants play a vital part in the ecosystem of the Earth. They protect the land from erosion by wind and water; they give cover to wildlife and provide people and animals with food and oxygen. Trees are one of the most valuable assets of this planet, yet we are cutting down tropical rain forests at the rate of 30 acres a minute, day and night.

Plants belong to the plant kingdom, called either *Plantae* or *Metaphyta*. Plant life is found on all parts of the Earth – even in the sea. Floating about in the upper layers of the oceans is a mass of tiny plants and animals, together known as plankton (from a Greek word meaning "floating"). These plants and animals are so small they are like dust. The plants of the plankton are eaten by the animals of the plankton, and both provide food for larger sea creatures, such as fish.

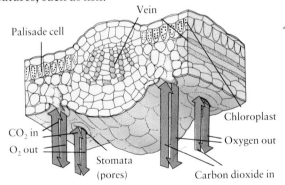

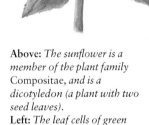

Above: *The sunflower is a member of the plant family* Compositae, *and is a dicotyledon (a plant with two seed leaves).*
Left: *The leaf cells of green plants make food from sunlight by photosynthesis.*

When biologists discuss the "who eats whom" of wild life, they refer to food chains. The reason that plants always come at the beginning of all food chains is that, unlike animals, green plants can make their own food. They draw in carbon dioxide from the air, and water and minerals from the ground, and convert them into fats, proteins, starches, and oxygen.

For this work plants need energy. They draw their energy from light. The light is absorbed and processed by *chlorophyll*, a pigment which colors plants green. Fungi – such as mushrooms and toadstools – which do not have chlorophyll, have to draw their food from other plants.

157

THE PLANT KINGDOM

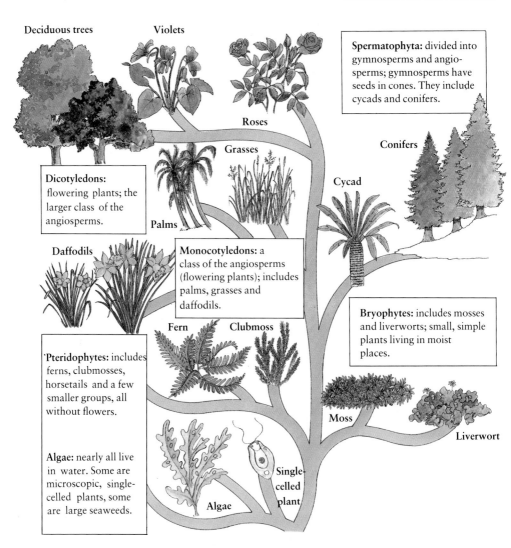

Deciduous trees

Violets

Roses

Spermatophyta: divided into gymnosperms and angiosperms; gymnosperms have seeds in cones. They include cycads and conifers.

Conifers

Grasses

Cycad

Dicotyledons: flowering plants; the larger class of the angiosperms.

Palms

Monocotyledons: a class of the angiosperms (flowering plants); includes palms, grasses and daffodils.

Daffodils

Fern   Clubmoss

Bryophytes: includes mosses and liverworts; small, simple plants living in moist places.

Pteridophytes: includes ferns, clubmosses, horsetails and a few smaller groups, all without flowers.

Moss

Liverwort

Algae: nearly all live in water. Some are microscopic, single-celled plants, some are large seaweeds.

Single-celled plant

Algae

The main divisions of the plant kingdom are the Algae, Bryophyta, Pteriodophyta, and the Spermatophyta phyla. The spermatopytes make up the largest division, consisting of over 350,000 different species which reproduce by bearing seeds. There are two kinds of seed-bearing plants: the gymnosperms, or "naked seed" plants, and the angiosperms, or "covered seed" plants, which include all flowering plants. The table above shows the classification of the plant kingdom.

When plants have finished making their food they release oxygen into the atmosphere. In this way they perform a valuable service to animal life, because animals must have oxygen to live. In turn, animals perform an essential service for flowering plants (and some other plants too) by pollinating them – that is, transferring *pollen*, the male cells of flowers, to the *stigmas*, the female parts of flowers. Most pollination is done by insects.

As well as emitting oxygen into the atmosphere, plants release a great deal of water. They draw this water from the ground through their roots and pump it up through their stems to the leaves, where it is given off in a process called transpiration. This is the evaporation of water through pores, called stomata, on the undersides of the leaves. In hot dry weather, transpiration will take place more quickly than a plant can draw water from the soil; it must then close its stomata to prevent further evaporation, or it will wilt.

Ash seeds

Plants use various ingenious methods of seed dispersal, including the wind, animals and birds. The poppy has a "sprinkler" system. The ripe ovary swells into a hollow container with holes around the lip. The wind shakes the seeds out through the holes.

Thistle seeds

Burdock

Poppy

Bird

Mouse

Blackberries

Dandelion seeds

Uncontrolled forest clearance can lead to ecological disaster. Rains can wash away fragile forest soil.

Plants also help to keep the soil together. Their roots bind it and help to hold water in the ground. Without plant cover, exposed land is at the mercy of wind and water. The wind blows loose dry soil away and water washes the soil down hill. Ignorant or wasteful farming practices and the removal of the natural plant cover created the Dust Bowl of America's Great Plains area during the 1930s. In a similar way, clearing large areas of Amazonian rain forest in Brazil in the 1980s damaged the soil of the region.

Diversity of plant life

Plants include the largest and oldest living things on Earth. The largest is a huge tree, a giant sequoia known as "General Sherman" which stands in Sequoia National Park, California. It has been estimated that it contains about 1,800 cubic yards (1,400 cubic meters) of timber.

By contrast, the plants of the plankton are so small that one drop of water can hold as many as 500 of them. Some land plants are also very tiny.

The "General Sherman" is thought to be about 3,500 years old, but it is barely middle-aged compared with the oldest known living tree. That is a bristlecone pine, named "Methuselah," which is also growing in California. "Methuselah" is 4,700 years old.

Plants can flourish in all sorts of extreme conditions.

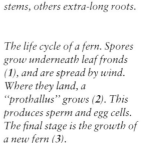

Cacti are desert plants which store water. Some have swollen stems, others extra-long roots.

The life cycle of a fern. Spores grow underneath leaf fronds (1), and are spread by wind. Where they land, a "prothallus" grows (2). This produces sperm and egg cells. The final stage is the growth of a new fern (3).

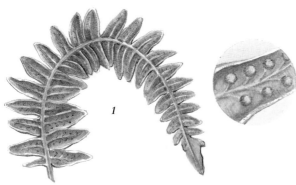

1

Spore-cases (sori)

Prothallus

2

There are plants growing in the cold of the Arctic, Antarctica, and high in the Himalayas of central Asia. Other plants can survive in all but the hottest deserts. Most desert plants are small or medium-sized, but the saguaro cactus of the California and Arizona deserts can reach a height of more than 50 feet (15 meters).

Plants can survive even when they seem to be dead. For example, when the apparently bare deserts of Israel receive a welcome shower of rain, plants spring up overnight from seeds lying in the soil, and soon provide the land with a rare carpet of flowers. Every year the frozen tundra of northern Canada and Siberia thaws out for a few weeks in the summer sunshine, and plants have a brief period of life before winter sets in.

The richest plant life is in the warm, wet tropical regions of Africa, Central and South America, and Southeast Asia. The rain forests which flourish there contain more diverse species of plants than any other parts of the world. Some of these forests have flourished for over 40 million years.

Young sporophyte

3

Flowering Plants

Flowering plants are not only the most beautiful plants; they are the most important. They provide food for herbivores – plant-eating animals – and for humans. There are about 285,000 species of flowering plants, against 148,000 for all other plants. Flowering plants form two groups. *Monocotyledons* produce a single seed leaf when they begin to grow; *dicotyledons* start with two seed leaves in the embryo.

When a flower has been fertilized it produces a fruit. Some fruits dry out as they ripen. Examples of these are peas, beans, and nuts. Others are fleshy fruits, such as bananas, grapes, squash, and tomatoes.

PARTS OF A FLOWER

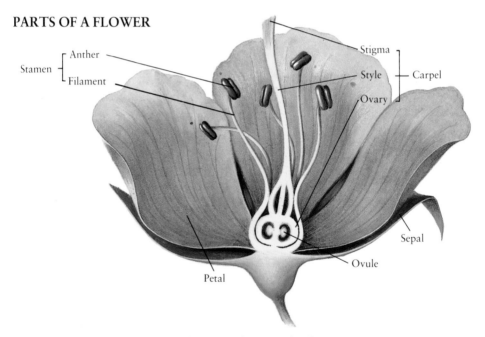

The scientific name for flowering plants is angiosperms, meaning "cased seeds," because their seeds are enclosed in the fruits. Some seeds are quite small, such as those of apples and oranges. Fruits of this type are pomes or berries according to how they are formed.

Cherries, peaches, and plums have a hard inner stone, inside which is the seed. Fruits of this type are called drupes. Many fruits that are known as berries, such as blackberries and raspberries, are actually several small drupes joined together.

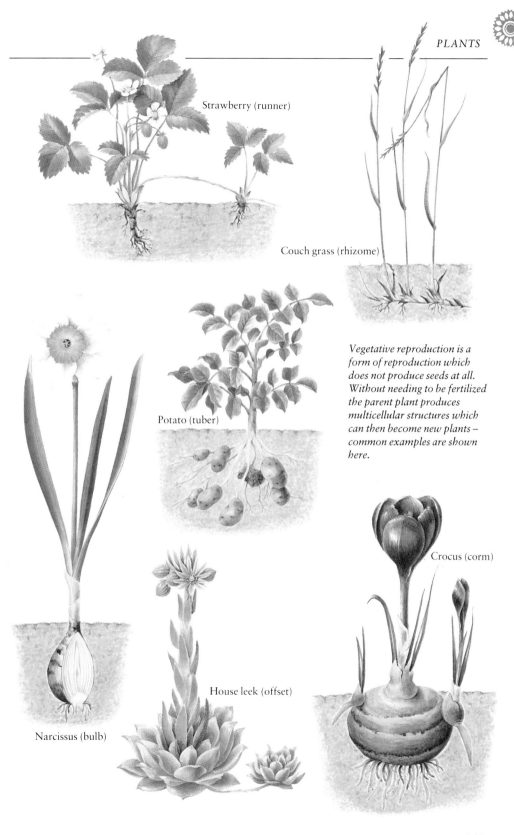

Strawberry (runner)

Couch grass (rhizome)

Potato (tuber)

Vegetative reproduction is a form of reproduction which does not produce seeds at all. Without needing to be fertilized the parent plant produces multicellular structures which can then become new plants – common examples are shown here.

Crocus (corm)

House leek (offset)

Narcissus (bulb)

FAMILIES OF FLOWERING PLANTS

There are more than 140 families (related groups) of flowering plants. Some families have only one or two species in them; others dozens. Quite often you would not expect some plants to be related – for example, the rose and the raspberry.

Amaryllis family daffodil, onion, snowdrop, narcissus.

Arum family arum, jack-in-the-pulpit.

Banana family banana, Bird-of-Paradise flower.

Beech family beech, chestnut, oak.

Birch family alder, birch, hazel.

Borage family Virginia cowslip, forget-me-not.

Buckwheat family dock, rhubarb, sorrel.

Cactus family cactus, prickly pear.

Cashew family mango, pistachio nut, sumac.

Composite family artichoke, chrysanthemum, daisy, dandelion, lettuce, sneezewort, thistle.

Crowfoot family anemone, larkspur, peony.

Ebony family ebony, persimmon.

Figwort family foxglove, toadflax.

Ginger family cardamom, turmeric.

Grass family bamboo, rice, rye, wheat.

Heath family azalea, briar, heath, rhododendron.

Laurel family avocado, baytree, laurel.

Lily family asparagus, crocus, lily, tulip.

Madder family bedstraw, coffee.

Mallow family cotton, hollyhock.

Mint family basil, lavender, rosemary.

Morning glory family bindweed, dodder.

Mulberry family fig, hop, mulberry.

Mustard family cabbage, sweet alyssum, turnip, wallflower.

Myrtle family clove, eucalyptus, pimento.

Nightshade family eggplant, henbane, nightshade, potato, tobacco, tomato.

Olive family ash, jasmine, privet.

Palm family coconut palm, date palm.

Parsley family carrot, dill, parsnip.

Pea family bean, brazilwood, clover, ground nut, laburnum, licorice, soya bean, vetch.

Pink family carnation, pink.

Primrose family European cowslip, pim-pernel.

Rose family rose, apple, bramble, nectarine, plum, raspberry, strawberry.

Rue family grapefruit, lemon, lime, orange.

Saxifrage family currant, gooseberry, hydrangea.

Spurge family cassava, rubber, teak.

Tea family camellia, tea.

Willow family aspen, osier, poplar.

Prickly juniper.

Cedar

TREES AND SHRUBS

Trees and shrubs differ from other plants in having woody stems. These stems support the plants and enable them to grow tall. A few plants, such as lianas and other creepers, have woody stems that are not strong enough to allow them to stand alone.

There are two main kinds of trees. Conifers are trees with needlelike leaves. They produce their seeds in cones. Most of them are evergreens – that is, they do not lose their leaves in the fall, but shed and renew a few all the year round. They often have a "pyramid" shape.

Broadleaved trees have wide leaves. They have flowers and produce their seeds in fruits. Most of them are deciduous – that is, they shed their leaves in the fall and grow new ones in the spring. But some, such as holly, rhododendron, and many trees of the rain forests, are evergreens.

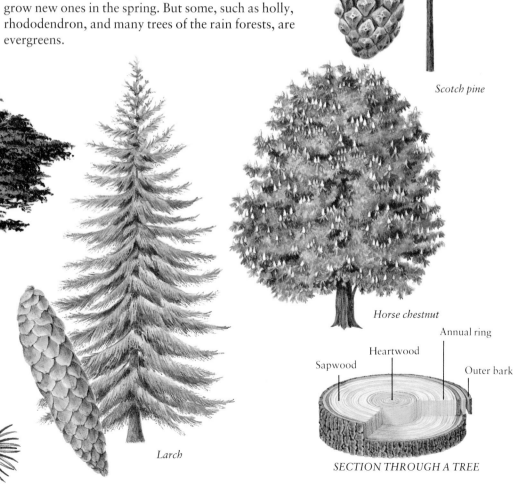

Scotch pine

Horse chestnut

Larch

Sapwood

Heartwood

Annual ring

Outer bark

SECTION THROUGH A TREE

Emergent layer   165ft.

THE MULTISTORY RAIN FOREST

Rain forest is dense forest, found on or near the
equator where the climate is hot and wet.
Although rain forests cover only 8% of the
Earth's surface they provide homes for at least
40% of the Earth's species of plants and
animals.
The Amazon rain forest has five main layers as
shown in the diagram (right).
The layers and their characteristics are:

Emergent layer A few trees grow high above
the others.

Canopy layer A thick mass of treetops which
break the heavy rain into fine spray. Many
plants and animals live here on nuts and fruit.

Middle Layer This layer, sometimes called the
understorey, is dark. Lianas (creepers) and
climbing plants grow and young trees
struggle toward the light.

Lower layer Some shrubs and young trees. Tall
trees have buttress roots. Dark.

Ground layer Little light but very damp.
Seedlings, herbs, and fungi grow in the fragile
soil.

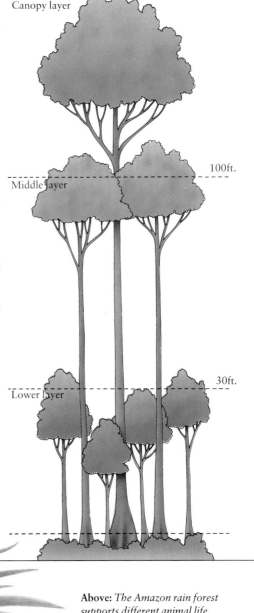

Canopy layer

100ft.
Middle layer

30ft.
Lower layer

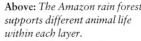

Above: *The Amazon rain forest
supports different animal life
within each layer.*
Left: *The South American
bromeliads are epiphytic
plants, growing on other plants
but able to make their own
food.*

166

THE PROTISTS

Some living things are difficult to classify as animals or plants. Today many biologists put them into a third kingdom, the "Protista." The name Protista comes from a Greek word meaning "the very first."

The protists include all the organisms that consist of one cell only, such as most algae, and other single-celled animals, most amoebas and small sea-dwelling creatures in the plankton such as diatoms, radiolarians, and sun animals. Many single-celled animals live in colonies.

Some biologists include the fungi in the Protista. Others list them with plants or give them their own kingdom, the Mycota. Biologists put the bacteria and the blue-green algae in yet another kingdom, the Monera.

Bladderwrack is a seaweed growing on rocky shores. These plants cling tightly to rocks, and have rubbery exteriors to prevent them drying out when exposed at low tide.

Death Cap

Fly Agaric

Chanterelle

ese Umber

Vividly colored, the Fly Agaric is often shown on greetings cards – although in fact it is toxic. The Death Cap is the most toxic toadstool of all. By contrast, the chanterelle is a highly prized edible mushroom.

Fungal mat

Loose fungal threads

Single-celled algae

Cross-section through a crusty lichen. The fungal threads make a dense mat on the outside, while inside the threads are looser, with green algal cells making food.

PLANT CELL

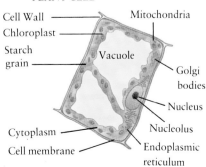

Cell Wall

Chloroplast

Starch grain

Cytoplasm

Cell membrane

Mitochondria

Vacuole

Golgi bodies

Nucleus

Nucleolus

Endoplasmic reticulum

167

DICTIONARY OF PLANTS

annual A plant which completes its life cycle in one season and then dies.

anther The part of the stamen that contains the pollen.

asexual reproduction Any form of reproduction that does not involve the fusing of male and female sex cells (gametes).

bark The outer layer of a woody stem.

berry A fleshy fruit with no hard inner layer and usually with several seeds, for example orange, gooseberry.

biennial A plant which completes its life cycle in two seasons and then dies.

bud An undeveloped shoot.

bulb An enlarged underground bud with fleshy leaves in which food is stored.

calyx The name for the sepals of a flower.

carbohydrate A food, for example sugar and starch, made up of carbon, hydrogen, and oxygen, produced in a plant by photosynthesis. Carbohydrate is "burned" to provide energy.

carpel The female reproductive organ of a flower, it is made up of stigma, style, and ovary.

cell Minute living unit. All living matter is made up of cells.

chlorophyll The green pigment that enables green plants to use the energy from light to make food (photosynthesis).

chromosome Minute threadlike structure in the nucleus of a cell containing the genes.

clone A group of plants with identical chromosomes and features, produced by vegetative reproduction, for example clusters of bulbs.

compound leaf One in which the blade is divided into separate leaflets.

corm A short fleshy underground stem in which food is stored.

cotyledon A seed leaf. The first leaf or pair of leaves of the embryo plant in a seed, often providing a food store.

deciduous Shedding all leaves at the end of each growing season.

dicotyledon (or dicot). A member of the class of flowering plants with two cotyledons in each seed.

drupe A fruit with a fleshy outer layer and a hard inner layer, for example peach, cherry.

ecology The study of the relations between living things and their environment.

embryo The young plant in the seed.

fertilization The combining of the male reproductive cell with the ovule to form a seed.

fruit A ripened carpel or group of carpels. It protects and helps in the dispersal of seeds.

gene Part of a chromosome, containing the coded hereditary information for a particular characteristic. Most characteristics involve many genes.

germination The beginning of growth of a seed or spore.

glucose The simple sugar produced in photosynthesis which is converted to starch and stored as a food reserve by some plants.

herb or **herbaceous plant** A non-woody seed plant in which the aerial parts (those exposed to the air) die (or die down) at the end of each growing season.

humus Decaying organic matter in the soil.

hybrid A plant produced when pollen from one species fertilizes the flower of different but usually very closely related species. Hybrids are usually sterile.

legume (or pod) A type of dry fruit formed from a single ovary, which splits down two sides when ripe, for example pea.

monocotyledon A member of the class of flowering plants with only one cotyledon (seed leaf) in each seed.

nectar The sweet liquid, produced in glands called nectaries, that attracts insects to a flower.

nucleus The part of a cell cotaining the chromosomes.

nut A one-seeded fruit with a hard woody wall.

organic Living; also used of material that was once part of a living thing.

osmosis The process whereby a solvent such as water diffuses through a semipermeable membrane, tending to equalize the strengths of the solutions on each side of the membrane.

ovary The hollow part of the carpel which contains the ovules. It may also be formed from the cavities of several carpels joined together.

ovule A structure inside the ovary which contains the female reproductive cell and which, after fertilization, develops into the seed.

parasite A living thing which lives on or in another living thing (the host), and which obtains all its food from the host.

perennial A plant that lives on from year to year.

photosynthesis The process by which green plants use the energy of light to make glucose from carbon dioxide and water.

pistil Another word for the female part of the flower – the carpel or group of carpels.

pollen Mass of grains produced in the stamens of a flower, carrying male reproductive cells.

pollination The transfer of pollen from stamen to stigma.

rhizoid Hairlike structure which anchors mosses in the ground.

rhizome A horizontal underground stem, sometimes containing stored food.

runner A creeping stem by which plants such as the strawberry reproduce.

self-pollination Transfer of pollen from the stamens to the stigma of the same flower.

sepals the outermost parts of a flower. They are usually green and protect the petals before the flower opens.

shrub A fairly short woody plant with many branches and no main trunk.

spore A single-celled reproductive body which grows into a new plant; found in algae, fungi, ferns, and mosses.

stamen Male reproductive part of a flower, made up of the pollen-producing anther and its supporting filament (stalk).

starch A type of carbohydrate food often stored in plants.

stigma The tip of the carpel that receives the pollen.

style Stalk-like part of the carpel with the stigma at its tip.

symbiosis A close association between two organisms in which both organisms benefit.

taproot The main root of the plant.

tendril A modified stem, leaf or leaflet used by some climbing plants. It is very thin, and coils around any support that it meets.

tuber A swollen stem (such as a potato) or root (for example a dahlia) used to store food.

Plant fossils, like these of a poplar and a fern, reveal much about the ecology of the prehistoric Earth. Plants are the planet's oldest life-forms.

PLANT RECORDS

Oldest surviving species of tree is the ginkgo or maidenhair tree of China. It first appeared about 160 million years ago.

Largest seeds are those of the coco-de-mer, a palm growing in the Seychelles. The nuts may weigh as much as 50 lb. (23 kg).

Longest seaweed is the Pacific Giant Kelp, which can grow nearly 200 ft (61 m) long.

Tallest grasses are the Thorney bamboos of India, which reach a height of120 ft. (37 m).

Most massive living thing is the giant sequoia tree "General Sherman," estimated to weigh 2,145 tons.

Largest flowers are those of the Southeast Asian plant *Rafflesia*, which reach more than 3 ft. (90 cm) across. Their smell gives them the popular name of stinking corpse lily.

Tallest trees are the coast redwoods of California. The tallest living specimen is over 364 ft. (111 m) high.

Earliest fossil land plants were of a primitive type called *Cooksonia*, which flourished in Ireland about 415 million years ago.

Earliest fossil flowers so far known were found at Scania, Sweden, in 1981 in deposits more than 65 million years old.

Science

The study of science is a quest for knowledge and the origins of life. By observation, measurement, and assessment of facts, scientists aim to discover answers to the questions How? and Why? Their research penetrates back into time, down into the depths of the ocean, and even beyond the reaches of our planet into outer space.

Aristotle (384–322 B.C.) laid the foundations of many of the modern sciences. He defined and classified the branches of knowledge.

A model of an early reflecting telescope. Invented in the 1600s, it was an enormous advance in scientific instrumentation. For the first time, scientists could study the stars and planets in detail.

Science is the study of the physical side of the universe. It is based on observation, measurement, and experiment. It is concerned with facts and with the methodical study of them.

Science may be divided into two disciplines: pure science, the study of things for their own sake; and applied science, using science for practical purposes. One aspect of applied science is technology, which is discussed in more detail on pages 190–191.

The story of science began long ago, before people could read and write. One of the earliest scientific discoveries was how to make and use fire. Even something as simple as the discovery that a sloping roof throws off the rain better than a flat one ranks as an early scientific advance.

When people began to settle down and build themselves cities to live in, science progressed by leaps and bounds. More than 5000 years ago the ancient Babylonians developed early mathematics and a calendar, and studied the stars. The Egyptians added geometry and surgery. At the same time the Chinese people made similar advances in science, but there was no exchange of scientific knowledge between China and Europe.

The biggest advances in science in ancient times were made by the Greeks, who not only learned a great deal but were able to write it down. One of the greatest Greek scientists, the philosopher Aristotle, developed the skills of observation and classifying knowledge in the 300s B.C., while Archimedes, a century later, established the principle of conducting experiments and by doing so discovered many facts we find useful today.

The Romans did not advance science much, and during the early Middle Ages people in Europe studied it hardly at all. However, the Arabs preserved much of the ancient Greek knowledge. In the Americas, the Aztec, Inca, and Maya Indians developed their own independent scientific knowledge but, like the Chinese, they had no influence on Europe.

The revival of science came in the 1500s, during the period which we call the Renaissance – "rebirth" – because there was a renewed interest in learning. The Greek books preserved by the Arabs were revived and studied. Since then science has progressed very fast.

The nineteenth century saw great leaps in scientific knowledge. Mendel revealed the laws of genetics, Darwin helped to develop the theory of evolution, and Babbage made the first mechanical computer. As the century closed, scientists studied the atom, and motion at the speed of light in space. The rules on gravity and motion which Newton had developed did not apply: Einstein's theory of relativity and Planck's laws of quantum mechanics were needed.

We are now living at a most exciting time in the story of science. Modern methods of research have enabled us to understand many things that were mysteries to our ancestors. With the aid of telescopes and space probes we are increasing our understanding of the universe. Special deep-sea submarines are enabling us to penetrate the secrets of the oceans and so add to our knowledge of our own planet and the origin of life.

But the more we find out, the more we realize how much there is still to learn. The main branches of science today are listed on the next page.

Top: *Ancient stone circles, such as Stonehenge, may have been used to observe movements of the stars and planets. Astronomers used these observations to work out calendars.*
Above: *Sumerian cuneiform writing. Writing enabled knowledge to be permanently recorded.*

BRANCHES OF SCIENCE

Science	Study of

EARTH SCIENCES

geology	Rocks, earthquakes, volcanoes, and fossils
meteorology	The atmosphere and weather
oceanography	Waves, tides, currents, trenches, and ocean life
paleontology	Plant and animal fossils

LIFE SCIENCES

anatomy	Structure, form, and arrangement of the body
bacteriology	Bacteria; their growth and behavior
biology	Animals and plants; origin, morphology, and environment
botany	The plant world
ecology	Relationship between living things and environment
medicine	Cause, prevention, and cure of disease
nutrition	Supply of adequate and correct foods to satisfy the body's requirements
pharmacology	Drugs; their preparation, use and effects
physiology	The function of living things
psychology	Behavior of humans and animals; working of the brain
zoology	Animal life

MATHEMATICAL SCIENCES

computing	The use of computers in mathematics and statistics
logic	Reasoning: especially as applied to and using mathematics
mathematics	The application of geometry, algebra, and arithmetic to concrete data
statistics	Numerical information and its analysis

PHYSICAL SCIENCES

astronomy	Heavenly bodies and their motions
chemistry	Properties and behavior of substances
electronics	Behavior of electrons in a vacuum, in gases and semiconductors

An optical microscope, with three lenses – each magnifying to a different degree. The microscope revolutionized the life sciences from the 1600s.

Eyepiece lens

Focusing knob

Turret

Objective lens

Specimen table

Condenser lens

Mirror

engineering	Application of scientific principles to industry
mechanics	The invention and construction of machines; their operation and the calculation of their efficiency
metallurgy	The working of metals; smelting and refining
physics	Nature and behavior of matter and energy

SOCIAL SCIENCES

anthropology	Origin, culture, development, and distribution of human beings
archaeology	Remains and monuments left by earlier people
economics	Use of natural resources to the best advantage
geography	Location of Earth's features and our relation to them
linguistics	Languages and their relationship to each other
political science	Function of states and governments
sociology	Relationship between groups and individuals

KEY DATES IN SCIENCE

c.400 B.C. Hippocrates devises the code of medical ethics – now the "Hippocratic oath."

1543 Nicolaus Copernicus argues that the Sun is at the center of the Solar System.

c.1600 Galileo Galilei develops and uses the scientific method.

1687 Sir Isaac Newton publishes his book, *Principia Mathematica*, setting out the laws of mechanics.

1789 Antoine Lavoisier writes *Elements of Chemistry*, the first modern textbook of chemistry.

1839 Matthias Schleiden and Theodor Schwann suggest that living things are made up of cells.

1858 Charles Darwin and Alfred Russel Wallace set out their theory of evolution.

1869 Dmitri Mendeleyev classifies the elements into the Periodic Table.

1900 Max Planck puts forward the quantum theory.

1905 Albert Einstein advances his Special Theory of Relativity.

1911 Ernest Rutherford discovers the nucleus and formulates the atomic theory.

1942 Enrico Fermi and others achieve the first successful nuclear chain reaction.

1953 Francis Crick and James Watson discover that DNA – "the molecule of life" – is a double helix, resembling a twisted ladder.

1957 Arthur Kornberg grows DNA in a test-tube.

1963 F.J. Vine and D.H. Matthews revolutionize geology by proving that the sea-floor spreads, so confirming the theory of continental drift.

1969 Neil Armstrong and Edwin Aldrin become the first men to explore the Moon.

1986 Spacecraft *Voyager 2* flies past Uranus, the planet seventh from the Sun, and takes the first close-up pictures of it.

1989 *Voyager 2* sends back pictures of Neptune, 2.8 billion miles away.

Above: *The equipment used in a modern chemistry laboratory has changed little over the years, though computers are now used widely to store the results of experiments. Some of the more common items found in a chemistry laboratory are shown here. They are **1.** Chemical balance; **2.** Bottles with ground glass stoppers; **3.** Centrifuge; **4.** Microscope; **5.** Burette; **6.** Conical flask; **7.** Filter funnel;*

8. Measuring cylinder; 9. Long-necked flask; 10. Pipette; 11. Flat-bottomed flask; 12. Beaker; 13. Test tube and holder; 14. Bunsen burner; 15. Mortar and pestle; 16. Condenser; 17. Tripod stand.

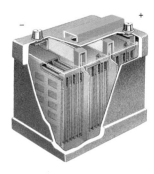

CHEMISTRY

Chemistry is the study of matter. Matter is made up of chemical elements – substances that differ from one another. The elements are made up of atoms, and the atoms of each element are different, too.

Each atom has a nucleus, or center, containing a number of protons – particles carrying a positive electrical charge. The atomic number of each element in the periodic table on pages 176–177 is the number of protons in the nucleus. Whirling around the nucleus are as many electrons (negatively charged particles) as there are protons.

In addition, the periodic table shows the elements arranged in periods (rows) according to their atomic numbers. The vertical columns contain elements that have similar characteristics; for example, the end column on the right contains a group of inert gases which are called the "noble gases."

Two groups of elements appear at the bottom of the table: the "Lanthanides" or rare-earth elements, and the "Actinides," which are all radioactive. Elements 1 (hydrogen) to 92 (uranium) are found in nature. Those from 93 onward are called trans-uranium elements, which have been made in laboratories.

HOW TO READ A CHEMICAL FORMULA

Chemists use a form of shorthand when writing out the formula of a chemical compound. It is very precise, and

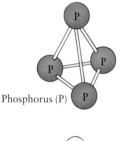

Phosphorus (P)

Methane (CH_4)

Carbon dioxide (CO_2)

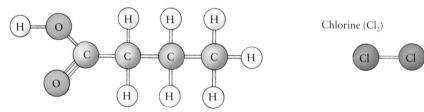

Butanoic acid (C_3H_7COOH)

Chlorine (Cl_2)

Above and right: *These molecules involve single and double bonds between two or more atoms. The diagrams also indicate the approximate shapes of the molecules.*

CHEMICAL RECORDS

Lightest element is the gas hydrogen.
Lightest metal is lithium, which is half the weight of an equal volume of water.
Hardest element is carbon when it occurs in the form of diamond.
Commonest element in the universe is hydrogen; in the atmosphere it is nitrogen; and in the Earth's crust it is oxygen.

tells them exactly what is in each molecule (unit) of the compound. It is based on standard abbreviations. A simple example is the formula for water, H_2O. H stands for hydrogen and O stands for oxygen. The subscript (lower) number after the letter H shows how many atoms of that element there are in each water molecule. So we know that each molecule of water contains two atoms of hydrogen and one of oxygen.

Many compounds consist of chains or webs of atoms. For example, butanoic acid (which gives rancid butter its smell), has the formula C_4H_7COOH.

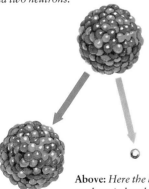

Above: *Many heavy atoms have unstable nuclei, which break down spontaneously in radioactive decay. As it breaks down, this heavy nucleus is emitting an alpha particle, which comprises two protons and two neutrons.*

Above: *Here the heavy unstable nucleus, in breaking down, emits a beta particle, identical with an electron. This form of radiation is more penetrating than alpha-particle radiation. More penetrating still is gamma radiation.*

CHEMICAL NAMES OF EVERYDAY SUBSTANCES

Many chemical substances have common names which we use every day. Chemists have more precise names for them which describe what they are. Here is a selection:

Substance	Chemical name
Baking soda	Sodium bicarbonate
Blue vitriol	Copper sulfate
Borax	Sodium borate
Caustic soda	Sodium hydroxide
Chalk	Calcium carbonate
Common salt	Sodium chloride
Corrosive sublimate	Mercuric chloride
Epsom salts	Magnesium sulfate
Glauber's salt	Sodium sulfate
Lime	Calcium oxide
Magnesia	Magnesium oxide
Oil of Vitriol	Sulfuric acid
Plaster of Paris	Calcium sulfate
Prussian blue	Ferric ferrocyanide
Red lead	Triplumbic tetroxide
Saltpeter	Potassium nitrate
Sal volatile	Ammonium carbonate
Vinegar	Dilute ethanoic acid
Washing soda	Crystalline sodium carbonate
Water glass	Sodium silicate

CHEMICAL INDICATORS

Indicators are chemicals which show how a chemical change is progressing, or whether a substance is an acid or a base (alkali). Two examples are litmus and methyl orange:

	Litmus	Methyl Orange
Acid	Turns red	Turns red
Base	Turns blue	Turns yellow

PERIODIC TABLE OF ELEMENTS

The elements, listed with their symbols and atomic numbers, lie horizontally in order of their atomic numbers. Those with chemically similar properties fall under one another in the columns. Elements with atomic numbers of 93 and over are made in the laboratory.

Scientists from both the United States and the former Soviet Union claim to have created elements 104 and 109 in the laboratory. All these elements have very short half lives, measured only in seconds.

1 Hydrogen H								

3 Lithium Li	4 Beryllium Be							
11 Sodium Na	12 Magnesium Mg							

19 Potassium K	20 Calcium Ca	21 Scandium Sc	22 Titanium Ti	23 Vanadium V	24 Chromium Cr	25 Manganese Mn	26 Iron Fe	27 Cobalt Co
37 Rubidium Rb	38 Strontium Sr	39 Yttrium Y	40 Zirconium Zr	41 Niobium Nb	42 Molybdenum Mo	43 Technetium Tc	44 Ruthenium Ru	45 Rhodium Rh
55 Caesium Cs	56 Barium Ba	57–71 Lanthanide series	72 Hafnium Hf	73 Tantalum Ta	74 Wolfram W	75 Rhenium Re	76 Osmium Os	77 Iridium Ir
87 Francium Fr	88 Radium Ra	89–103 Actinide series	104 Rutherford-ium Rf	105 Element 105	106 Element 106	107 Element 107	108 Element 108	109 Element 109

57 Lanthanum La	58 Cerium Ce	59 Praseodym-ium Pr	60 Neodymium Nd	61 Prometheum Pm	62 Samarium Sm	63 Europium Eu	64 Gadolinium Gd	65 Terbium Tb
89 Actinium Ac	90 Thorium Th	91 Protactinium Pa	92 Uranium U	93 Neptunium Np	94 Plutonium Pu	95 Americium Am	96 Curium Cm	97 Berkelium Bk

Russian chemist Dmitri Mendeleyev (1834–1907) laid the foundation for the modern periodic classification of the chemical elements. He allowed gaps in the table to represent undiscovered elements.

					2 Helium He
5 Boron B	6 Carbon C	7 Nitrogen N	8 Oxygen O	9 Fluorine F	10 Neon Ne
13 Aluminium Al	14 Silicon Si	15 Phosphorus P	16 Sulphur S	17 Chlorine Cl	18 Argon Ar

28 Nickel Ni	29 Copper Cu	30 Zinc Zn	31 Gallium Ga	32 Germanium Ge	33 Arsenic As	34 Selenium Se	35 Bromine Br	36 Krypton Kr
46 Palladium Pd	47 Silver Ag	48 Cadmium Cd	49 Indium In	50 Tin Sn	51 Antimony Sb	52 Tellurium Te	53 Iodine I	54 Xenon Xe
78 Platinum Pt	79 Gold Au	80 Mercury Hg	81 Thallium Tl	82 Lead Pb	83 Bismuth Bi	84 Polonium Po	85 Astatine At	86 Radon Rn

66 Dysprosium Dy	67 Holmium Ho	68 Erbium Er	69 Thulium Tm	70 Ytterbium Yb	71 Lutecium Lu
98 Californium Cf	99 Einsteinium Es	100 Fermium Fm	101 Mendelev-ium Md	102 Nobelium No	103 Lawrencium Lr

Albert Einstein, one of the greatest scientists, put forward the theory of relativity which was a new way of looking at time, space, matter, and energy. His explanations made possible many developments, one of which was nuclear energy and through it the atomic bomb. Despite this, he also campaigned passionately for world peace.

PHYSICS

Physics is the study of matter and energy. It is basic to the study of many other branches of science, including chemistry and the Earth sciences. Knowledge of its laws has enabled people to put satellites into orbit around the Earth, land men on the Moon, and send space probes to the most distant planets. And it also helps us with more simple actions here on Earth.

BRANCHES OF PHYSICS

acoustics The study of sound and sound waves
atomic physics The study of the behavior, properties, and structure of atoms
biophysics The physics of biological processes
crystallography The study of the formation, structure, and properties of crystals
cryogenics The study of very low temperatures
electrodynamics The study of the relation between electrical and mechanical forces
fluid physics The study of gases and liquids
geophysics The study of the physical properties of the Earth
mechanics The study of bodies in motion and at rest
nuclear physics The study of the atomic nucleus and nuclear reactions
optics The study of light
rheology The study of the flow of matter
solid-state physics The study of the effect of such things as temperature and pressure on properties of solid materials
thermodynamics The study of work and energy
tribology The study of friction and lubrication

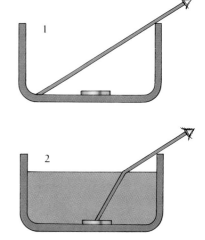

Above: *A coin invisible in a dish becomes visible when the dish is filled with water – because the light from it bends.*

Right: *By bending light rays, refraction causes images to be displaced. This paintbrush seems to bend because light from it is refracted as it passes from the air into water. The brush also looks enlarged, since the glass gives the water a curved shape, like a magnifying lens.*

NEWTON'S LAWS OF MOTION

The movement of objects, both in space and on Earth, was explained by the English scientist Sir Isaac Newton in 1687, in the following three laws of motion:

The first law states that a stationary object remains still, and a moving object continues to move in a straight line, unless some external force acts on them.

The second law states that how much a force makes an object accelerate depends on the mass of the object and the strength of the force. The same force will move an object of twice the mass at half the acceleration.

The third law states that for every action there is an equal and opposite reaction. This is the law that governs rocket motors: when the burning gases escape from the back end of the rocket, they press against the rocket, driving it forward.

Sir Isaac Newton (1642–1727).

THE LAWS OF THERMODYNAMICS

Heat is a form of energy, stored in the motions and vibrations of the atoms which make up materials; the amount of vibration determines the temperature of the material. Larger objects contain more heat energy than smaller objects at the same temperature. The molecules of an object are affected by heat energy, and the most obvious effect is a change of state: from solid to liquid, and from liquid to gas.

The study of the relationship between heat and work, and how one can be transformed into the other, is called "thermodynamics." There are four laws, numbered from 0 to 3:

Law 0 states that no heat will flow between two bodies at the same temperature.

Law 1 states that energy cannot be created or destroyed. So energy, in the form of heat, may be transformed into another form of energy, such as motion, as in an automobile engine, but the amount of energy stays the same.

Law 2 says that heat can never pass spontaneously from a colder body to a hotter one.

Law 3 states that it is impossible to cool anything down to absolute zero, the lowest possible temperature, because heat from it would have to be transferred to an even colder body.

LAWS AFFECTING GASES

The tiny molecules that make up matter are held in constant motion. In a gas, the molecules are more loosely held together than they are in a solid or liquid, and can move around freely.

Thus a gas will always expand to fill its container. It takes its space from its container, but does not take up a definite amount of space – it has no fixed volume. The molecules in a gas move rapidly and randomly and bump into each other and into the inside of a container, exerting pressure.

Boyle's Law At a constant temperature, the volume of a gas is inversely proportional to its pressure – that is, the higher the pressure, the smaller the space occupied by the gas (described by the Irish physicist Robert Boyle in 1662).

Charles's Law At a constant pressure, the volume of a gas is proportional to its absolute temperature – that is, the higher the temperature, the greater the volume (described by the French chemist Jacques Charles in 1787).

Avogadro's Law states that equal volumes of different gases, at the same pressure and temperature, all contain the same number of molecules (described by the Italian scientist Amedeo Avogadro in 1811).

ELECTRICITY AND ELECTRONICS

Electricity is a form of energy. In addition to the electricity we are familiar with as power in the home and at work, it is a part of everything. Each atom contains electrically-charged particles, including protons with a positive charge and electrons with a negative charge.

Electronics is an important part of the study of electricity. It deals with the way in which electrons control the flow of electricity. It is largely a matter of pulses of current. The current is controlled by devices such as semiconducting transistors.

Today, electronics is involved in many of our daily activities. It is found in factories controlling robot machines; in the home, in the form of radio and TV sets, and controlling dish-washers and washing machines; in transportation, controlling railroad signals and electric trains, regulating car engines and controlling the engines of airplanes. An important application of electronics is the production of new and increasingly powerful calculators and computers.

Electronically controlled robots that duplicate human actions are now widely used in industrial processes.

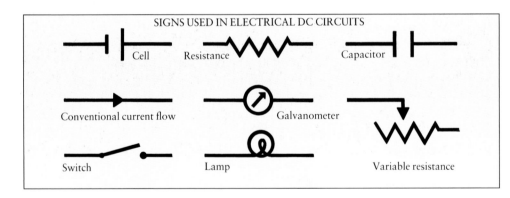

SIGNS USED IN ELECTRICAL DC CIRCUITS

Cell   Resistance   Capacitor

Conventional current flow   Galvanometer

Switch   Lamp   Variable resistance

MODERN TRENDS IN ELECTRONICS

1982 Capacity of the most powerful memory chips is increased to 256 kilobits (256,000 bits).

1983 Compact discs (CDs) come on to the market.

1984 Capacity of memory chips is increased to 1 megabit (a million bits).

1986 A two-way wrist radio weighing only 2 oz (57 g) is developed in Japan.

An electronic pacemaker which can vary the heartbeat rate to suit a patient who is taking exercise is developed in the United States.

1987 Memory chips with capacities of 4 megabits and 16 megabits are developed in Japan. "Smart cards" – credit cards with built in computers to prevent forgery and overspending – are tested in the U.S. First 3-D video systems are introduced.

1986 The development of CD-ROM is announced in the U.S. CD-ROM – Compact Disc Read Only Memory – is a sophisticated optical data storage and retrieval device.

1988 First pocket-sized color television sets.

Computers

The first working electronic computer was built at the University of Pennsylvania in 1945. It was called ENIAC (Electronic Numeral Integrator And Calculator). It weighed 30 tons and occupied a large hall. It contained more than 18,000 tubes. Today's personal computers occupy just a small amount of desk space, and have as much power as ENIAC. Even smaller computers are used to play games.

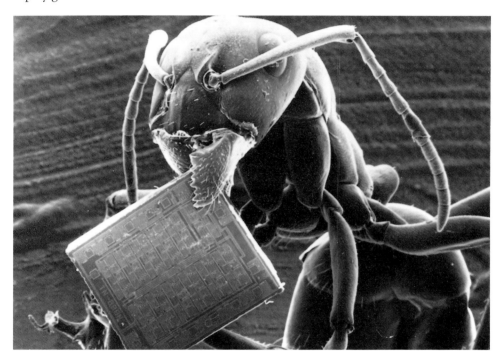

Today's computers can produce three-dimensional pictures (or graphics) of high quality, making them a useful tool for graphic artists. Graphics are also increasingly popular in business and educational programs because drawings and color can provide a computer user with information far more quickly than hundreds of words. Powerful computers can produce very high quality images.

Computer Aided Design (CAD) uses graphics to help in designing objects from shoes to spacecraft. In some cases the design computer is linked to manufacturing machinery: this is known as Computer Aided Manufacture (CAM). When a design is agreed, the system can produce samples and finally the finished product.

Microminiaturization has made the silicon chip smaller and smaller, as this comparison with an ant demonstrates.

COMPUTER LANGUAGE

access To connect to a remote computer database (usually by telephone line).

A.I. Artificial Intelligence; theoretical intelligence that would give computers humanlike reasoning abilities. True artificial intelligence has yet to be attained.

ALGOL A mathematically-oriented programming language; short for ALGOrithmic Language.

analog A representation of numerical or physical quantities by means of physical variables such as voltage or resistance.

ASCII Short for American Standard Code for Information Interchange, a system of codes used by most computers to represent the alphabet, the numbers 0 to 9, and some punctuation.

assembler A program that translates an assembly language into machine language.

assembly language A computer language that uses symbols as well as words, more difficult to use than a high-level language.

backup A copy of a program or file, made for safety.

BASIC Beginner's All-purpose Symbolic Instruction Code: a computer programming language using common English terms. Developed in the 1960s and widely used throughout the world.

binary A number system with a base of 2, using the symbols 0 and 1; it can be represented electronically by a current on or off in a computer.

bit Binary DigiT: A numeral in binary notation, that is 0 or 1.

bug An error in a program, causing it to fail.

byte A space in a computer's memory occupied by one character.

COBOL COmmon Business Orientated Language: a programming language designed for business and commercial use.

compatible Used to describe a computer or program able to work with another computer.

compiler A program that translates a high-level language into machine language.

continuous stationery A continuous sheet of paper folded into pages.

CP/M Control Program for Microcomputers: an operating system used by some computers.

cursor An area of highlighting on screen which picks out the character or block which is being worked on.

daisywheel A kind of printer which has the characters arranged on a daisylike wheel.

data General term for information processed by a computer.

debug To remove the bugs from a program.

default The drive, program, or other material that is entered automatically if there is no other command.

desk-top publishing Producing material for commercial printing using a micro-computer.

disk The most commonly used means of storing programs and data; a hard disk is rigid, a floppy disk is not.

dot matrix A kind of printer in which the characters are built up from a system of dots.

draft quality Low-quality text produced at high speed by a dot-matrix printer, using only a relatively few dots.

drive Part of a computer that accepts disks, writes to them and reads from them.

field A specific set of characters treated as a whole, or the recording area used for some particular kind of data.

file A collection of data or the contents of a document, as stored in memory or on disk.

file-name A collection of characters which an operating system identifies as the file.

format Electronically marking up a disk so that it will receive data, and erasing any previously entered data.

FORTRAN FORmula TRANslation: a programming language for scientific use.

graphics Pictures or diagrams on screen and printed out; as distinct from text.

hacker A person who does programming as a hobby, often breaking into other people's programs and computer systems.

hard copy A printout of a document held in a computer.

hardware The physical working units of a computer system.

high-level language Any computer language which enables the user to write instructions in everyday terms, such as "read" or "stop."

highlighting Also called reverse video: a method of reversing light and dark areas of a screen to show something up.

high quality The best quality of print produced by a dot matrix printer, using more dots at a slower speed than draft quality.

K Short for kilobytes: 1 K = 1024 bytes.

language A defined set of characters for communication with a computer.

Logo A program language specially designed to allow young children to program using a device called a turtle.

loop Repeated execution of a series of commands.

These children are using a computer to draw. Graphics are used to make designs, maps, and graphs.

machine language The language of binary digits – representing codes and symbols – which a computer works with.

mainframe computer A powerful high-speed computer, usually with a large storage capacity, to which one or more work stations have access.

memory Part of a computer in which programs or data are stored.

micro Abbreviation for micro-computer, a small computer for individual use.

microchip A small silicon chip which provides memory for a computer.

modem A device that enables one computer to communicate with another over a telephone line; from MOdulator-DEModulator.

monitor A cathode-ray tube similar to a television set, on which data is displayed.

mouse A small pointing device which, when rolled across the desktop, causes a pointer to move across the computer screen.

MSDOS An operating system for business microcomputers.

NLQ Near Letter Quality: another term for high quality on dot matrix printers.

printer A typewriter-like machine that produces printed copy from a computer.

printout The output of a printer.

program A complete sequence of instructions for a task to be carried out by a computer.

programming Writing a program to carry out a specific task.

RAM Random Access Memory, the computer's memory in which both a program and data are held ready for processing. Whatever is stored in it is lost when the computer is switched off.

ROM Read Only Memory: permanent instructions or programs kept in the computer's memory, retained when the computer is switched off.

screen The visible part of a monitor.

software Programs for use in a computer to simplify programming and operations, usually available on disk.

string A sequence of zero or more characters.

terminal Another name for a work station.

VDU Visual Display Unit: a monitor for use with a computer.

window Small section of the screen that has a separate display from the main section.

word processor A program to store and edit text typed on a computer's keyboard, effectively a superior form of typewriter; the machine itself.

work station A setup of screen, keyboard, and printer linked to a mainframe computer.

zero suppression Elimination of non-significant zeros either on screen or in a print-out.

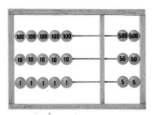

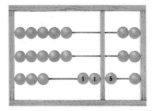

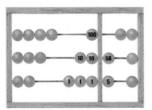

The abacus has been used in calculation since ancient times, and is still in use today.

MATHEMATICS

Mathematics is the science of numbers. It plays an important part in all the other sciences. There are three basic branches of mathematics.

Pure mathematics studies what mathematics can do without any particular practical use.

Applied mathematics relates mathematics to other activities.

Statistics deals with collecting large numbers of figures and analyzing them – for example, taking the United States census every ten years and looking at what its figures tell us about our country.

NUMERATION

The three types of numbers in common use today are the decimal or Arabic system, with the base 10 and using the symbols 0–9; the Roman system, based on the letters I, V, X, L, C, D, and M; and the binary system used by computers, with the base two and using just two symbols, 0 and 1.

In the Roman system I stands for 1, and is repeated to make 2 (II) and 3 (III). V stands for 5, X for 10, L for 50, C for 100, D for 500, and M for 1,000. These letters are combined to make other numbers. A lower symbol before a higher one subtracts from it; a lower symbol after a higher one adds to it; for example XL is 40, while LX is 60. Lines over the top are used for higher figures in the thousands. For example, V̄ is 5000, X̄ is 10,000 and C̄ is 100,000.

DECIMAL MULTIPLES

Prefix	Symbol		Multiplication factor
tera	T	10^{12}	1,000,000,000,000
giga	G	10^{9}	1,000,000,000
mega	M	10^{6}	1,000,000
kilo	k	10^{3}	1,000
hecto	h	10^{2}	100
deca	da	10	10
deci	d	10^{-1}	0.1
centi	c	10^{-2}	0.01
milli	m	10^{-3}	0.001
micro	μ	10^{-6}	0.000001
nano	n	10^{-9}	0.000000001
pico	p	10^{-12}	0.000000000001
femto	f	10^{-15}	0.000000000000001
atto	a	10^{-18}	0.000000000000000001

In binary, the base of the system is two (written as 10). And, just as 10 to the power of three is written as 1 followed by three zeros (1,000), so two to the power of three (8 in decimal) is written 1,000 in binary. To write a number in binary you break it up into powers of two.

EQUIVALENT NUMBERS

Arabic	Roman	Binary	Arabic	Roman	Binary
1	I	1	50	L	110010
2	II	10	60	LX	111100
3	III	11	64	LXIV	1000000
4	IV	100	90	XC	1011010
5	V	101	99	XCIX	1100011
6	VI	110	100	C	1100100
7	VII	111	128	CXXVIII	10000000
8	VIII	1000	200	CC	11001000
9	IX	1001	256	CCLVI	100000000
10	X	1010	300	CCC	100101100
11	XI	1011	400	CD	110010000
12	XII	1100	500	D	111110100
13	XIII	1101	512	DXII	1000000000
14	XIV	1110	600	DC	1001011000
15	XV	1111	900	CM	1110000100
16	XVI	10000	1,000	M	1111101000
17	XVII	10001	1,024	MXXIV	10000000000
18	XVIII	10010	1,500	MD	10111011100
19	XIX	10011	2,000	MM	11111010000
20	XX	10100	4,000	M$\bar{V}$	111110100000
21	XXI	10101	5,000	$\bar{V}$	1001110001000
30	XXX	11110	10,000	$\bar{X}$	10011100010000
32	XXXII	100000	20,000	$\bar{X}\bar{X}$	100111000100000
40	XL	101000	100,000	$\bar{C}$	11000011010100000

MATHEMATICAL FORMULAE

Note: r = radius, h = height; $\pi = 3.14159$

CIRCUMFERENCE

Circle	$2\pi r$

AREA

Circle	πr
Surface of sphere	$4\pi r$
Ellipse, semi-axes a, b	πab
Triangle, base b	$\frac{1}{2}bh$
Rectangle, sides a, b	ab
Trapezium, parallel sides a, c	$\frac{1}{2}h\,(a+c)$
Regular pentagon, side a	$1.721a^2$
Regular hexagon, side a	$2.598a^2$
Regular octagon, side a	$4.828a^2$

VOLUME

Sphere	$\frac{4}{3}\pi r$
Cylinder	$h\pi r$
Cone	$\frac{1}{3}h\pi r$
Rectangular prism, sides a, b, c	abc
Pyramid, base area b	$\frac{1}{3}hb$

ALGEBRAIC

$$a^2 - b^2 = (a+b)(a-b)$$
$$a^2 + 2ab + b^2 = (a+b)^2$$
$$a^2 - 2ab + b^2 = (a-b)^2$$

For quadratic equation $ax^2 + bx + c = 0$,

$$x = \frac{-b \pm \sqrt{b^2 - 4ac}}{2a}$$

ANGLES

second(")	
60"	1 minute (')
60'	1 degree (°)
90°	1 quadrant, or right angle
4 quadrants	1 circle = 360°
1 radian	57.2958° = 57°17'44.8"
2† radians	1 circle = 360°
1°	0.017453 radian

WEIGHTS AND MEASURES

There are two main systems of weights and measures in use in the world: the metric system, based on the number ten, and an older system, called "imperial" in Britain, where it originated, and "customary" in the United States. The customary system is more difficult to use because the units are so varied. The revolutionary government of France devised the metric system in the 1790s. It is now used by people in most countries of the world.

LENGTH

Metric units
millimeter (mm)
10 mm = 1 centimeter (cm)
100 cm = 1 meter (m)
1,000 cm = 1 kilometer (km)
1 micron (μ) = 10^{-6}m (i.e. 1 micrometer)
1 millimicron (mμ) = 10^{-9}m (i.e. 1 nanometer)
1 ångstrom (Å) = 10^{-10}m (i.e. 100 picometers)

Customary units
inch (in.)
12 in. = 1 foot (ft.)
3 ft. = 1 yard (yd.)
1,760 yd. = 1 mile = 5280 ft.
1 link = 7.92 in.
100 links = 1 surveyor's chain = 22 yd.
1 rod, pole, or perch = 5½ yd.
4 rods = 1 chain
10 chains = 1 furlong = 220 yd.
8 furlongs = 1 mile

AREA

Metric units
square millimeter (sq. mm)
100 sq. mm = 1 square centimeter (sq. cm)
10,000 sq. cm = 1 square metre (sq. m)
100 sq. mm = 1 are (a) = 1 square decameter
100 a = 1 hectare (ha) = 1 square hectometer
100 ha = 1 square kilometer (sq. km)

Customary units
square inch (sq. in)
144 sq. in. = 1 square foot (sq. ft.)
9 sq. ft. = 1 square yard (sq. yd.)
4840 sq. yd. = 1 acre
640 acres = 1 square mile (sq. mile)
625 square links = 1 square rod
16 square rods = 1 square chain
10 square chains = 1 acre
36 square miles = 1 township

VOLUME

Metric units
cubic millimeter (cu. mm)

1000 cu mm	1 cubic centimeter (cu. m)
1000 cu cm	1 cubic decimeter (cu. dm) = 1 liter
1000 cu dm	1 cubic meter (cu. m)
1,000,000,000 cu m	1 cubic kilometer (cu. km)

Customary units
cubic inch (cu. in.)

1728 cu. in.	1 cubic foot (cu. ft.)
27 cu. ft.	1 cubic yard (cu. yd.)
5,451,776,000 cu. yd.	1 cubic mile (cu. mile)

The kitchen measuring jug is customarily marked in fluid ounces/pints and sometimes in cu.cm/liters.

CAPACITY

Metric units
milliliter (ml)

1000 ml	1 liter (l)
1001	1 hectoliter (hl)

Customary units
gill

4 gills	1 pint
2 pints	1 quart
4 quarts	1 gallon = 231 cu in.

Dry

4 pecks	1 bushel
8 quarts	1 peck
2 pints	1 quart

WEIGHT

Metric units
milligram (mg)

1000 mg	1 gram (g)
1000 g	1 kilogram (kg)
100 kg	1 quintal (q)
1000 kg	1 metric ton, or tonne (t)

Customary units (Avoirdupois)
grain (gr.); dram (dr.)
7,000 gr. = 1 pound (lb.)
16 dr. = 1 ounce (oz.)
16 oz. = 1 lb.
25 lb. = 1 quarter
100 lb. = 1 hundredweight (cwt.)
20 cwt. = 1 ton (short) = 2,000 lb.
2,240 lb. = 1 ton (long)

Troy weight
24 gr. = 1 pennyweight (dwt.)
20 dwt. = 1 (troy) ounce = 480 gr.
12 oz. = 1 lb.

Apothecaries' weight
20 gr. = 1 scruple
3 scruples = 1 dram
8 drams = 1 (apoth.) ounce = 480 gr.

Crude oil (petroleum)
1 barrel = 35 imperial gallons
= 42 U.S. gallons

Paper (writing)
24 sheets = 1 quire
20 squires = 1 ream = 480 sheets

HISTORICAL UNITS

Where used	Current equivalent
Cubit (elbow to finger tip)	
Egypt (2650 B.C.)	20.6 in. (52.4 cm)
Babylon (1500 B.C.)	20.9 in. (53.0 cm)
Hebrew	17.7 in. (45 cm)
Black Cubit	
(Arabia A.D. 800s)	21.3 in. (54.1 cm)
Mexico (Aztec)	20.7 in. (52.5 cm)
Ancient China	20.9 in. (53.2 cm)
Ancient Greece	18.2 in. (46.3 cm)
Ancient Rome	17.4 in. (44.4 cm)
England	18.0 in. (45.7 cm)
Northern Cubit	26.6 in. (67.6 cm)
(c.3000 B.C.–A.D. 1800s)	
Foot (length of foot	
Athens	12.44 in. (31.6 cm)
Rome	11.66 in. (29.6 cm)
Northern	13.19 in. (33.5 cm)
England (Medieval)	13.19 in. (33.5 cm)
France	12.79 in. (32.5 cm)

Ancient Roman units

1 digitus	0.73 in. (1.85 cm)
4 digiti	2.9 in. (1 palmus = 7.4 cm)
4 palmi	11.7 in. (1 pes = 29.6 cm)
5 pes	4.86 ft. (1 passus = 1.48 m)
125 passus	202.3 yd. (1 stadium = 185 m)
8 stadia	0.92 mi. (1 millar = 1480 m)

TIME

Second (s, or sec)
60 s = 1 minute (min)
60 min = 1 hour (h or hr)
24 h = 1 day (d)
7 days = 1 week
365¼ days = 1 year
10 years = 1 decade
100 years = 1 century
1,000 years = 1 millennium
1 mean solar day = 24 h 3 min 56.555 s
1 sidereal day = 23 h 56 min 4.091 s
1 solar, tropical, or equinoctial year =
365.2422 d (365 d 5 h 48 min 46 s)
1 sidereal year = 365.2564 d (365 d 6 h 9 min
9.5 s)
1 synodic (lunar) month = 29.5306 d
1 sidereal month = 27.3217 d
1 lunar year = 354.3672 d = 12 synodic months

CONVERSION FACTORS

If measurements are customary, multiply by the conversion factors given below to find the metric equivalent; if they are in metric, divide by the conversion factors to find customary.

1 acre	0.4047 hectares
1 bushel (cust.)	36.369 liters
1 centimeter	0.3937 inch
1 chain	20.1168 meters
1 cord	3.62456 cubic meters
1 cubic centimeter	0.0610 cubic inch
1 cubic decimeter	61.024 cubic inches
1 cubic foot	0.0283 cubic meter
1 cubic inch	16.387 cubic centimeters
1 cubic meter	35.3146 cubic feet
	1.3079 cubic yards
1 cubic yard	0.7646 cubic meter
1 fathom	1.8288 meters
1 fluid oz. (apoth.)	28.4131 milliliters
1 fluid oz.	28.4 milliliters
1 foot	0.3048 meter
	30.48 centimeters
1 foot per second	0.6818 mph
	1.097 km/h
1 gallon (customary)	4.5461 liters
1 gallon (U.S. liquid)	3.7854 liters
1 gill	0.142 liter
1 gram	0.0353 ounces
	0.002205 pound
	15.43 grains
	0.0321 ounce (Troy)
1 hectare	2.4710 acres
1 hundredweight	50.80 kilograms
1 inch	2.54 centimeters
1 kilogram	2.2046 pounds
1 kilometer	0.6214 mile
	1093.6 yards
1 knot (international)	0.5144 meters/sec
	1.852 km/h
1 liter	0.220 gallon (imperial)
	0.2642 gallon (U.S.)
	1.7598 pints (imperial)
	0.8799 quarts
1 meter	39.3701 in
	3.2808 ft
	1.0936 yd
1 metric tonne	0.9842 ton
1 mile (statute)	1.6093 kilometers
1 mile (nautical)	1.852 kilometers
1 millimeter	0.03937 inch
1 ounce	28.350 grams
1 peck (customary)	9.0922 liters
1 pennyweight	1.555 grams
1 pica (printer's)	4.2175 millimeters
1 pint (imperial)	0.5683 liter
1 pound	0.4536 kilogram
1 quart (imperial)	1.1365 liters
1 square centimeter	0.1550 square inch
1 square foot	0.0929 square meter
1 square inch	6.4516 square centimeters
1 square kilometer	0.3860 square mile
1 square meter	10.7639 square feet
	1.1960 square yards
1 square mile	2.5900 square kilometers
1 square yard	0.8361 square meter
1 ton	1.0160 square meter
1 yard	0.9144 meter

INTERNATIONAL PAPER SIZES*

	mm	in.
A0	841 × 1189	33.11 × 46.81
A1	594 × 841	23.39 × 33.11
A2	420 × 594	16.54 × 23.39
A3	297 × 420	11.69 × 16.54
A4	210 × 297	8.27 × 11.69
A5	148 × 210	5.83 × 8.27
A6	105 × 148	4.13 × 5.83
A7	74 × 105	2.91 × 4.13
A8	52 × 74	2.05 × 2.91
A9	37 × 52	1.46 × 2.05
A10	26 × 37	1.02 × 1.46

*The sizes are based on a rectangle of area 1 sq meter (AO), with sides in the ratio 1: ×2.

MISCELLANEOUS MEASURES

Nautical

1 span	9 in. = 23 cm
8 spans	1 fathom = 6 ft.
1 cable's length	¹⁄₁₀ nautical mile
1 nautical mile (old)	6080 ft.
1 nautical mile (international)	6076.1 ft. = 1.151 statute miles (= 1852 meters)
60 nautical miles	1 degree
3 nautical miles	1 league (nautical)
1 knot	1 nautical mile per hour
1 ton (shipping)	42 cubic feet
1 ton (displacement)	35 cubic feet
1 ton (register)	100 cubic feet

Timber
1,000 millisteres = 1 stere = 1 cu. m
1 board foot = 144 cu. in (12 × 12 × 1 in.)
1 cord foot = 16 cu. ft.
1 cord = 8 cord feet

Horses (height)
1 hand = 4 in. = 10 cm

Knitting needle sizes

metric	American
2 mm	0
2¼ mm	1
2¾–3 mm	2
3¼ mm	3
—	4
3¾	5
4 mm	6
4½ mm	7
5 mm	8
5½ mm	9
6 mm	10
6½–7 mm	10½
7½–8 mm	11
9 mm	13
10 mm	15

TEMPERATURES

The following table shows comparative temperatures in the Celsius (Centigrade) scale and in the Fahrenheit scale. Note that freezing point in Celsius is 0°C, and in Fahrenheit is 32°, while boiling point in the two scales is respectively 100° and 212°. The scales coincide on just one temperature – minus 40°.

°Celsius	°Fahrenheit
100	212
90	194
80	176
70	158
60	140
50	122
40	104
30	86
20	68
10	50
0	32
−10	14
−20	−4
−30	−22
−40	−40
−50	−58

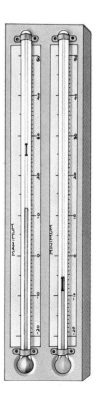

*Maximum and minimum thermometers (right)
are of the alcohol type, with metal markers.
The bimetal thermometer relies on the
different expansion rates of two metals.*

TECHNOLOGY

Technology is defined as the application of practical science to industry. We live in the age of technology. Its benefits are everywhere – in the home, the factory, the office, at school, in hospital.

The most obvious benefits of modern technology are the public services – suppliers of water, gas, and electricity; modern sewage and refuse disposal; telephone, radio, and television services. To travel from home to school or work there are cars, trains, and buses – even the humble bicycle is a technological achievement.

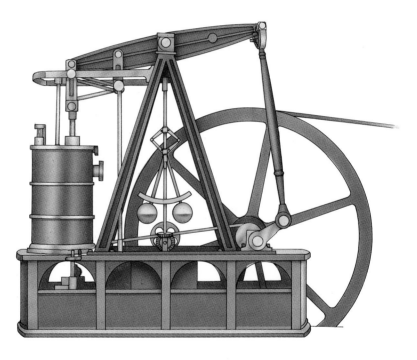

James Watt's steam engine (1761) was more efficient than earlier designs. It was quickly adopted in factories to drive machinery, such as looms in textile mills.

Modern factories are equipped with a range of machines, many of them controlled by computers. Offices have such business machines as typewriters, photocopiers, word processors, and computers. Schools are equipped with laboratories, computers, television, and video. Hospitals have a range of equipment to detect disorders and treat them, ranging from electrocardiographs, which monitor heart conditions, to X-ray machines and ultrasonic scanners which can peer inside a person's body.

This technology is mostly very recent. It all began in the 1700s in what is known as the Industrial Revolution – a

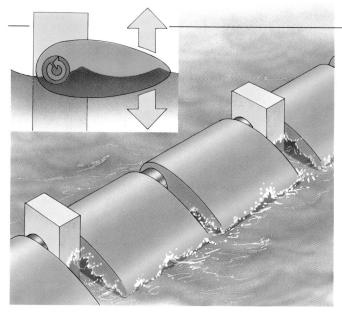

Wave power is one projected answer to future "clean energy" requirements. Each "beak" of the nodding boom or "duck" contains a small generator. As the waves move the "beak" up and down (inset) the generator turns to produce electricity.

peaceful revolution which is still going on. The revolution began in Britain, where conditions were right – a period of internal peace and prosperity.

The start was in the textile industry, with machines to spin thread and weave cloth. Early factories were set up beside rivers, which provided power through waterwheels to drive the new machines. At the same time the steam engine was being developed and, by the end of the 1700s, steam was driving much of the machinery. It became easier to build machines because iron was now freely available.

Although the Industrial Revolution began in Britain, it spread almost at once to the rest of Europe and to North America. Inventors in these lands were quick to help the revolution along.

The combination of steam and iron made railroads and fast steamships possible in the 1800s, thus speeding up communications. During that century the electric telegraph, the telephone, and radio made their appearance, and airplanes followed early in the 1900s. The latest revolution has been brought about by the computer which has speeded up work in offices and factories.

But all these technological advances have been bought at a price: damage to the environment in which we live by pollution of air, water, and soil – especially from factories and cars. Chemicals released into the atmosphere are even damaging the layer of ozone high above us which protects us from the more harmful rays of the Sun. Now we are having to harness the resources of technology to preserve the Earth we live on, before it is too late.

ENGINEERING

Engineering is the term used to cover construction of all kinds. The ancient Egyptians were the first real engineers. When the pyramids were being built, about 2500 B.C., Egyptian workmen were already using tools such as the lathe. They smelted and cast metals, and their quarrying and stoneworking techniques were so advanced that they could fit blocks of stone 40 feet (12 m) long so closely together that a hair couldn't be passed between them.

Today there are several branches of engineering:

Mechanical engineering is concerned with the making of machines, from airplanes to power plants.

Civil engineering covers the construction of buildings, canals, dams, highways, railroads, and tunnels.

Mining engineering and metallurgy includes the construction of mines, the extraction of minerals, and refining metals.

Oil-based chemicals are used in the manufacture of thousands of products – among them, the items illustrated here. Plastics, (vinyl, polyester, polyurethane, and polyethylene for example) are all by-products of the petro-chemical industry, which relies on oil (and to a lesser extent coal) as its raw material.

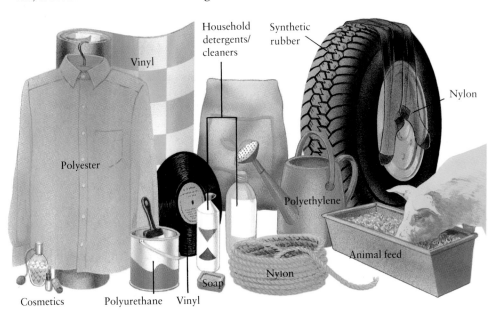

Chemical engineering includes all the manufacturing processes which involve chemicals, such as making medicines, plastics, and soap.

Electrical and electronic engineering is concerned with any processes using electricity, and more and more those using electronic equipment, such as computers, radio, and television.

ENGINEERING RECORDS

First successful solar furnace was built in the 1960s at Odeillo, in the French Pyrenees. It produces a heat of 6,300°F (3,500°C) – enough to melt a steel plate in one minute.

World's biggest hydroelectric plant is the Itaipu power plant, on the Paraná River between Brazil and Paraguay. It produces enough power to supply a city twice the size of New York.

Largest man-made hole is the Bingham Canyon Copper Mine near Salt Lake City, Utah. It is 2,543 ft. (775 m) deep and covers more than 2¾ sq. miles (7.2 sq km).

Deepest mine is the Western Deep Levels gold mine at Carletonville, South Africa. It is 12,390 ft. (3,777 m) deep.

Largest movable flood barrier is the Thames River Barrier at Woolwich, completed in 1983. It is 1,706 ft. (520 m) wide.

Most massive vehicles are the two Marion "Crawler" transporters used to carry U.S. space shuttles to their launch pads. They measure 131 ft. × 114 ft. (40 m by 34.7 m)..

Largest scientific instrument ever built is the LEP (Large Electron-Positron Collider) which went into operation in August 1989. It is in a circular tunnel, 16.6 miles (26.56 km) in circumference, which passes beneath the Jura mountains along the border between France and Switzerland. It is designed to help scientists explore the nature of matter.

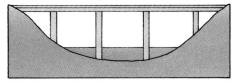

Beam

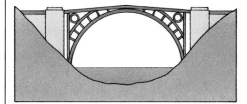

Arch

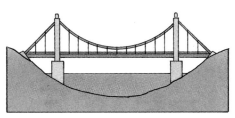

Suspension

Three common bridge designs. The beam is the simplest, with the weight borne on vertical piers. Suspension bridges have the longest individual spans.

HOW TUNNELS ARE BUILT

Many tunnels are dug with special machines called moles, which are like huge drills that push slowly through the ground. At the head of the mole, rotating cutters dig out the rock which is carried away along a conveyor belt.

Powerful jacks act like springs to force the mole forward as it digs away the rock and soil. As the mole advances, engineers fix lining panels in place to form the walls of the tunnel. For both power and safety, the mole is driven by electric motors and hydraulic jacks, which are supplied with high-pressure fluid.

In good conditions, a mole can burrow through the ground at 16 ft. (5 m) an hour for a train-sized tunnel. To prevent waterlogged soil from slowing down the rate of progress, the head of the mole is contained in a sealed compartment.

DAMS: HIGHEST AND LARGEST

HIGHEST	Location	Type	(m)	(ft.)	Completed
Rogunsky	Tajikistan	earthfill	335	1098	*
Nurek	Tajikistan	earthfill	317	1040	1980
Grande Dixence	Switzerland	gravity	284	932	1962
Inguri	Georgia	arch	272	892	*
Vaiont	Italy	multi-arch	262	858	1961
Mica	Canada	rockfill	242	794	1973
Mauvoisin	Switzerland	arch	237	777	1958

LARGEST	Location	(cu. m)	(cu. yd.)	Completed
Syncrude Tailings	Canada	540,000,000	706,000,000	*
Chapetón	Argentina	296,200,000	387,400,000	*
Pati	Argentina	238,180,000	311,527,000	*
New Cornelia Tailings	Arizona	209,506,000	274,026,000	1973
Tarbela	Pakistan	105,570,000	138,100,000	1979
Fort Peck	Montana	96,050,000	125,630,000	1940
Lower Usuma	Nigeria	93,000,000	121,650,000	*

Under construction.

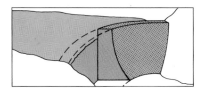

An arch dam curves so the weight of water pushes against the sides of the valley.

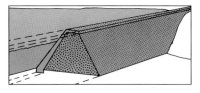

Earth embankment dams are triangular in section with a skin of concrete.

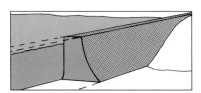

A gravity dam of concrete or stone is usually massive.

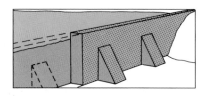

Buttress dams have relatively thin walls strengthened by buttress supports.

TALLEST BUILDINGS

Name	Location	Height (m)	Height (ft.)	Date
CN Tower	Toronto, Canada	553	1815	1976
Sears Tower	Chicago	443	1454	1974
World Trade Center	New York City	411	1350	1973
Empire State Building	New York City	381	1250	1931
Chrysler Building	New York City	319	1046	1930
Woolworth Building	New York City	241	792	1913

LONGEST BRIDGE SPANS

	Location	Longest span (ft.)	(m)	Opened
SUSPENSION				
Akashi-Kaiko	Japan	6,496	1,980	*
Humber Estuary	England	4,626	1,410	1980
Verrazano Narrows	New York	4,260	1,298	1964
Golden Gate	California	4,200	1,280	1937
CANTILEVER				
Quebec Railroad	Canada	1,800	549	1917
Forth Rail	Scotland	1,710	521	1890
STEEL ARCH				
New River Gorge	W. Virginia	1,700	518	1977
Bayonne	New Jersey	1,652	504	1931
Sydney Harbour	Australia	1,650	503	1932
CABLE-STAYED				
Vancouver	Canada	1,526	465	1986
St. Nazaire	Loire, France	1,325	404	1975
Sunshine Valley	Florida	1,200	366	1986
CONTINUOUS TRUSS				
Astoria	Oregon	1,232	376	1966
CONCRETE ARCH				
Gladesville	Australia	1,000	305	1964
LONGEST BRIDGE (total length)				
Pontchartrain Causeway	Louisiana	23.9 miles	38.4 km	1969

*Under construction.

LONGEST TUNNELS

RAILROAD*

Seikan (Japan)	33 miles 862 yds.	53.9 km	Opened 1988
Eurotunnel (England/France)	31 miles 53 yds.	49.94 km	Due to open 1993
Oshimizu (Japan)	13 miles 1397 yds.	22.2 km	**
Simplon II (Switz/Italy)	12 miles 559 yds.	19.823 km	Opened 1922

ROAD

St. Gotthard (Switzerland)	10 miles 246 yds.	16.32 km	Opened 1980
Arlberg (Austria)	8 miles 1232 yds.	14.0 km	Opened 1978
Mont Blanc (France/Italy)	7 miles 350 yds.	11.59 km	Opened 1965

UNDERWATER

Seikan (Japan)†	14 miles 880 yds.	23.3 km	Opened 1988
Shin Kanmon (Japan)	11 miles 1073 yds.	18.7 km	Opened 1974

*Longest continuous rail tunnel is the Belyaevo-Medvedkovo stretch of the Moscow Metro subway, opened in 1979: it is 19 miles 123 yds. (30.7 km) long.

**Under construction.

†Length of the underwater section of the tunnel.

INVENTIONS

B.C.
7000   *POTTERY* in Iran
6000   *BRICKS* at Jericho, Palestine
4000   *WRITING* in Mesopotamia
3750   *COSMETICS* in Egypt
3200   *THE WHEEL* in Mesopotamia
3000   *GLASS* in Egypt
2600   *GEOMETRY* in Egypt
747   *CALENDAR* by the Babylonians
700   *DENTURES* by the Etruscans of Italy
100s   *PAPER* in China
A.D.
767   *PRINTING* in Japan
950   *GUNPOWER* in China
1280   *CANNON* in China
1280s   *SPECTACLES* in Italy
1440s   *PRINTING PRESS AND METAL TYPE* Johannes Gutenberg (Ger)
1589   *KNITTING MACHINE* William Lee (Eng)
1590   *MICROSCOPE* Hans and Zacharias Janssen (Neth)
1592   *THERMOMETER* Galileo (It)
1608   *TELESCOPE* Hans Lippershey (Neth)
1620   *SUBMARINE* Cornelius van Drebbel (Neth)
1644   *BAROMETER* Evangelista Torricelli (It)
1679   *PRESSURE COOKER* Denis Papin (Fr)
1698   *STEAM PUMP* Thomas Savery (Eng)
1712   *STEAM ENGINE* Thomas Newcomen (Eng)
1733   *FLYING SHUTTLE* John Kay (Eng)
1752   *LIGHTNING CONDUCTOR* Benjamin Franklin (U.S.)
1767   *SPINNING JENNY* James Hargreaves (Eng)
1785   *POWER LOOM* Edmund Cartwright (Eng)
1792   *COTTON GIN* Eli Whitney (U.S.)
1800   *BATTERY* Alessandro Volta (It)
1816   *CAMERA* Nicéphore Niépce (Fr)
1823   *ELECTROMAGNET* William Sturgeon (Eng)
1827   *FRICTION MATCHES* John Walker (Eng)
1831   *DYNAMO* Michael Faraday (Eng)
1834   *REAPING MACHINE* Cyrus McCormick (U.S.)
1838   *SINGLE-WIRE TELEGRAPH* Samuel F.B. Morse (U.S.)

Above: *Hargreaves's spinning jenny was hand-operated but spun eight threads simultaneously.*
Below: *The first practical typewriter was invented by Christopher Latham Sholes.*

1839   *BICYCLE* Kirkpatrick Macmillan (Scot)
1841   *VULCANIZATION* Charles Goodyear (U.S.)
1845   *SEWING MACHINE* Elias Howe (U.S.)
1849   *SAFETY PIN* Walter Hunt (U.S.)
1852   *GYROSCOPE* Léon Foucault (Fr)
1852   *ELEVATOR* Elisha Otis (U.S.)
1858   *WASHING MACHINE* Hamilton Smith (U.S.)
1862   *RAPID-FIRE GUN* Richard Gatling (U.S.)
1866   *DYNAMITE* Alfred Nobel (Swe)
1868   *MOTORCYCLE* Michaux brothers (Fr)
1872   *TYPEWRITER* Christopher Scholes (U.S.)
1873   *BARBED WIRE* Joseph Glidden (U.S.)

Edison's original phonograph played cylindrical records.

Baird's televisor (1930) lost out to the Marconi-EMI electronic television system.

The Polaroid camera.

1876	*TELEPHONE* Alexander Bell (Scot/U.S.)
1876	*CARPET SWEEPER* Melville Bissell (U.S.)
1877	*PHONOGRAPH* Thomas Edison (U.S.)
1878	*MICROPHONE* David Hughes (Eng/U.S.)
1879	*INCANDESCENT LAMP* Thomas Edison (U.S.)
1884	*FOUNTAIN PEN* Lewis Waterman (U.S.)
1885	*AUTOMOBILE ENGINE* Karl Benz (Ger) and Gottlieb Daimler (Ger), independently
1885	*TRANSFORMER* William Stanley (U.S.)
1892	*VACUUM BOTTLE* James Dewar (Scot)
1892	*DIESEL ENGINE* Rudolf Diesel (Ger)
1893	*ZIP FASTENER* Whitcomb Judson (U.S.)
1895	*RADIO* Guglielmo Marconi (It)
1895	*SAFETY RAZOR* King C. Gillette (U.S.)
1898	*TAPE RECORDER* Valdemar Poulson (Den)
1901	*VACUUM CLEANER* Herbert Booth (Eng)
1903	*AIRPLANE* Wright Brothers (U.S.)
1924	*FROZEN FOOD PROCESS* Clarence Birdseye (U.S.)
1925	*TV* John L. Baird (Scot) and others
1930	*JET ENGINE* Frank Whittle (Eng)
1935	*NYLON* Wallace Carothers (U.S.)
1938	*BALL POINT PEN* Ladislao Biro (Hung)
1945	*ELECTRONIC COMPUTER* J. Presper Eckert (U.S.) and John W. Mauchly (U.S.)
1947	*POLAROID CAMERA* Edwin Land (U.S.)
1948	*TRANSISTOR* John Bardeen (U.S.), Walter Brattain (U.S.) and William Schockley (U.S.)
1948	*LONG-PLAYING RECORD* Columbia (U.S.)
1960	*LASER* Theodore Maiman (U.S.)
1961	*SILICON CHIP* Texas Instruments (U.S.)
1971	*MICROPROCESSOR* Intel Corp (U.S.)
1981	*SPACE SHUTTLE* NASA (U.S.)

SCIENCE GLOSSARY

absolute zero Lowest temperature possible in theory; zero on absolute scale is $-459.6°F$ $(-273.15°C)$.

acceleration Rate of change of velocity; measured in distance per second per second.

acid Chemical substance that when dissolved in water produces hydrogen ions, which may be replaced by metals to form salts.

alkali Base consisting of a soluble metal hydroxide.

alloy Metal composed of more than one element; e.g. brass (copper and zinc).

Bronze, an alloy of tin and copper, was widely used in the ancient world. These bronze-tipped spears are nearly 2,000 years old and the bronze vessel was made in China in about 1100 B.C.

alternating current Electric current that rapidly goes from maximum in one direction through zero to maximum in the other direction.

ampere (A) Unit of electric current equivalent to flow of 6×10^{18} electrons per sec (i.e. 6 million million million electrons).

anode Positive electrode through which current enters an electrolytic cell or a vacuum tube.

Archimedes' principle When a body is immersed or partly immersed in a fluid, the apparent loss in weight is equal to the weight of the fluid displaced.

atom Smallest fragment of an element that can take part in a chemical reaction. See also isotope.

base Substance that reacts chemically with an acid to form a salt and water.

battery Device that converts chemical energy into electrical energy.

boiling point Temperature at which liquid turns into vapor throughout its bulk.

calorie Unit of heat equal to amount needed to raise the temperature of one gram of water through one degree C.

catalyst Substance that markedly alters the speed of a chemical reaction without appearing to take part in it.

cathode Negative electrode through which an electric current leaves an electrolytic cell or a vacuum tube.

Celsius Temperature scale on which $0°C$ is the melting point of ice and $100°C$ is boiling point of water; often called centigrade.

circuit, electrical The complete path taken by an electric current.

combustion (burning) Chemical reaction in which a substance combines with oxygen and gives off heat and light.

compound Substance consisting of two or more elements in chemical combination in definite proportions.

condensation Change of vapor into liquid that takes place when pressure is applied to it or the temperature is lowered.

conductor, electric Substance that permits the flow of electricity; e.g. metal.

crystal Substance that has been solidified in a definite geometrical form. Some solids do not form crystals.

current Flow of electrons along a conductor.

decibel Unit for comparing power levels or sound intensities.

diffraction The spreading out of light by passing it through a narrow slit or past the edge of an obstacle.

direct current Current that always flows in the same direction.

elasticity Property of a material that makes it go back to its original shape after a force deforming it is removed.

electrode Metal plate through which electric current enters or leaves an electrolysis cell, battery, or vacuum tube. See anode and cathode.

electromagnet Magnet that produces magnetism because of current in a wire.

electron Negatively charged subatomic particle.

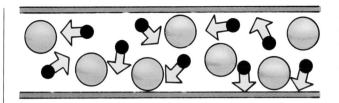

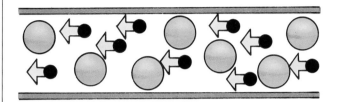

In a flowing current, all the electrons in the wire move in the same direction – from negative terminal to positive terminal.

element Substance made up entirely of exactly similar atoms (all with the same atomic number).

energy Capacity for doing work.

evaporation Phenomenon in which liquid turns into vapor without necessarily reaching the boiling point.

fission (splitting) In atomic or nuclear fission, the nuclei of heavy atoms split and release vast quantities of energy.

fluid Substance (liquid or gas) that takes the shape of part or all of the vessel that contains it.

focus The point at which converging rays of light meet.

force Anything that can act on a stationary body and make it move, or make a moving body change speed or direction.

frequency Of a wave motion, the number of oscillations, cycles, vibrations, or waves per second.

friction Force that resists sliding or rolling of one surface in contact with another.

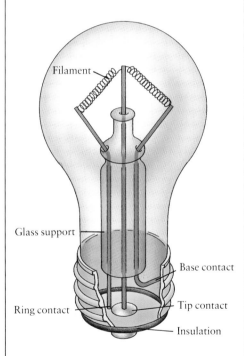

In a light bulb an electric current flows through a thin coil of wire called a filament. Because the filament has a high electrical resistance, it gets so hot that it glows white and gives off light. By contrast, in strip lighting the electric current excites gas molecules in the tube which then emit light.

The tread on a tire increases friction, and so reduces slipping or skidding. Without friction, a vehicle would stand still, no matter how fast its wheels turned.

fulcrum The point of support of a lever when it is lifting something.

fusion, nuclear The joining of nuclei of light atoms together with the release of vast amounts of energy; this is the process that occurs in stars.

gas A fluid that, no matter how little there is, always takes up the whole of the vessel containing it.

gravitation Force of attraction between any two objects because of their masses.

inclined plane Simple machine consisting of smooth plane sloping upwards; used for moving heavy loads with a relatively small force.

inertia Property of an object that makes it resist being moved or its motion being changed.

infrared rays Electromagnetic radiation of wavelengths just longer than those of visible light; invisible heat radiation.

insulator Substance that does not conduct electricity.

ion Atom or group of atoms carrying an electrical charge.

isotope One of two or more forms of an element with the same atomic number (i.e. number of protons in the nucleus), but different relative atomic masses (due to different numbers of neutrons in the nucleus).

joule Unit of work or energy.

laser Device that produces an intense, thin beam of light; abbreviation for light amplification by stimulated emission of radiation.

latent heat Heat absorbed, without a rise in temperature, when a substance is changed from solid to liquid or liquid to gas.

lens Device that affects light passing through it by converging (bringing together) or diverging (spreading apart) the rays.

lever Simple machine consisting of a rigid beam pivoted at one point, called the fulcrum; effort applied at one point on the beam can lift a load at another point.

liquid Substance that without changing its volume takes up the shape of all, or the lower part of, the vessel containing it.

mass Amount of matter in an object.

melting point Temperature at which solid turns to liquid; equal to freezing point of the liquid.

metal Element or alloy that is a good conductor of heat and electricity and has a high density.

mixture More than one element or compound together, but not in chemical combination.

molecule Smallest amount of chemical substance that can exist alone; it is made up of two or more atoms.

momentum The product of the mass and velocity of a moving body.

motion, Newton's laws of (1) A stationary object remains still or a moving object continues to move in a straight line unless acted on by an external force. (2) The force producing acceleration in an object is proportional to the product of the object's mass and its acceleration. (3) Every action has an equal and opposite reaction.

neutron Uncharged atomic particle found in the nuclei of all atoms except hydrogen.

newton Unit of measurement of a force. The weight of an apple is approximately 1 newton.

nucleus, atomic The positively charged center of an atom; consists of one or more protons and, except for hydrogen, one or more neutrons. See also atom.

ozone Form of oxygen containing three atoms in each molecule; O_3.

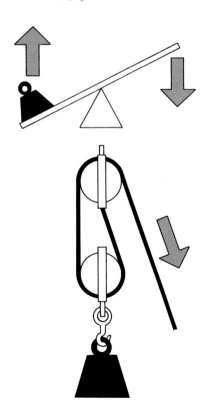

The lever (top) and pulley are two of the most important simple machines.

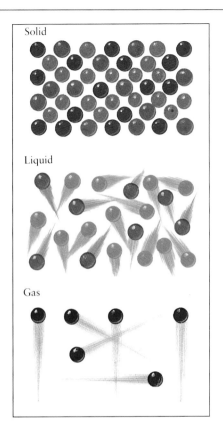

The three states of matter. In each state, molecules are arranged differently.

proton Positively charged atomic particle found in the nuclei of all atoms.

radiation, heat Transfer of heat by means of waves; infrared rays.

radioactivity Emission of radiation, such as alpha particles, beta particles, and gamma rays, from unstable elements by the spontaneous splitting of their atomic nuclei.

refraction Bending of a light ray as it crosses the boundary between two media of different optical density.

salt Chemical compound formed, with water, when a base reacts with an acid; a salt is also formed, often with the production of hydrogen, when a metal reacts with an acid.

solid State of matter that has a definite shape and resists having it changed; a crystalline solid melts to a liquid on heating above its melting point.

solubility Quantity of a substance (solute) that will dissolve in a solvent to form a solution.

speed Distance traveled by a moving object divided by the time taken.

static electricity Electricity at rest (not flowing), in contrast to current.

superconductor Material which conducts current at very low temperatures with virtually no resistance.

surface tension Property of the surface of a liquid that makes it behave as though it were covered with a thin elastic skin.

ultrasonic waves "Sound" waves beyond the range of human hearing.

ultraviolet rays Electromagnetic radiation of wavelengths just shorter than those of visible light. The Sun's radiation is rich in ultraviolet rays.

vacuum In practice, a region in which pressure is considerably less than atmospheric pressure.

vapor Gas that can be turned into a liquid by compressing it without cooling.

velocity Rate of change of position equal to speed in a particular direction.

volt (V) Unit of electromotive force; (emf).

volume Measurement of the space occupied by an object.

watt (W) Unit of electrical power, defined as the rate of work done in joules per second; equal to the product of current in amperes (A) and potential difference in volts (V). $W = AV$.

wavelength Of a wave motion, the distance between crests (or troughs) of two consecutive waves.

waves Regular disturbances that carry energy. Light and radio travel as electromagnetic waves.

X rays Very short wavelength electro-magnetic waves.

Ultraviolet rays from the Sun tan pale skin. Most UV light is absorbed by the atmosphere.

Transportation

One of the world's greatest inventions is the wheel, most likely developed from the notion of transporting heavy loads on rolling logs. Logs floating downstream probably provided inspiration for the first rafts and boats. A man watching steam lift the lid off a kettle got the idea for a steam engine, which revolutionized transportation in the 1700s. Since then, people have discovered how to fly and have penetrated the ocean depths and outer space, but in many parts of the world we still rely on faithful beasts of burden to get us and our belongings from one place to the next.

Transportation and the need for it have grown up together over the centuries. At first, people had to rely on their own two feet for moving from place to place, and had to carry any loads themselves.

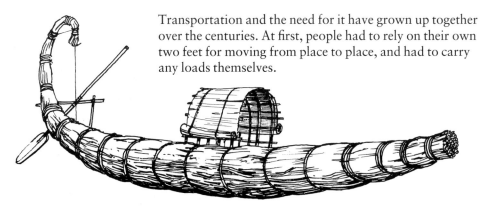

Ancient Egyptian boat made from bundles of reeds.

Water was probably the first means of transportation that people used. Logs floating in rivers would have put the idea into their heads. It seems likely that river transportation has been used for hundreds of thousands of years because, when migrating over the land, people must have had to cross streams many times.

The first craft to be used were undoubtedly rafts – logs lashed together with vines, or bundles of reeds tied together. By 6,000 years ago, people were building boats and had invented sails.

The big change in land transportation came with the domestication of animals, which began less than 10,000 years ago. The most important animal for carrying loads and riders was the horse, in use in the Middle East more than 5,000 years ago. Horses remained the chief means of transportation until the development of railroads in the early 1800s.

Important as horses were for carrying people and loads, as draft animals – that is, animals used for pulling loads –

oxen of various kinds were preferred because with the primitive harness then in use they could draw larger and heavier weights.

The harness consisted of a wooden yoke attached to the shoulders and neck of the ox. An ox pulls with its head whereas a horse uses the base of its neck. Therefore, the yoke tended to throttle horses. When the horse collar came into use in Europe, from about 500 B.C. onward, the full power of the horse for pulling heavy loads could be exploited.

Leonardo da Vinci sketched this helicopter-like flying machine in the early 1500s. It never flew, for there was no engine able to power it.

Horses are not suited to desert conditions. There the camel is the most important beast of burden. It can travel for days without water and can feed on plants that other animals reject, such as thorn trees. Its feet are large and do not sink into soft sand. The main disadvantage is that camels seem to have a grudge against everything, even other camels, and especially work!

In the 1980s researchers in Egypt, Israel, Pakistan, Saudi Arabia, and Syria were studying camels with the idea of extending their uses in areas of Africa and Asia where severe drought and famine are common, and other animals such as horses and cattle do not manage well.

The Industrial Revolution

The Industrial Revolution, which began in Britain in the 1700s, changed the methods and speed of transportation. In the 1700s people began constructing networks of canals, especially in Europe. Canal travel was cheap and ideal for shipping heavy loads.

Above: *An ordinary bicycle, or penny-farthing, of the 1880s.*
Below: *An early submarine: The* Turtle *of 1776. This tiny one-man craft tried to sink a British warship during the Revolutionary War.*

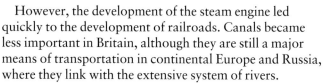

Liner Lengths

Great Western (1837)

Great Eastern (1858)

Mauretania (1906)

Normandie (1932)

Queen Elizabeth (1940)

United States (1952)

France (1962)

Queen Elizabeth 2 (1968)

Above: *The evolution of the ocean liner: as engine power increased, so did the size, speed, and luxury of passenger ships.*
Below: *An early raft constructed from logs tied together with reeds.*

However, the development of the steam engine led quickly to the development of railroads. Canals became less important in Britain, although they are still a major means of transportation in continental Europe and Russia, where they link with the extensive system of rivers.

Railroads dominated land travel until the advent of the car, in the late 1800s and early 1900s. Today, cars and trucks form the main means of transportation for millions of people.

At sea, steam, and later diesel engines, made sea travel faster. For the first 50 years of the 20th century, the oceans were dominated by the giant passenger liners, such as the *Queen Mary* and *Queen Elizabeth*, which made regular journeys across the Atlantic and other oceans.

Although the great liners have had their heyday, giant ships still ply the seas, but now they are bulk carriers for oil and other freight.

Air transportation developed rapidly after World War II and now most long-distance passenger traffic and some freight is carried by air.

Modern transportation

Transportation today is a combination of many means of travel and freighting. On land, roads provide the basic means of transportation, because they run from door to door. All over North America and Europe, trucks carry freight, while cars and buses carry passengers.

Other means of transportation provide a service only to and from certain places – seaports, airports, railroad stations – and depend on road vehicles to carry people and loads to their final destinations. The modern transportation network is a miracle of organization.

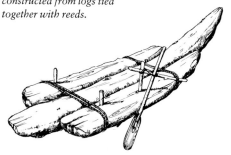

Right: *Last of its line: Atlantic 4-4-2 steam locomotive.*

Milestones

B.C.

4000 Earliest known canals were constructed in Mesopotamia (modern Iraq).

c. **3200** First wheeled vehicles, with solid disk wheels, are used in Mesopotamia.

c. **2000** Spoked wheels come into use.

1800 Hittites develop war chariots.

540 Chinese begin the Grand Canal, from Beijing to Hangzhou (completed A.D. 1327).

312 Roman engineers build the Appian Way from Rome to Capua.

c. **200** China develops a system of roads.

Above: *Cugnot's steam carriage of 1769 had a top speed of just over 3 mph (5 km/h).*

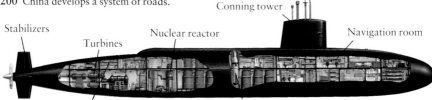

Conning tower · Stabilizers · Turbines · Nuclear reactor · Navigation room · Living quarters · Missile

Above: *A nuclear submarine, showing the reactor and the steam turbine engines.*

A.D.

c. **1100** Magnetic compass comes into use.

1400s The first three-masted ships are built.

1474 Four-wheeled coaches are built in Germany.

1662 Blaise Pascal (France) invents the first (horse-drawn) omnibus.

1783 Marquis Jouffroy d'Abbans (France) builds the first successful steamboat.

1802 First paddle steamer, the *Charlotte Dundas*, sails on the Forth and Clyde Canal, Scotland.

1815 John L. McAdam (Scotland) develops macadam paving for roads.

1819 First iron passenger vessel, the barge *Vulcan*, goes into service on the Forth and Clyde Canal.

1831 First passenger railroad opens (UK).

1835 Screw propellor invented.

1839 First pedal-driven bicycle.

1852 Henri Giffard (France) flies first airship.

1863 First underground railway opens in London.

1869 Suez Canal opens.

1869 U.S. transcontinental railroad completed.

1876 Nikolaus Otto improves the four-stroke gasoline engine.

1890 First electric-powered tube railroad.

1897 First diesel engine built.

1903 First power flight in heavier-than-air craft.

1914 Panama Canal is opened.

1925 First diesel locomotive goes into regular service in the U.S.

1936 Prototype helicopter successfully tested.

1939 First jet aircraft.

1954 First nuclear-powered submarine (U.S.).

1961 First man in space.

1987 Work begins on the Channel Tunnel between England and France.

TRAVEL BY ROAD

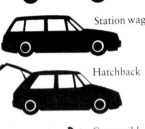

Notchback

Fastback

Station wagon

Hatchback

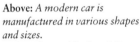

Convertible

In 1769 the *Fardier*, the world's first horseless carriage, rumbled onto the road. The brainchild of Capitaine Nicolas Cugnot of the French army, it was a steam cart designed to haul guns. Its top speed was 3 mph (5 km/h), and it had to stop every 15 minutes to take in water and raise steam pressure. It was not a success.

From such unlikely beginnings came the modern automobile and truck. Steam proved unreliable and it was not until nearly a century later, after the invention of the internal combustion engine, that Karlz Benz in 1885 and Gottlieb Daimler in 1886 produced the first successful cars. Mass production of cars was begun in the United States by Eli Ransom Olds, whose Oldsmobiles began rolling off the production lines in 1901.

Today, there are more than 411 million vehicles on the world's roads. The United States has about 40 percent of the world's total.

Above: *A modern car is manufactured in various shapes and sizes.*
Right: *The world's first fully enclosed car, the Renault of 1898. Renault put the engine at the front of the car, driving the read wheels through a gearbox and propeller shaft, with no chains or belts.*

Induction   Compression   Ignition   Exhaust

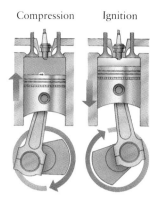 

How a gasoline engine works. Induction: *Piston moves downward and petrol/air mixture is drawn into cylinder.* Compression: *Piston rises, compressing mixture.* Ignition: *Spark plug sparks, igniting compressed mixture. Gases force piston downward.* Exhaust: *Piston moves upward, forcing out burned gases.*

DATES IN ROAD TRAVEL HISTORY

1888 First successful electric trolley cars run in Richmond, Virginia, in the United States.

1901 A car with front-wheel drive, the Korn and Latil Voiturette, is built in France.

1901 A new model Daimler is named the Mercedes, after the daughter of one of the firm's agents. The name has persisted to this day.

1902 A nine horsepower Napier car is built in Britain with an all-steel body.

1902 Belgium's Dechamps cars are built with an electric starter as standard.

1902 Renault of France introduces drum brakes, and Frederick Lanchester of Britain experiments with disc brakes.

1903 A Dutch Spyker is the first car to be fitted with four-wheel drive and brakes.

1904 The Hon. Charles Rolls and Henry Royce found the firm of Rolls-Royce.

1904 First car with a silencer is built in the United States.

1905 Gasoline-driven buses are introduced in London.

1908 Henry Ford produces his first Model T – over the next 19 years he sells 15,007,033 of them. It originally cost $850.00; car ownership now possible for the masses.

1916 First automatic windshield wipers are fitted to a Willys Knight in the United States.

1919 The world's first traffic lights are installed in Detroit, Mich.

1921 The first hydraulic brakes are fitted to an American Duesenberg.

1924 The world's first expressway opened, an *autostrada* between Milan and Varese, Italy.

1926 The Soviet Union builds its first car, the "Nami 1."

1927 White lines down the center of the road are first used in Britain.

1928 The first transcontinental bus service in the United States begins a San Francisco–New York service.

1929 A U.S. Cadillac is the first production car to be fitted with a synchromesh gearbox.

1934 Citroen of France introduces monocoque construction – building body and chassis in one.

1934 Percy Shaw invents "Cat's eyes" – reflecting road studs – in England.

1938 Automatic direction signaling is introduced.

1948 Tubeless tires are introduced.

1967 First car with a Wankel rotary engine is built in Germany.

1980 General Motors begin fitting computers in some cars to reduce fuel consumption.

1988 Lead-free gasoline is introduced in the European Community.

The Ford Model T, known as the "Tin Lizzie."

THE MIGHTY ENGINE

The heart of the car is the internal-combustion engine, whose development in the 19th century made the car possible. Here are some of the terms used in describing an engine.

accelerator Pedal that regulates engine speed by controlling the flow of fuel.

air-cooled engine Engine cooled by air drawn into the engine compartment by a fan.

choke Means of enriching the fuel/air mixture going to the cylinder.

crankshaft Shaft that is turned by the connecting rods from the pistons. The up-and-down motion of the pistons is converted into rotary motion.

cylinder Broad tube in the engine in which each piston moves up and down.

dipstick Rod for measuring the amount of oil in the crankcase.

distributor Unit that distributes high-voltage current from the coil to each of the spark plugs in turn.

exhaust system Pipes that carry exhaust gases away from the engine.

fan belt Belt that drives the cooling fan from a pulley on the crankshaft.

four-stroke cycle Operating cycle of the internal combustion engine. The strokes (up or down movements of the piston) are induction, compression, power, and exhaust.

ignition Firing of the fuel/air mixture in the cylinders.

radiator Device for cooling the water in the car's cooling system.

spark plug Device that, using high-voltage current from the distributor, generates a spark to ignite the fuel/air mixture in the cylinder.

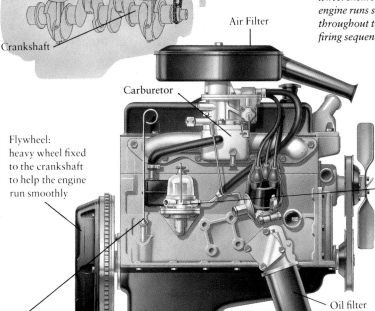

Cutaway of a car engine. The engine may have as many as 150 moving parts. The flywheel ensures that the engine runs smoothly throughout the cylinder-firing sequence.

Rocker Shaft

Valves

Camshaft

Piston

Crankshaft

Air Filter

Carburetor

Flywheel: heavy wheel fixed to the crankshaft to help the engine run smoothly

Pump, to pump gasoline from the tank to the carburetor

Oil filter

Dipstick, to check the oil level

Crankcase, full of oil

Travel by Rail

Railroads first came into use in the 1500s in Britain and other parts of Europe, where they were used to haul coal from underground mines. The wagons were drawn by horses or people, women as well as men.

The steam locomotive was developed in Britain in the 18th and 19th centuries. The first practical steam railroad was built by Richard Trevithick, a Cornish inventor and professional wrestler.

The first public railroad, the Stockton and Darlington Railway, opened in the north of England in 1825. It was engineered by George Stephenson, and carried coal and freight, hauled by the engine *Locomotion No 1*. The first passenger line ran between Liverpool and Manchester; it opened in 1830. The first American steam-powered railroad was built in South Carolina in 1831. By 1860 there were 30,000 miles (48,000 km) of track in the United States.

Since World War II, the steam engine has been replaced by electric and diesel-fueled engines.

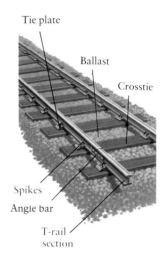

Tie plate

Ballast

Crosstie

Spikes

Angle bar

T-rail section

Most of the world's railroads use track laid in the traditional manner.

RAILROAD TERMS

arrester Trackside device to slow or stop shunted vehicles.

ballast Gravel or crushed stone on which the crossties are laid.

brake car Car manned by a brakeman and containing a screw brake, marshaled at the rear of a freight train.

buffers Sprung metal "studs" at the ends of a vehicle to absorb the shocks of minor collisions in shunting.

bufferstop Set of buffers mounted at the end of a length of track.

classification Sorting vehicles into the correct order for a train.

coupling Hooking device for joining railroad vehicles to a train.

crossties Usually wooden members that carry the tie plates.

double-heading Using two locomotives to pull one train.

fishplate (joint bar) Metal plate used to join rails end to end.

freight train Train of wagons for carrying freight.

frog X-shaped casting that allows rails to "cross" at points.

gauge Width of track, measured between the inside edges of the rails.

hump yard A downgrade after a hump in the track to move railroad vehicles.

light engine Locomotive traveling without pulling a train.

loading guage Maximum permitted height of a railroad vehicle.

monorail A railroad that runs on a single rail. Most modern monorails are of the straddle type where the cars hang from the top of the rail.

shoe Steel collector on electric train for collecting electricity from a third rail.

shunting Pushing uncoupled vehicles along the track.

siding Branch track for holding stationary vehicles.

standard gauge in Britain, most of Europe and North America, 4 ft 8½ in (1.44 m)

switches Sets of movable rails laid where trains need to switch from one track to another.

tie Wood or concrete tie across and beneath the rails to form the track.

vacuum brake Type of railroad vehicle brake held *off* by low air pressure (vacuum).

welded rail Rail made continuous by welding together shorter lengths.

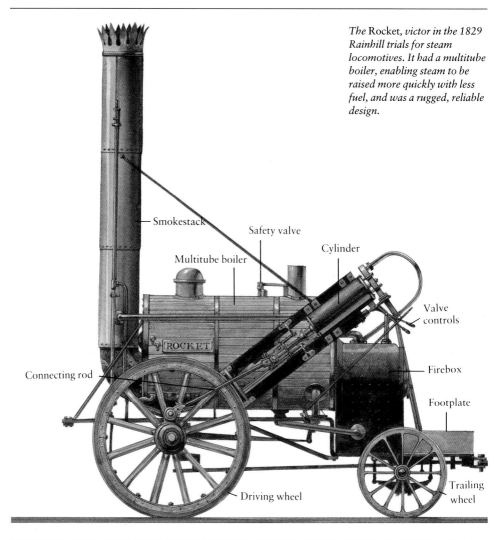

The Rocket, *victor in the 1829 Rainhill trials for steam locomotives. It had a multitube boiler, enabling steam to be raised more quickly with less fuel, and was a rugged, reliable design.*

Smokestack

Safety valve

Cylinder

Multitube boiler

Valve controls

ROCKET

Connecting rod

Firebox

Footplate

Driving wheel

Trailing wheel

GOING UNDER

London Underground has the longest route in the world, 254 miles (408 km), serving 272 stations. It carries about 770 million passengers a year, more than 350 thousand commuters being carried each working day. The Victoria Line can carry 50 thousand people per hour in trains spaced at two-minute intervals. Its Northern Line Morden to East Finchley has 17½ miles (28 km) of tunnel, the longest in Britain.

The Moscow Metro carries about two billion passengers a year, making it the world's busiest. It has 123 miles (198 km) of track and 123 spacious stations finished in black and white marble.

The New York City Subway has more stations – 458 – than any other underground railroad in the world. It runs for a total of 232 miles (373 km). It carries approximately 1,1 billion passengers a year. The first sections of New York's subway were opened in 1904.

Boston was the first U.S. city to build a subway. Its 1½-mile (2.4-km) line opened in 1897. Today, subways operate in Atlanta, Baltimore, Chicago, Philadelphia, San Francisco, and Washington, D.C.

Travel by Sea

Today, when people fly everywhere, it is hard to realize that until recently it was necessary to travel by ship for any journey overseas. Before the days of rail it was often quicker, if you were near the coast, to sail along it than to travel overland.

It is still often easier to send freight along the coast and, for all except perishable freight, which must be transported quickly, the sea is still the most satisfactory means of transporting goods long distances across the world.

A supertanker (foreground) and a container ship, loaded with containers destined for onward movement by road or rail.

SHIP'S LOG

A ship's log book is a day-by-day account of everything that happens during a voyage, including her course, speed, and weather encountered. This "log" is a chronology of the sea and sea travel.

pre-8000B.C. Old Stone Age people use form of dugout canoe.

***c.* 7250B.C.** Earliest form of seafaring – trade in Mediterranean between Melos and Greek mainland.

***c.* 3000B.C.** First known ships – Egyptian galleys.

***c.* 1000B.C.** Phoenicians develop bireme, galley with two rows of oars on each side.

A Viking longship of around A.D.900.

211

FAMOUS VOYAGES

1487 Bartolomeu Dias of Portugal sailed south in search of a route to India and discovered the Cape of Good Hope.

1492 Christopher Columbus sailed from Spain to find a westward route to the Indies, landed instead on a Caribbean island.

1497–1499 Vasco da Gama of Portugal found the sea route to India around the Cape of Good Hope. The round trip took him two years and two months.

1519–1521 Ferdinand Magellan of Portugal, sailing with Spanish backing, found the way westward into the Pacific Ocean by sailing through the Magellan Strait. He died on the voyage, but 18 members of his expedition led by Sebastián Del Cano completed the first voyage around the world.

1577–1580 Francis Drake of England made the second voyage around the world, leaving with five ships and returning with one.

1642 Abel Janszoon Tasman of the Netherlands sailed southward from Java and discovered Tasmania and New Zealand.

1768–1779 James Cook of Britain made three voyages to explore the Pacific and discovered Hawaii.

1895–1898 Joshua Slocum of the U.S. made the first single-handed world voyage.

1947 Thor Heyerdahl of Norway with five companions sailed a balsa wood raft, the *Kon-Tiki*, from Peru to the Tuamoto Islands in Polynesia, to prove that some Pacific Islands could have been settled by people from America.

Above: *Columbus's first voyage to the New World, 1492. He landed on a Caribbean island.*

Above: *Vasco da Gama was the first European to sail around Africa to India, 1497–99.*
Above, opposite: *Magellan's voyage (1519–21) ended with his death in the Philippines. One ship completed the circumnavigation.*

---

c. 200B.C. Romans build huge galleys, with as many as 200 oars.

c. A.D.1100 Sailors in the Mediterranean and in the China Seas navigating by means of magnetic compass.

1400s Portuguese develop three-masted ship; facilitates sailing against wind.

1571 The Battle of Lepanto was the last major naval battle fought by rowing galleys. The sea power of the Ottoman Empire was destroyed.

1620 Dutch scientist Cornelius van Drebbel demonstrates "submarine," a leather-covered rowing boat, in England.

1783 Steam propulsion first achieved, by Marquis Jouffroy d'Abbans (France), with 180-ton paddlesteamer *Pyroscaphe*.

1790s Sailing ships built with iron hulls.

1801 Robert Fulton (U.S.) builds 21 ft. (6.4 m) submarine *Nautilus*.

1801 First successful power-driven vessel, the *Charlotte Dundas*, built by William Symington (UK).

1807 Robert Fulton (U.S.) builds the *Clermont*, first regular passenger steamer.

1822 First iron-built steamship, the *Aaron Manby*; also first prefabricated ship.

1939 British steamer *Archimedes* first to use screw propeller successfully.

1845 *Rainbow* (U.S.), first true clipper ship.

1897 Charles Parsons (UK) demonstrates first turbine-driven ship, *Turbinia*.

1912 First oceangoing diesel-driven ships.

Columbus's Santa Maria *may have looked like this.*

The SR-N4 hovercraft's four propellers give the ferry a speed of up to 60 knots as it skims over the sea on its cushion of air.

1955 First nuclear-powered submarine, *Nautilus* (U.S).

1959 First hovercraft, SR-N1, invented by Christopher Cockerell (UK).

1959 First nuclear-powered surface ship, Russian ice-breaker *Lenin*.

1962 *Savannah* (U.S.) goes into service as first nuclear-powered merchant ship.

1962 First public hovercraft service, inaugurated in Britain.

1979 First helicopter-carrying patrol vessel in operation with Danish Fisheries Protection.

1986 World's largest dry cargo ship, the Norwegian *Berge Stahl*, launched.

1988 Catamaran *Jet Services 5* makes fastest Atlantic crossing under sail.

TRAVEL BY AIR

People have been trying to fly for thousands of years. The ancient legend of Daedalus and his son Icarus, who set out to fly from Crete to Sicily, may well have a foundation in experiments with artificial wings and gliding. The 16th century artist Leonardo da Vinci designed several flying machines, which were never built.

People first sailed through the skies in 1783 when two French brothers, the Montgolfiers, made a balloon. Balloons are at the mercy of the wind, and it was not until the Wright Brothers made their historic flight in 1903 that people conquered the air. And man-powered flight came in the 1970s. *Gossamer Albatross*, with a pedal-driven propeller powered by biologist and cyclist Bryan Allen, made the first flight across the English Channel.

Below: *In July 1909 Louis Blériot made the first cross-channel flight, in a monoplane he built himself.*

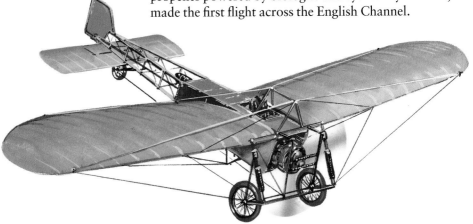

Right: *Bryan Allen made the first man-powered flight across the English Channel in* Gossamer Albatross *(1979).*

214

In 1783 the first human ascent was made in the Montgolfier brothers' hot-air balloon.

FIRSTS IN FLIGHT

1783 First human ascent, made in a captive Montgolfier hot air balloon by J. F. Pilâtre in Paris.

1783 First flight in a hydrogen balloon, made by J. A. C. Charles and M. Roberts.

1785 First air crossing of the English Channel, in a hydrogen balloon, by J. P. Blanchard and J. Jeffries.

1852 First (steam) powered airship, flown by Henri Giffard (France).

1853 First successful airplane (glider), built by Sir George Cayley (UK).

1890s First successful glider flights, made by Otto Lilienthal (Germany).

1903 First controlled flights in a heavier-than-air machine, made by Wilbur and Orville Wright (U.S.).

1909 First flight across the English Channel, by Louis Blériot (France).

1919 First transatlantic flight by flying-boat by Albert C. Read (U.S.).

1919 First non-stop transatlantic airplane flight by J. Alcock and A. W. Brown (UK).

1923 First autogyro, flown by Juan de la Cierva (Spain).

1927 First non-stop transatlantic solo flight, by Charles Lindbergh (U.S.).

1928 First transatlantic passenger flight, by a German airship.

1930 First patented design for jet aircraft engine, by Frank Whittle (UK).

1930 Amy Johnson becomes first woman to fly solo from England to Australia.

1933 First solo round-the-world flight, made by Wiley Post (U.S.).

1939 First transatlantic passenger service begun by Pan American Airways.

1939 First jet-propelled plane, built by Heinkel (Germany).

1939 First flight of a single-rotor helicopter, made by Igor Sikorsky.

1947 First supersonic flight by Charles Yeager (U.S.).

1949 First non-stop round-the-world flight, in a Boeing *Superfortress* bomber.

1969 Supersonic airliner *Concorde* makes first flight.

1979 Bryan Allen (U.S.) makes first man-powered cross-Channel flight.

1986 Richard Rutan and Jeana Yeager (U.S.) make first nonstop round-the-world flight without refueling.

Communications

The Ancient Egyptians wrote using pictures. We call this script hieroglyphs, a Greek word meaning sacred carvings. The Egyptians used the script on monuments, temples, and tombs. The scribes had to learn about 700 different signs. Some words, such as Sun, were represented by one sign – a picture of the Sun. Most words were made up from several signs.

All living creatures communicate with one another – whales sing, bees dance, and cats scent-mark their territory. People communicate by speech, laughter, gesture, and touch. They advanced further by inventing the written word, and this has formed the basis of our civilization. Today's technology means that words and pictures, in the form of electronic signals, can be transmitted across continents and bounced from satellites in outer space. The method is there – the message is up to us!

All animals communicate in one way or another – dogs bark, birds sing to mark out their territories, female moths emit pheromones (scent-like chemical messengers) to lure males from many miles away. But human beings have developed the art of communication far beyond that of animals.

We can communicate with one another not only from city to city, but across the oceans and out into space. We can send and receive messages from far out in space. Communications can be instant: someone in London can chat by telephone to a friend in California as readily as to a friend in the next street. Interesting events such as a royal wedding can be seen as they happen on television in every country in the world.

Perhaps the most important way in which we communicate is by storing and sharing knowledge. If you go into a big library, you will find books containing the knowledge and experience collected over thousands of years.

People invented writing only about 5,500 years ago. They had accumulated knowledge and passed it on to others long before that. They passed on their news and knowledge orally – that is, by word of mouth. Bards used to memorize and chant stories of bygone days. The great poems the *Iliad* and the *Odyssey*, attributed to the Greek minstrel Homer who lived around 2,800 years ago, were undoubtedly passed on in this way for a long time before they were written down.

The earliest visual form of communication that has survived is the paintings we seen on the walls of caves, particularly those in France and Spain. Some of those paintings are more than 30,000 years old. Writing gradually evolved from just such paintings.

People have always been travelers. From their beginnings in Africa they spread first through Europe and Asia, and then to the Americas and across the ocean to the islands of the Pacific. Wherever they went, they carried with them their knowledge and the ability to communicate and receive knowledge in return.

Modern methods of communication developed only in the past 500 years or so. The first real breakthrough was the invention of printing in the 1400s. Books and, later, newspapers, have poured off the presses ever since. The next breakthrough came less than 200 years ago, when the discovery of electricity enabled people to send messages instantly over long distances. The telegraph and the telephone made possible quick communication between distant places.

The world's earliest postal services were set up by kings to send messages to distant parts of their lands. One of the most efficient was that of the Persian ruler Darius the Great in the 500s B.C. He had couriers galloping along specially built post roads, carrying his orders. Similar services were organized by the Mongol emperors of China, Genghis Khan and his grandson Kublai Khan.

In Europe the first Roman emperor, Augustus, organized an efficient postal system during the first century A.D. After the end of the Roman empire, postal services lapsed. They were revived in Russia in the 1200s, and in England and France in the 1400s. Charles I set up England's first public postal service in 1635, and in 1680 William Dockwra, an English merchant, set up a short-lived penny postal service in London. The first American postal service was started in Massachusetts in 1639.

Today every country has a postal service, linked by the Universal Postal Union, established in 1874, which is now an agency of the United Nations.

The importance of sending news quickly is shown by the War of 1812 between Britain and the United States. The cause of the quarrel was British interference with U.S. shipping during war with France. The British agreed on June 16, 1812, to end this interference, but because Congress did not know this it declared war on Britain on June 18. The peace treaty ending that war was signed on December 24, 1814. The news took so long to reach America that the Battle of New Orleans, which cost 1,500 British lives, took place 15 days after the treaty was signed.

Now, thanks to radio, television, and satellite link-ups, it would be much more difficult for this kind of tragic error to happen.

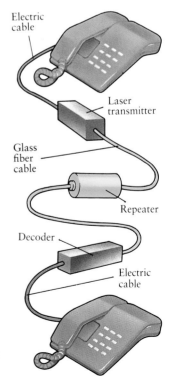

Two electric wires are needed for each telephone conversation, whereas one glass fiber can transmit nearly one million calls at the same time.

Electric cable

Laser transmitter

Glass fiber cable

Repeater

Decoder

Electric cable

WRITING

The earliest way in which people tried to write was by drawing pictures. The cave paintings of the Stone Age showed the animals the men were hunting, possibly as an indication to the gods that the hunters needed help to find their prey.

Soon people started using drawings to describe not just things but ideas, such as "front" and "God." From there it was a step to make the drawings stylized – symbols or signs rather than pictures. People used signs for words, as in written Chinese. Then they used them to stand for syllables. Finally the alphabet was invented. Each letter of an alphabet stands for a single sound. The first proper alphabet was used in Ugarit in Syria in around 1300 B.C. Gradually this alphabet spread to other people who made their own adaptations.

Konrad Gesner's pencil (1565) shown alongside a modern ballpoint pen, fountain, and felt tip pens.

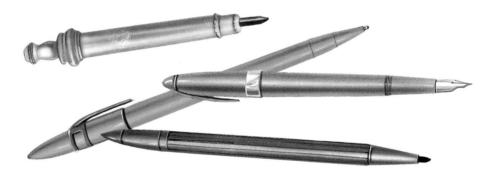

TERMS IN THE HISTORY OF WRITING

alphabet A set of letters used in writing; the name comes from the first two letters of the Greek alphabet, alpha and beta.

cuneiform Wedge-shaped writing inscribed with a stylus on clay tablets. It was invented by the Sumerians about 3000 B.C.

Cyrillic Form of alphabet used in Russian and Bulgarian, derived from the Greek alphabet.

Greek Form of alphabet was adapted about 1000 B.C. from the writing systems of the Middle East. Modern alphabets are derived from it.

hieroglyphics Picture writing, especially the picture writing used by the Egyptians and by early Native Americans, such as the Aztec.

letter A symbol representing a sound.

logogram A symbol representing a complete word or phrase; the sign $, dollar, is a logogram.

pictographs Pictures of objects; used in the ancient Middle East and by the Aztec and Maya of North America.

quipu Knotted strings used by the Inca of Peru, mostly for keeping accounts.

rebus A mixture of words and pictures, the pictures representing syllables or words.

runes Letters of an alphabet used by the Teutonic peoples of northern Europe before A.D.1000.

stylus Tool made from a reed for impressing cuneiform characters into clay tablets.

syllabary A set of symbols representing syllables, as in Japanese writing.

tally Split stick used for keeping accounts, according to the number of notches cut in it.

Greek			Hebrew			Russian		
Letter	Name	Transliteration	Letter	Name	Transliteration	Letter		Transliteration
A	α	alpha	a	א	aleph†	'	А	а	a

Greek:

Letter	Name	Transliteration
A α	alpha	a
B β	beta	b
Γ γ	gamma	g
Δ δ	delta	d
E ε	epsilon	e
Z ζ	zeta	z
H η	eta	ē
Θ θ	theta	th
I ι	iota	i
K κ	kappa	k
Λ λ	lambda	l
M μ	mu	m
N ν	nu	n
Ξ ξ	xi	x (ks)
O o	omicron	o
Π π	pi	p
P ρ	rho	r
Σ σ,ς*	sigma	s
T τ	tau	t
Υ υ	upsilon	u, y
Φ φ	phi	ph
X χ	chi	kh, ch
Ψ ψ	psi	ps
Ω ω	omega	o

Hebrew:

Letter	Name	Transliteration
א	aleph†	'
ב	beth	b
ג	gimel	g
ד	daleth	d
ה	heh	h
ו	waw	w
ז	zayin	z
ח	heth	ḥ
ט	teth	ṭ
י	yod	y
כך*	kaph	k, kh
ל	lamed	l
מם*	mem	m
נן*	nun	n
ס	samekh	s
ע	ayin	'
פף*	peh	p, ph
צץ*	sadhe	ṣ
ק	qoph	q
ר	resh	r
שׁ	shin	sh
שׂ	sin	ś
ת	taw	t

Russian:

Letter		Transliteration
А	а	a
Б	б	b
В	в	v
Γ	г	g
Д	д	d
E	е	e, ye
Ж	ж	zh
З	з	z
И	и	i
Й	й	i
К	к	k
Л	л	l
М	м	m
Н	н	n
О	о	o
П	п	p
Р	р	r
С	с	s
Т	т	t
У	у	u
Ф	ф	f
Х	х	kh
Ц	ц	ts
Ч	ч	ch
Ш	ш	sh
Щ	щ	shch
	ы	i
	ь	'
Э	э	e
Ю	ю	yu
Я	я	ya

PRINTING

Printing was one of the world's most important inventions because it brought knowledge within the reach of ordinary people. For thousands of years before printing, books were made by scribes laboriously writing out each copy by hand. Such books were rare and expensive. Printing using type began in Europe in the 1440s. A German printer, Johannes Gutenberg began to cast letters in metal. The letters could be moved around to form words and could be used more than once. Today most typesetting is done by computer.

The invention of printing in the 15th century revolutionized the spread of learning and knowledge.

PRINTING GLOSSARY

electrotype A copy of engravings and type made by an electroplating process.

engraving A plate engraved for printing, or a printed illustration.

halftone A printing process in which a picture is made up of tiny black dots.

intaglio Printing from a design cut into a metal plate; ink stays in the cutaway part when the rest of the plate is wiped clean.

lithography A form of planographic printing, originally using a piece of linestone.

photogravure A form of intaglio printing from a plate made photographically.

planographic printing Printing from a flat surface with the design in a greasy medium; the ink clings only to the greasy part.

relief printing Printing from an inked design which is raised above the background.

stereotype A copy of a page of type made with the aid of a mold.

Keyboard

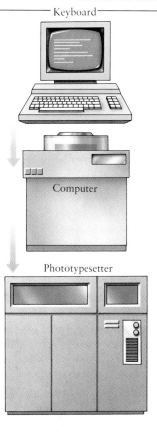

Computer

Phototypesetter

Computerized phototypesetting system.

CHRONOLOGY OF PRINTING

B.C.

c. 1320 The Chinese use inked engraved seals to stamp documents.

A.D.

868 The earliest known printed book is produced in China, using a carved wood block.

c. 1040 The Chinese alchemist Pi Sheng invents movable type made of pottery.

1403 T'ai Tsung, king of Korea, establishes a foundry for casting metal type.

1423 The earliest known European printed picture is produced from a wood block.

c. 1440 Johannes Gutenberg, a goldsmith of Mainz, Germany, invents a system of casting type, a printing press, and suitable ink.

1451 Gutenberg prints his first book, a Latin grammar, using a black-letter (Gothic) type.

1457 First book printed in two colors, black and red, is produced in Mainz.

1470 Nicolas Jensen, a French printer working in Venice, invents Roman type.

1475 William Caxton sets up the first printing press in England.

1477 Intaglio printing from engraved metal plates is introduced.

1501 Francesco Griffo of Bologna, Italy, invents *italic* type.

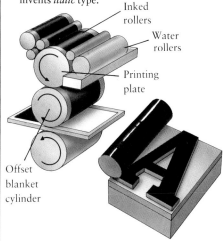

Inked rollers

Water rollers

Printing plate

Offset blanket cylinder

In offset lithography (top), *inked rollers transfer ink to the large cylinder holding the printing plate. Ink is then transferred or "offset" from the plate to a rubber blanket and onto the paper.*
Printing by letterpress (bottom) *using inked, raised type.*

1719 Full color printing is pioneered in Frankfurt, Germany.

1798 Bavarian actor Alois Senefelder invents lithography.

1800 Earl Stanhope, an English amateur printer, makes the first iron-framed press.

1810 German printer Friedrich König, makes a steam-powered press.

1839 Electrotyping is invented in the United States, Britain, and Russia.

1845 Richard Hoe of New York makes the first high-speed rotary press.

1880 The first half-tone picture is printed in the New York *Daily Graphic.*

1886–7 Linotype and Monotype machines speed up typesetting, hitherto done by hand.

1939 American William C. Huebner invents the first photocomposition machine.

1965 Computer typesetting is introduced in Germany.

1980s Complete pages are produced by computers, transferred to paper by laser, and then photographed onto a printing plate.

221

PHOTOGRAPHY

There is an old Chinese saying that a picture is worth a thousand words, but before the advent of photography pictures were expensive and not always accurate. Pictures depended on the ability of the artist – and only a few people can draw and paint well.

Since the first photograph was taken in 1826 that has changed. Anyone can take a photograph. Communication by pictures has proved of immense importance in science and education as well as in everyday life.

Photography has many applications in industry, including the production of the miniature circuits needed for the silicon chips in computers and pocket calculators. In medicine it has enabled doctors to examine the interior of the body from the outside by means of X-ray photography, and to photograph inside by inserting long tubes incorporating fibre optics.

Photographs have even been taken in Space. Scientists have sent probes to visit the other planets and take photographs, thus solving many mysteries of Space.

GLOSSARY

aperture Opening of variable size made by the diaphragm. It helps to control the amount of light entering the camera.

exposure The amount of light reaching the film, controlled by the aperture size and the shutter speed.

f-number (or f-stop) One of a collection of numbers on a camera showing the aperture size after adjusting the diaphragm.

focus To make an image clear and sharp on the viewing screen and the film.

image The upside-down picture captured on the film when the shutter is released.

lens Several specially shaped pieces of glass focusing the image.

negative An image fixed on a film. Light tones appear dark; dark tones appear light.

print Image made on paper from a negative.

processing Turning the invisible image exposed on a film into a visible photograph.

reflex camera Camera with a mirror or mirrors inside to reflect light entering through the lens onto a viewing screen.

shutter Device which opens and shuts to let light through the lens of a camera.

transparency A true-to-life colour picture made on transparent film.

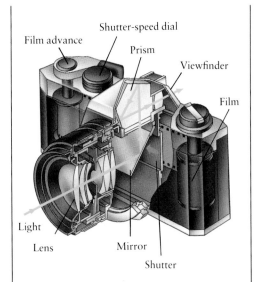

How a camera works. Opening the shutter lets light from the object through a lens, which directs the light through an aperture (the iris). The light is focused onto the film by a second set of lenses, forming an inverted (upside-down) image.

KEY DATES IN PHOTOGRAPHY

c1000 Arab astronomers use the camera obscura, a tiny aperture in a darkened room.

1725 Johann Schulze of Germany discovers that some silver compounds darken on exposure to light.

1826 Joseph Nicéphore Niépce, a French inventor, takes the earliest known surviving photograph.

1839 Louis Jacques Daguerre, a French artist, invents a process of making photographs on copper plates.

Daguerreotype camera, 1839.

Powell's stereoscopic camera, 1858, produced 3-D photographs.

The cheap Brownie camera, 1900, made the snapshot universal.

Leitz camera, 1925, was the first reliable hand-held camera using fast film.

1839 William Henry Fox Talbot, an English scientist, produces the Calotype negative, from which prints can be made.

1851 Frederick Scott Archer, an English sculptor, invents the wet glass plate.

1855 Roger Fenton of England photographs the Crimean War.

1858 First aerial photograph is taken from a captive balloon.

1861 Matthew Brady begins photographing the American Civil War.

1873 Bromide printing paper is introduced.

1888 George Eastman introduces flexible paper roll film and the Kodak camera in which to use it.

1889 Eastman replaces the paper film by celluloid.

1895 X-ray photography is introduced.

1903 French brothers Louis and Auguste Lumière invent the first practical three-colour process.

1914 Panchromatic black and white film, sensitive to all colours, comes into use.

1925 A German firm, Leitz, produces the first miniature camera, the Leica.

1931 Harold Edgerton of the United States invents electronic flash.

1935 Kodak introduces the Kodachrome process.

1942 Agfa in Germany and Kodak in the United States introduce colour prints.

1945 The zoom lens is introduced.

1947 Edwin Land of the United States invents the Polaroid camera, producing instant black and white prints.

1963 Polaroid produces instant colour film.

1963 Holography – three-dimensional photography – is introduced in the United States.

1970s Automatic focusing is introduced.

1989 Ultra high speed flash, producing an output of 40 joules in 1/250,000 second, becomes commercially available.

RADIO AND TELEVISION

Radio and television are the two quickest means of communication. They depend on electromagnetic waves, which travel through space as fast as light. There are several kinds of electromagnetic waves, including radio waves (the longest), infrared rays, visible light, ultraviolet light, X-rays and gamma rays (the shortest). Radio and television both use radio waves. These were discovered by the German physicist Heinrich Hertz in 1887, though their existence had been predicted by James Clerk Maxwell, a Scottish scientist, 23 years earlier.

The first radio signals for communications were transmitted in 1895 by the Italian inventor Guglielmo Marconi. Radio was used for communicating to ships at sea from 1903 onwards, and first saved lives in 1909 when two ships collided in the Atlantic.

Radio telephones came into use in the 1920s to cross the Atlantic Ocean, before the first permanent cable was laid in 1956. From 1962 radio signals relayed by satellites carried phone calls and radio programmes all over the world. Soon after, citizens' band radio began, first in North America and then in Europe. In the 1980s, radio came into use for mobile telephones.

Television received its first practical demonstration in 1926 from a Scottish inventor, John Logie Baird, though

A VCR records the incoming signal in a diagonal pattern of strips across the tape.

Left *Radio pioneer Guglielmo Marconi with his 1901-style transmitter.*

John Logie Baird pioneered TV with a mechanical system that produced flickering images. Light from the object (a doll's head) passed through holes in a spinning disc and was turned into electrical signals. These signals were then turned back into a light beam projected onto a screen to produce pictures.

Baird's system was not the one finally adopted. Regular broadcasting began in the 1930s.

Both radio and television have an important role in communicating news and 'entertainment' directly into people's homes. This ranges from popular music to comedy shows, drama and informative talks. They also have an important part in education, beaming learning material to schools, colleges, and people's homes.

Below *A huge radio telescope reflecting dish.*

RADIO AND TV FACTS

Biggest TV manufacturer is Japan, producing around 13 million sets a year.

Biggest radio manufacturer is Hong Kong, making about 42 million sets a year.

The Coronation of Queen Elizabeth II in 1953 was the first major international TV broadcast.

Earliest transatlantic radio transmission was the Morse signal for 'S', sent in 1901.

Earliest transatlantic TV transmission was made in 1928 by Baird to a liner at sea; it was picked up in Hartsdale, New York State.

First public radio broadcast was by Professor Reginald A. Fessenden, Massachusetts, 1906.

First stereo broadcasts on radio were made in the United States in 1961.

Geostationary satellites orbit the Earth in step with Earth rotation, introduced in 1963, making constant radio links possible.

The ionosphere, a region of electrified air between 130 km and 160 km (80–100 miles) above the Earth, 'bounces' radio waves around the world.

Most TV sets in use. China claimed 600 million sets in use in 1988.

Ninety-eight per cent of United States households owned at least one TV set in 1988.

Satellite TV began in Europe in 1989, with signals beamed via the Astra satellite to home receivers.

Score, launched by the United States in 1958, was the first communications satellite.

Teletext, transmission of pages of information by television using spare lines not normally seen, was pioneered in Britain in 1973.

Telstar, launched in 1962, was the first successful communications satellite.

Videotape recording was first demonstrated in 1956.

225

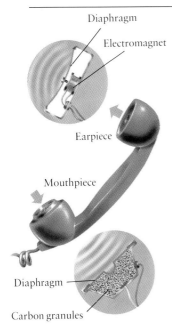

Diaphragm

Electromagnet

Earpiece

Mouthpiece

Diaphragm

Carbon granules

Above *How a telephone works. As the caller speaks, a microphone vibrates and the vibrations are turned into electrical signals which travel along cables. At the earpiece, these signals set up vibrations in the diaphragm, which reproduces the caller's voice.* **Right** *A teletext machine.*

BUSINESS COMMUNICATIONS

The main advances in communications have come in the realm of business, which can increasingly be carried on at a distance.

Electronic mail is an international series of computer networks, through which a subscriber can send messages to other subscribers by addressing them to mailboxes. A mailbox is an electronic store with a code number. Messages can be sent and stored, or retrieved, at any time.

Electronic offices enable staff of a company to work at home or in small branch offices. The basis of the system is either a computer terminal linked to a mainframe at the head office, or personal computers linked by fax or another form of electronic mail.

Electronic paging is a radio system which enables key workers to be contacted quickly. It is used extensively in factories and hospitals. Each person on the system carries a small pocket 'bleeper' which can be activated, calling them to the nearest telephone.

Fax – short for 'facsimile' – machines enable people to send copies of documents or pictures over telephone lines or radio links. The document to be transmitted is scanned by a photoelectric cell, which turns tones of black and white into electronic signals.

Telephones have come a long way since their invention in 1876 and business as we know it would be impossible without them. **Mobile telephones** allow people to be contacted while travelling. One kind operates within a building, enabling the user to move about freely carrying a small telephone receiver. Many countries now have networks of transmitters and receivers enabling people to use telephones in their cars, on trains, and even in passenger aircraft.

Photocopying is a method of making quick copies of documents. An image of the document is recorded temporarily on an electrically charged plate, which prints it on to paper by means of powder.

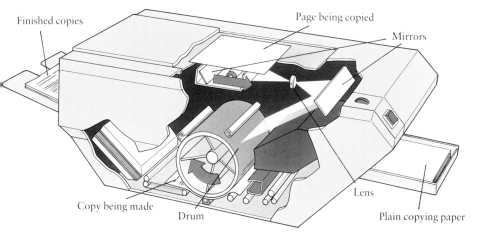

Telex is an older system of quick communication, and is an advance on simple telegraph systems. Each subscriber has a teleprinter machine, like a large typewriter. Any message is typed on the machine and recorded on a punched tape. When the tape is fed through the machine it transmits the message to a similar machine at the receiving end at about 100 words a minute. This system is used by newspapers and agencies for transmitting "copy" quickly.

Teletext is a faster form of telex that links word processors through a telephone line. It was developed in Europe in the 1980s. The message is encoded on a floppy disk and is transmitted electronically to the receiving station.

Viewdata is a system by which information can be stored at a central point and retrieved by means of a telephone line, linked to word processors. A subscriber to the system can call up thousands of pages of information, ranging from stock market prices to encyclopedia-style material.

A photocopier reproduces images electrostatically. Light is reflected from the original onto a light-sensitive material charged with static electricity. An image forms, and is fixed when dusted with powdered ink and heat-transferred onto paper.

227

Arts and Entertainment

Neapolitan Fisherboy, *a marble sculpture by Carpeaux (1800s).*

Since the dawn of civilization, people have been moved to express their feelings and relate their experiences in pictures, words, music, and dance. Twenty thousand years ago Stone Age people painted on the walls of caves scenes of life at that time; they also made primitive musical instruments. Literature began when stories were told around the hunters' fire; ballet was born in ritual dances to appease or thank the gods. All art is a celebration of life, in sorrow and in happiness. Today we can enjoy art and entertainment in our homes through television, video, radio, and compact disc.

Throughout the history of mankind, people have been involved in those activities which we now call "the arts". Having met their basic needs for food, warmth, and shelter, they have used their creative skills and imagination to satisfy a need for decoration, color, and entertainment.

The earliest carvings and paintings we know of were produced by Stone Age people over 20,000 years ago. Archaeologists have discovered primitive musical instruments made during the Stone Age. Decorated pottery of baked clay has been found dating from the Neolithic period (6000–3000 B.C.). The Greeks and Romans had theaters where plays were performed, and the plays and poetry of ancient Greece are considered to be the world's first important literature.

Some 4,500 years ago, the Egyptians built huge stone temples for their gods and tombs (pyramids) for their kings and queens. These are the first major works of architecture, and many can still be seen today.

Across the Atlantic, in Central and South America, Indian civilizations had developed their own types of art, architecture, pottery, and stone carving by about 1000 B.C.

This section covers the traditional arts of painting and sculpture, pottery and porcelain, architecture, classical music, opera and ballet, the theater and literature. It also includes a new range of media which the scientific advances of the 20th century have brought into being. These are the motion picture, radio and television, and popular music. They can be seen as arts in their own right, especially the movie. The use of satellites in space to relay television signals means that events happening in one country can be shown on TV, as they happen, on the other side of the world.

The motion picture was developed in the early years of this century and the first film with a sound track came out only in 1927. The development of radio and television came even more recently. The first public radio broadcasting services did not begin until the 1920s and the world's first television service began in Britain in 1936. Very few people in Britain or America had television sets until the 1950s.

In the 1970s video became popular. Video is a way of recording pictures and sounds on magnetic tape, which is simpler to use than film. Many people now have video cassette recorders (VCRs), which enable them to record television programs and to play video cassettes. Easy-to-use video cameras make it simple for people to make their own home movies. Film companies also release films on video which people can buy or borrow to watch at home instead of in a movie theater.

A Phoenician ivory carving dating from about the 1800s BC.

Towards the end of the nineteenth century, the phonograph (gramophone) was invented by an American, Thomas A. Edison. Soon afterwards the wax-coated, grooved disc which we call "a record" was invented. The development of the gramophone record and the coming of radio brought about the growth of the huge popular music industry. Now records are being replaced by tapes and, latest of all, by compact discs.

Modern sound systems have stereo speakers. Now people can listen to their favorite music in their own home and it sounds as if the musicians on the tape, disc, or record are in the room.

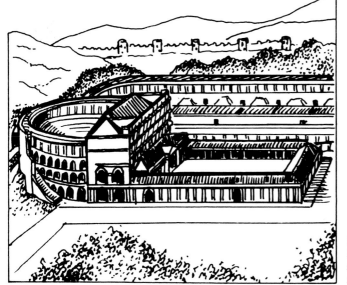

Roman theater at Orange, France. Actors wore large masks denoting the character they were playing.

PAINTING

The earliest paintings we know of are cave paintings in France and Spain. Some beautiful wall paintings still survive from ancient Egypt, Greece, and Rome. In western Europe, the subjects of medieval paintings were religious. They were followed by the real flowering of art which came with the Renaissance. Painters such as Leonardo da Vinci began to make their subjects look more lifelike.

Picasso's Weeping Woman *(1937) Picasso introduced the style known as Cubism.*

Later, Dutch painters such as Rembrandt and Vermeer began to portray everyday scenes. In the late 19th century an important new style of painting called "Impressionism" developed. Artists such as Monet and Renoir painted from nature, studying the effects of different lights on a subject. Painting in the 20th century became even freer. Pablo Picasso, one of the most famous artists of the 20th century, and Georges Braque invented a style of art called Cubism. Its aim was to express the idea of something rather than to paint a likeness.

SOME PAINTING TERMS

abstract art Art form that represents ideas (by means of geometric and other designs) instead of natural forms.

airbrush Device used by artist to spray paint, varnish or fix, worked by compressed air.

aquarelle A watercolor painting.

cartoon Originally, a full-size plan for a work of art which is then traced onto the final surface to be painted.

cave paintings Pictures (mostly animals) painted by prehistoric artists on the walls of caves.

chiaroscuro ("light-dark") Balance of light and shade in a picture.

Cubism Important movement in modern French painting started by Picasso and Braque in 1907. Cubists aimed to reduce objects to basic shapes of cubes, spheres, cylinders, and cones.

distemper Cheap and impermanent method of painting in which powdered colors are mixed with glue.

Dutch School Art and artists of Netherlands in 1600s. Leaders were Rembrandt, Hals, Van der Velde.

egg tempera A painting medium in which the colors are ground with pure egg yolk; one of the most permanent media available.

Expressionism Movement that aims at expressing the artist's inner feelings and experiences. It began in the late 1800s.

Fauves ("wild beasts") Group of Parisian painters of early 1900s (Dufy, Matisse, Rouault, Vlaminck, etc.) who shocked the critics by their brilliant use of color.

finger painting Chinese watercolor technique using finger instead of a brush.

fresco Method of great antiquity but perfected during Italian Renaissance; uses pigments ground in water applied to a fresh lime-plaster wall or ceiling.

gouache Non-transparent watercolor paint that provides easy way of obtaining oil-painting effects.

icon Religious picture (usually painted on wood or ivory) associated with Eastern Church.

Impressionism Important movement that developed among French painters just after mid-1800s. Impressionists were concerned with light and its effects. They included Renoir, Manet, Degas, Monet, Pissarro, and Sisley.

landscape painting Picture whose main subject is pure landscape without human figures.

miniature Tiny painting (less than 6 in., or 15 cm, across), usually a portrait.

mural Wall-painting, usually executed in fresco, oil, or tempera.

narrative painting One that tells a story; popular in Victorian England.

oil painting Technique of covering a slightly absorbent surface with pigment ground in oil.

op art (optical art) Modern technique with which painter creates optical illusions by means of dazzling patterns.

palette Range of colors available to a painter; usually arranged on little board for easy mixing, with thumb-hole for holding.

pastel Painter's coloring medium consisting of crayon of pure pigment or pigment mixed with chalk and other materials.

pigments Dry paints or dyes that are mixed with oil, water, or other material.

portrait painting Representation in painting of a human being. First portraits were usually of kings and other leaders.

Post-impressionism Work of French painters that followed Impressionism between 1885 and 1905. Typified by Cézanne, Gauguin, Van Gogh, and Seurat.

Renaissance Rebirth in arts and learning that took place in Europe (especially Italy) from 1300s to 1500s. Among the masters of this period were Botticelli, Leonardo da Vinci, Michelangelo, Titian, and Raphael.

representational art Type of painting that shows objects as nearly as possible as they actually are; the opposite of abstract art.

rococo European art style (about 1735–1765) characterized in painting by lavish decoration and extravagant ornament.

still life Art form in which subject of picture is made up of inanimate objects; favorite form of Dutch School.

tempera Binding medium for powder colors, made up of egg yolk, sometimes thinned with water. Tempera mixtures last longer than oil colors.

triptych Series of three painted panels or doors that are hinged or folded.

Venetian School Painters who worked in Venice during High Renaissance. They included Titian, Veronese, Tintoretto, and Giorgione.

watercolor Technique of painting with colors that have been mixed with water-soluble gum; paints are applied to paper with soft, moistened brush. English painters such as Turner, Cozens, Sandby, Cotman, and Girtin were supreme at the art.

GREAT ARTISTS

Botticelli, Sandro (1444–1510) Italian painter who spent most of his life in Florence. Most of his work consisted of religious pictures.

Braque, Georges (1882–1963) French painter and sculptor; one of the founders of Cubism.

Brueghel, Pieter (1520?–1569) Flemish artist renowned for lively pictures of village life.

Cézanne, Paul (1837–1906) French painter famous for his landscapes and still lifes.

Goya, Francisco (1746–1828) Spanish court painter representing people realistically rather than in a flattering light.

Greco, El (1541–1614) Nickname meaning "The Greek," born in Crete, but worked in Venice and Spain. His pictures often contain strange, thin, brightly colored figures.

Hals, Frans (1580?–1666) Dutch painter who was one of the greatest portraitists.

Degas is famous for his paintings of the ballet.

Constable, John (1776–1837). One of the greatest English landscape painters.

Degas, Edgar (1834–1917) French artist of the Impressionist period, noted for his pictures of ballet dancers.

Dürer, Albrecht (1471–1528) German artist who made many fine woodcuts and engravings for book illustrations.

Gauguin, Paul (1848–1903) French painter who escaped from European civilization to paint in the peaceful Pacific island of Tahiti.

Giotto (1266?–1337) Italian painter who greatly influenced Renaissance art. His style was more realistic than that of the formal painters of his time, and he is considered the father of modern painting.

Hogarth, William (1697–1764) English artist who satirized the cruelty and vice which he saw around him in London.

Holbein, Hans, the Younger (1497?–1564) German portrait painter who created realistic likenesses of his subjects.

Leonardo da Vinci (1452–1519) Italian painter, architect, sculptor, and musician, as well as a brilliant inventor and scientist.

Michelangelo Buonarroti (1475–1564) Italian painter, sculptor, and architect. Possibly his finest work was painted on the ceiling of the Sistine Chapel, in the Vatican.

Leonardo da Vinci's Portrait of a Musician.

Monet, Claude (1840–1926) French artist who developed the impressionist technique of using light to change the nature of a painting.

Picasso, Pablo (1881–1973) Spanish painter whose early paintings were dominated by the color blue. In 1907 he introduced the style known as Cubism, that changed the whole course of art.

Raphael (1483–1520) Italian artist whose pictures are notable for their peaceful beauty and perfect composition.

Rembrandt van Rijn (1606–1669) One of the finest Dutch portrait painters; a master at capturing the character of his subjects, and in the dramatic use of light and shade (chiaroscuro).

Renoir, Pierre Auguste (1841–1919) French Impressionist painter who used rich colors; particularly known for his nudes.

Rubens, Peter Paul (1577–1640) Flemish artist who became court painter in Antwerp after spending eight years in Italy. Known for his love of rich color and fleshy nudes.

Titian (1487–1576) One of the greatest Venetian painters. He painted many religious works for churches.

Toulouse-Lautrec, Henri de (1864–1901) French artist, best remembered for his Parisian cabaret posters and his pictures of music hall performers.

Turner, Joseph Mallord William (1775–1851) English painter especially noted for his water-colors and his magnificent sunsets.

Van Gogh, Vincent (1853–1890) Dutch painter whose early pictures were somber, but in his later work he used bright, swirling colors. His later paintings reflect his growing insanity.

Velázquez, Diego Rodríguez de Silva (1599–1660) Spanish court painter; renowned for his portraits of Philip IV and the courtiers.

Vermeer, Jan (1632–1675) Dutch painter, a master of painting interior scenes, often portraying women working at quiet household tasks.

The Umbrellas *by Pierre Auguste Renoir.*

SCULPTURE

The Kiss, *by Constantin Brancusi. In his work Brancusi carved only the essential form of a subject.*

The earliest pieces of sculpture we know of were carved by Stone Age people some 30,000 years ago. The ancient Egyptians made fine sculptures between 2,000 and 4,000 years ago – many were huge statues of their kings and queens. Some of the world's most beautiful carvings were done by the sculptors of ancient Greece and Rome. All over the world, in China, India, Africa, and many other countries, people have made three-dimensional images. During the Renaissance, especially in Italy, the art of sculpture advanced rapidly. Michelangelo carved superb statues, such as his *David*. Today, sculptors work in stone, marble, wood, metal, even fiberglass. They often carve sculptures in which the general shape is more important than the likeness of the figure or object.

As well as carving statues and abstract shapes, sculptors through the ages have also decorated buildings. They have carved figures and scenes from flat stones and these are called reliefs. The best relief sculptures have usually been carved on religious buildings and monuments.

SOME SCULPTURAL TERMS

armature Wood or metal framework used to support sculptor's model.

bronze Alloy of copper and tin used by sculptors in ancient Greece, Rome, China, and Africa; revived in modern times.

bust Sculpture of the upper part of the human body.

cast Figure made from mold of original model. See cire perdue; plaster cast, sand cast.

cire perdue (French, "lost wax") Traditional method for casting bronze sculptures: model with wax surface is enclosed in mold; wax is melted and runs out through holes at bottom; molten metal poured through holes at top, filling up space left by wax.

figurine Miniature figure.

free-stone An easily worked fine-grained limestone or sandstone.

genre sculpture Style that reflects everyday or rustic life; hallmark of Etruscan art and of biblical subjects in Middle Ages.

heroic Any figure or group of figures carved larger than life.

maquette (French, "small model") Small wax or clay model made by sculptor in preparation for larger work.

marble Popular stone for sculpture because of its extreme durability; found in all colors ranging from nearly pure white to nearly pure black. Pure white marble from Carrara, Italy, valued by sculptors since classical times.

mobile Movable sculpture of shapes cut out of wood or sheet metal, linked by wires or rods in order to revolve easily or move up and down; invented by American sculptor, Alexander Calder (1932).

modeling Building-up of forms in three dimensions by means of plastic material such as clay or wax.

plaster cast Intermediate stage in bronze sculpture from which final mold is made.

polychromatic sculpture Sculpture painted in naturalistic colors to make it more lifelike; mostly pre-1500s.

relief Sculpture not free-standing from background; various degrees, from *bas-relief* (low relief) to *alto-relievo* (high relief).

sand cast Mold of special sand made from plaster model and from which bronze cast is made.

sculpture-in-the-round Sculpture that can be seen from all sides.

stabile Sculpture that does not move, as opposed to mobile.

FAMOUS SCULPTORS

Bernini, Gianlorenzo (1598–1680) Italian Renaissance sculptor. As well as owing much to classical tradition, his figures appear almost to be living people.

Brancusi, Constantin (1876–1957) Romanian sculptor, most famous for a series of bird sculptures made of different materials, but also for bronzes such as the powerful Prodigal Son.

Calder, Alexander (1898–1976) American sculptor, known particularly for his moving sculptures made from flat metal disks suspended from wires. These were given the name "mobiles."

Donatello (1386–1466) Italian Renaissance sculptor who carved realistic figures. He developed a new form of relief sculpture where the feeling of depth is created without cutting deep into the surface of the marble.

Epstein, Sir Jacob (1880–1959) English sculptor influenced by primitive art. At the beginning of his career, people were shocked by the directness of his work.

Gabo, Naum (1890–1977) Russian sculptor who made new use of industrial materials such as glass, metal, plastics, and wire.

Ghiberti, Lorenzo (1378–1455) Italian painter and sculptor. Famous for his bronze doors for the baptistery in Florence.

Giacometti, Alberto (1901–1966) Swiss sculptor and painter, best-known for his tall, spindly figures cast in bronze.

Hepworth, Barbara (1903–1975) British sculptor, created abstract carvings in wood and stone, huge shapes broken by holes with wires stretched across them.

Lipschitz, Jacques (1891–1973) Cubist Lithuanian sculptor, most famous for his powerful, angular animals and figures.

Michelangelo Buonarroti (1475–1564) Italian Renaissance sculptor, painter, and architect, famous for many fine carvings including the Pietà, David, and a series of slaves who seem to be trying to escape from the rock from which they are carved.

Modigliani, Amedeo (1884–1920) Italian sculptor and painter. Influenced by Cézanne and by African art, he carved elongated faces from wood.

Moore, Henry (1898–1986) British sculptor best known for his large reclining nudes and for groups of figures. He was influenced by both primitive African and Mexican art.

The Prodigal Son,
by Rodin.

Phidias (c 490–c 417 BC) Influential Greek sculptor. He designed and supervised the Parthenon sculptures, as well as a sculpture of Zeus at Olympia.

Rodin, Auguste (1840–1917) French sculptor who worked in bronze and marble. His work includes The Thinker, The Kiss, and The Burghers of Calais. His work treated the human figure realistically, and did not idealize it.

Jane Austen (1775–1817), drawn by her sister.

LITERATURE

Literature – the art of the written word – has existed as long as people have been able to express themselves in writing. In western Europe the first great ages of literature were those of ancient Greece and Rome. The works of Homer, Virgil, and others, which became known as "the classics," have influenced writers up to the present day. The Renaissance brought another great explosion of literary activity, with writers such as Chaucer, Dante, and, perhaps greatest of all, Shakespeare. Poems and plays are both very ancient forms of literature, but the novel is relatively new. It was only fully developed at the end of the 18th century and reached a peak of popularity in the 19th century. Today the novel is the major form of literature.

SOME LITERARY TERMS

allegory A story in which the obvious meaning symbolizes a hidden meaning.

ballad A poem describing a historical or legendary event or deed. Ballads were very popular in the late Middle Ages.

blank verse A form of poetry based on unrhyming ten-syllable lines with alternate syllables stressed.

couplet Two successive lines of verse that rhyme with one another.

drama A story written as a dialogue, in conversational form, so that it can be spoken and acted.

elegy A poem mourning a death or on some other solemn theme.

epic A long narrative poem about heroic, historical or legendary events and people. An example is Homer's *Odyssey*.

essay A short piece of prose on any subject.

fable A short tale with a moral lesson in which animals act and talk like people.

limerick A kind of comic, nonsense poem in five lines, usually rhyming *a a b b a*. Edward Lear wrote many limericks.

ode A medium-length poem, usually in praise of something. It has various forms.

rhyme Agreement in sound of two syllables, but with differing preceding consonants.

romantic Belonging to the Romantic period, the early 1800s, when writers stressed liberty and chose exotic themes and settings.

satire A style using sarcasm or irony to attack some form of human behavior.

science fiction A form of literature that uses possible future scientific developments as the basis for fantasy.

sonnet A 14-lined poem with various rhyming schemes. Italian sonnets rhyme *abba abba cde cde*. Elizabethan sonnets rhyme *abab cdcd efef gg*.

An illustration from Don Quixote, *one of the earliest novels, by the Spanish writer Cervantes.*

GREAT WRITERS

Andersen, Hans Christian (1805–75), Danish writer, best known for his fairy tales. Some of the most loved are *The Tinder Box*, *The Emperor's New Clothes*, and *The Snow Queen*.

Austen, Jane (1775–1817), English novelist, wrote about comfortably-off country people, who led lives bound by strict rules of behavior. Her books include *Sense and Sensibility*, *Pride and Prejudice*, and *Emma*.

Balzac, Honoré de (1799–1850), French novelist, wrote a series of 90 realistic stories about everyday life in France called the *Human Comedy*.

Blake, William (1757–1827), English poet and artist. His *Songs of Innocence* and *Songs of Experience* show the same world from the viewpoints of innocence and disillusioned experience.

Brontë Family name of three English novelist sisters: **Charlotte** (1816–55), **Emily Jane** (1818–48), and **Anne** (1820–49). Charlotte included many personal experiences in her most famous novel, *Jane Eyre*. *Wuthering Heights*, a dramatic love story, is probably Emily's best work.

Above: *Chaucer's* Canterbury Tales *remained unfinished at the author's death.*
Top: *Danish storyteller, Hans Christian Andersen (1805–1875).*

Bunyan, John (1628–88), English preacher and religious writer, best known for his allegory *The Pilgrim's Progress*, most of which he wrote while in jail.

Burns, Robert (1759–96), Scottish poet who wrote poems in Scottish dialect and composed many songs, including *Auld Lang Syne*.

Byron, Lord George (1788–1824), English Romantic poet, wrote several long narrative poems. Probably the finest is *Don Juan*.

Carroll, Lewis (Charles Lutwidge Dodgson 1832–98), best remembered for his stories *Alice's Adventures in Wonderland* and *Through the Looking Glass*.

Cervantes, Miguel de (1547–1616), Spanish novelist, playwright and poet, author of the novel *Don Quixote*, story of a gentleman who imagines he can put right all the evil in the world.

Chaucer, Geoffrey (1340?–1400), English poet, famous for his *Canterbury Tales*, a collection of stories told by travelers on a journey.

Coleridge, Samuel Taylor (1772–1834), English Romantic poet and friend of Wordsworth, wrote the famous poem *The Rime of the Ancient Mariner*.

GREAT WRITERS

CVIC CÆLVM CECINIT MEDIVMQVE IAVAMQVE TRIBVNAL ⁘ LVSTRAVIT QVE ANIMO CVNCTA POETA SVO ⁘ DOCTVS ADES T DANTES SVA QVEM FLORENTIA SÆPE ⁘
SENSIT CONSILIIS AC PIETATE PATRE M ⁘ NIL POTVIT TANTO MORS SÆVA NOCERE POETÆ ⁘ QVEM VIVVM VIRTVS CARMEN IMAGO FACIT ⁘

Dante Alighieri (1265–1321), Italian poet, wrote *Divine Comedy*, a poem in three parts about a man's role on Earth.

Dickens, Charles (1812–70), English novelist, wrote stories about the harsh lives of ordinary people in industrial England. The best-known include *Great Expectations*, *David Copperfield*, and *Oliver Twist*.

Dostoevsky, Fyodor (1821–81), Russian novelist, wrote powerful stories. Among the finest are *Crime and Punishment*, *The Idiot*, and *The Brothers Karamazov*.

Eliot, George (Marian Evans 1819–80), English novelist, wrote *The Mill on the Floss* and other novels including *Middlemarch*.

Eliot, T.S. (Thomas Stearns 1888–1965), American-born British poet, dramatist and critic, wrote poetry expressing his frustration and despair.

Hemingway, Ernest (1898–1961), American novelist, wrote stories about adventurous and violent lives. Best-known include *A Farewell to Arms* and *For Whom the Bell Tolls*.

Dante, painted amid scenes from the Divine Comedy.

Charles Dickens, one of Britain's greatest novelists.

Homer (700s B.C.), great and influential Greek poet, wrote the *Iliad* which tells the story of the siege of Troy, while the *Odyssey* describes the wanderings of the hero Odysseus after the war.

Johnson, Dr. Samuel (1709–84), English poet and essayist, wrote on English poetry and compiled a *Dictionary of the English Language*.

Joyce, James (1882–1941), Irish novelist, wrote stories about people in conflict with their surroundings.

Keats, John (1795–1821), English Romantic poet, composed narrative poems. The finest include *Ode to Autumn* and *Ode to a Nightingale*.

Kipling, Rudyard (1865–1936), an Indian-born English novelist, wrote of the British Empire, and adventure stories for children which include *Kim, The Jungle Book*, and the *Just So Stories*.

Lawrence, D.H. (David Herbert 1885–1930), English novelist; much of his work is about working-class life, including growing up and natural love. He wrote *Sons and Lovers* and *Lady Chatterley's Lover*.

Melville, Herman (1819–91), American novelist, best known for his adventure tale *Moby Dick*, a symbolic study of good and evil in Captain's Ahab's search for a great white whale.

Milton, John (1608–74), English poet and religious and political writer. His most important works were the long poems *Paradise Lost* and *Paradise Regained*.

Poe, Edgar Allan (1809–49), American short-story writer, poet and critic, is best known for his tales of mystery.

Rabelais, François (1494?–1553?), French priest and doctor, poked fun at life in his day in his four books about Gargantua and Pantagruel.

Scott, Sir Walter (1771–1832), Scottish novelist and poet, author of romantic adventures often set in the Middle Ages. They include *Waverley* and *Ivanhoe*.

Shelley, Percy Bysshe (1792–1822), English Romantic poet, wrote idealistic poems including *Ode to a Skylark* and *The Cloud*.

Stevenson, Robert Louis (1850–94), Scottish novelist, wrote *Treasure Island* and *Kidnapped*, both adventure stories, and *Dr. Jekyll and Mr. Hyde*, a mystery.

Swift, Jonathan (1667–1745), Irish clergyman, wrote satirical pamphlets on religion and politics, but is best known for his story *Gulliver's Travels*.

Tennyson, Alfred, Lord (1809–92), English poet, wrote *Break, Break, Break, The Charge of the Light Brigade*, and *Idylls of the King*.

Tolstoy, Count Leo (1828–1910), Russian novelist and playwright, wrote one of the world's greatest novels, *War and Peace*. It traces the lives of several families during Napoleon's invasion of Russia.

Twain, Mark (Samuel Langhorne Clemens 1835–1910), American novelist, wrote many books about American life. His best-known *The Adventures of Huckleberry Finn*, describes life along the Mississippi River.

Virgil (Publius Vergilius Maro 70–19 B.C.), a Roman poet, wrote the *Aeneid*, a long epic poem about the founding of Rome.

Wordsworth, William (1770–1850), an English poet, expressed his deep love of nature in poems often written in beautiful, simple language.

Portrait of John Keats by Benjamin Haydon.

Friction between the strings of a viola and a bow cause the vibrations that make sound.

MUSIC

We know that people have been making some kind of music all through history – for example, paintings of musicians have been found in Egyptian tombs – but we do not know what early music sounded like because there was no way of writing it down. As instruments improved through the centuries, new ones were added to the orchestra. Bach and Handel, both born in 1685, used orchestras with mostly stringed instruments such as violins but they also had flutes, oboes, trumpets, and horns. The first man to use the orchestra as a whole was Haydn, who established the symphony. The piano was not developed until the early 19th century. Early this century new kinds of music were produced by composers such as Stravinsky. Recently, composers have used electronic systems to produce sounds which are often strange to our ears.

Both popular and classical music have a long history in the U.S. The music of Charles Ives and Aaron Copland has a "New World" flavor, including fragments of folk music. Jazz influenced the work of George Gershwin, Leonard Bernstein, and others.

SOME MUSICAL TERMS

accelerando Gradually faster.
adagio At a slow pace.
allegro At a fast pace.
alto Highest adult male voice.
andante At a quiet, peaceful pace.
arpeggio Notes of chord played in rapid succession.
bar Metrical division of music bounded by vertical bar-lines.
baritone Male voice higher than bass and lower than tenor.
bass Lowest male voice.
brass instruments Metal instruments sounded by blowing through mouthpiece and altering tension of lips (French horn, trumpet, euphonium, trombone, tuba).
choir A body of singers.
chord Three or more notes sounded together.
chorus Main body of singers in choir; words and music repeated after each stanza of song.
classical music Music that aims at perfection of structure and design (period of Bach to Brahms).

clef Sign in musical notation that fixes pitch of each note written on the stave.
concerto Substantial work for one or more solo instruments and orchestra.
contralto Lowest female voice.
counterpoint Two or more melodies combined to form a satisfying harmony.

J. S. Bach, the greatest of his distinguished musical family.

crescendo Increasing in loudness.
descant The addition of a second melody above a given melody. This is a form of counterpoint.
diminuendo Gradually softer.
flat Conventional sign showing that pitch of a certain note has been lowered by a semitone.
forte Played or sung loudly.
fortissimo Very loud (loudest).
harmony Combining of chords to make musical sense.
key Classification of the notes of a scale.

The Emperor Maximilian I of Germany traveled with an impressive entourage of court musicians.

largo At a slow pace.
lied German word for "song" (plural lieder).
major One of the two main scales, with semitones between 3rd and 4th and 7th and 8th notes.
measure Another term for bar.
melody A tune; series of musical sounds following each other, as distinct from harmony.
mezzo Half or medium.
mezzo-soprano Female voice between contralto and soprano.

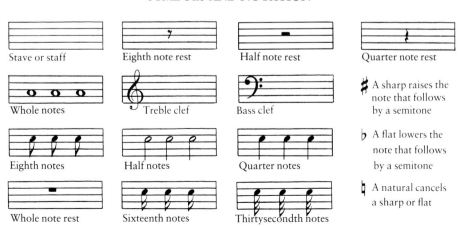

SYMBOLS AND NOTATION

Stave or staff

Eighth note rest

Half note rest

Quarter note rest

Whole notes

Treble clef

Bass clef

♯ A sharp raises the note that follows by a semitone

Eighth notes

Half notes

Quarter notes

♭ A flat lowers the note that follows by a semitone

Whole note rest

Sixteenth notes

Thirtysecondth notes

♮ A natural cancels a sharp or flat

241

minor One of the two main scales. Harmonic minor scales have a semitone between 2nd and 3rd, 5th and 6th, and 7th and 8th notes.

movement Complete section of larger work (such as symphony).

nocturne A "night-piece," tuneful but sad.

octave Interval made up of eight successive notes of scale, from one note to note of same name, above or below.

oratorio Religious musical composition for soloists, chorus, and orchestra, but without costume or scenery.

percussion instruments Instruments that are struck; they include drums, tambourine, cymbals, bells, glockenspiel, xylophone, vibraphone, marimba, triangle, gong, and castanets.

piano Played or sung softly.

pitch Highness or lowness in sound of one note compared with another.

plainsong Unaccompanied vocal melody used in medieval church music.

presto At a fast pace.

romantic music Music (mainly 19th century) that plays on the emotions.

scale Progression of successive notes ascending or descending.

score Written music showing all parts (vocal and instrumental) of composition on separate staves.

semitone A half-tone; smallest interval commonly used in western music.

sharp Conventional sign indicating that note referred to has been raised in pitch by a semitone.

sonata Musical piece, usually for one or two players, following the sonata-form; made up of exposition, development, and recapitulation.

soprano Highest female voice.

stave or **staff** Framework of lines and spaces on which music is usually written.

stringed instruments Instruments that are played with a bow (violins, violas, cellos, double basses).

symphony Large orchestral piece of music of a serious nature, usually in four movements.

tempo Pace or speed of piece of music.

tenor Highest natural male voice.

treble Upper part of a composition; a high voice, usually of children.

virtuoso Musician of outstanding technical skill.

woodwind instruments Instruments that are blown and are traditionally, but not always, made of wood; they include flute, oboe, clarinet, piccolo, recorder, saxophone, bassoon, and English horn (cor anglais).

The harpsichord was a keyboard instrument popular in the 16–18th centuries.

THE TONIC SOL-FA

The tonic sol-fa is a method of musical notation using letters and syllables instead of notes on a stave. It was devised by the English musician John Curwen (1816–1880), who based it on the system known as solmization used in the Middle Ages.

The eight notes of a major scale are denoted by the syllables doh, re, mi, fah, soh (or sol), lah, te, doh. It works for any scale by just changing the note which represents doh. Sharpened and flattened notes are indicated by changing the vowel sounds (for example, sol sharp is se and te flat is taw).

GREAT COMPOSERS

Bach, Johann Sebastian (1685–1750) German composer born at Eisenach; the most distinguished in a long line of musicians. Bach's vast output can be divided into three groups: organ works; instrumental and orchestral works; and religious choral works.

Beethoven, Ludwig van (1770–1827) German composer, one of the outstanding figures of Western music. His symphonies, overtures, concertos, piano sonatas, and string quartets are considered some of the world's greatest.

Brahms, Johannes (1833–97) German composer. His works include four symphonies, two piano concertos, a violin concerto and a double concerto (violin and cello), chamber music, piano music, and many songs and choral compositions.

Chopin, Frédéric (1810–49) Polish piano virtuoso and composer, known almost entirely for piano music.

Dvořák, Antonín (1841–1904) Czech composer. From 1892–5 was in the United States as Director of the National Conservatory in New York, where he wrote his best-known work, the symphony *From the New World*.

Gershwin, George (1898–1937) American composer and pianist whose combination of American styles (jazz and blues) with impressionist harmony was a major influence on 20th century American music.

German composer, George Frideric Handel.

Handel, George Frideric (1685–1759) German-born composer of Italian operas and, later, oratorios (music dramas) mainly on religious themes; *Messiah* is the most famous. Handel also wrote many instrumental compositions.

Haydn, Franz Joseph (1732–1809) Prolific Austrian composer whose development of the sonata-symphony form and style earned him the title of "Father of the Symphony."

Mahler, Gustav (1860–1911) Bohemian-born composer noted for his symphonies, written in late German-romantic style.

Mozart, Wolfgang Amadeus (1756–1791) Austrian composer, born in Salzburg. As a child prodigy, he toured Europe giving piano recitals with his sister and father. For speed and ease of composition Mozart was unrivaled, producing in his short life over 600 works.

Schubert, Franz Peter (1797–1828) Austrian composer. In a career even shorter than Mozart's, Schubert achieved a large output ranging from symphonies and operas to chamber music and over 500 songs.

Stravinsky, Igor (1882–1971) Russian-born composer and one of the key figures of 20th century music. Made his reputation with a series of remarkable ballets, including *The Firebird, Petrushka*, and *The Rite of Spring*.

Tchaikovsky, Peter Ilyich (1840–93) Russian composer, the first to become widely popular outside his country. His work was notable for its melodic flair and vivid orchestration.

Beethoven's early music was influenced by Mozart and Haydn.

OPERA

An opera is a play with music. The actors are singers who sing all or many of their words. An orchestra accompanies them. The first operas were performed in Italy nearly 400 years ago. Famous composers of serious operas include Mozart (*The Marriage of Figaro*, *The Magic Flute*); Verdi (*Aida*, *La Traviata*); Puccini (*Tosca*, *Madame Butterfly*); Wagner (*The Ring of the Nibelung*).

American opera has never enjoyed as much popularity as American musical comedy. A notable exception is George Gershwin's popular *Porgy and Bess* (1935), which has many features of the Broadway musical.

SOME OPERATIC TERMS

aria (Italian, "air") A solo.

ballad opera Simple kind of opera, made up of popular tunes interspersed with spoken dialogue.

comic opera Opera with a farcical plot.

finale Closing portion of act or opera; usually whole company sings together.

folk opera Opera based on folk tales.

grand opera Opera with libretto entirely set to music.

intermezzo Instrumental piece interposed between scenes or acts of opera, also called interlude.

Leitmotiv (German, "leading motive") Short theme in opera that emphasizes by repetition an individual character, object, or idea.

libretto Text of opera.

opera buffa Humorous opera, but not farcical as comic opera; typical is Rossini's *Barber of Seville*.

opera seria Serious opera, as distinct from opera buffa.

operetta Light opera based on amusing subjects and implying some spoken dialogue; nowadays often synonymous with musical comedy.

patter song Comical song made up of string of words and sung at high speed; Gilbert and Sullivan's operas include many of this type.

prima donna (Italian, "first lady") Principal female singer in cast; or, more often, most famous or most highly paid; also called diva.

The Opera House, Paris.

BALLET

The ballet as it is danced today began in France, and during the reign of King Louis XIV (1600s) it was officially recognized as a form of art. Traditional or classical ballet follows strict rules – the five basic ballet positions were devised over 300 years ago. Some of the most famous classical ballets have been danced for many years. *Giselle*, for example, was first performed in 1841. Other long-time favorites are *Swan Lake* and *Sleeping Beauty*. Modern ballets include freer dance steps and often illustrate a mood or theme rather than telling a story.

Above: *Modern ballet tends to interpret a theme, rather than tell a story.*
Left: Swan Lake *performed by the London Festival Ballet.*

SOME BALLET TERMS

arabesque Position in which dancer stands on one leg with arms extended, body bent forward from hips, while other leg is stretched out backward.

attitude Position in which dancer stretches one leg backward, bending it a little at the knee so that lower part of leg is parallel to floor.

ballerina Female ballet dancer.

barre Exercise bar fixed to classroom wall at hip level; dancers grasp it when exercising.

battement Beating movement made by raising and lowering leg, sideways, backward, or forward.

choreography Art of arranging the steps, movement, and pattern in the composition of a ballet.

corps de ballet Main body of ballet dancers, as distinct from soloists.

enchainement Series of steps.

entrechat Leap in which dancer rapidly crosses and uncrosses feet in air.

fouetté Turn in which dancer whips free leg around.

glissade Gliding movement.

jeté Leap from one foot to another.

pas Any dance step.

pas de deux Dance for two.

pas seule Solo dance.

pirouette Movement in which dancer spins completely around on one foot.

plié Bend – done at the barre as a warming up exercise.

pointes Tips of dancer's toes, on which many movements are executed.

positions Five positions of feet on which ballet is based.

tutu Short, stiff, spreading skirt worn in classical ballet.

RADIO AND TELEVISION

Television and radio broadcasting has developed even more recently than the movies. The first advertised radio broadcast in the United States came in 1906, and in Great Britain in 1920. The world's first television service (from London's Alexandra Palace) did not begin until 1936. Now, nearly every home in the U.S. has both TV and radio, and for many people they are the main source of both news and entertainment.

The final episode of M*A*S*H, shown in February 1983, was watched by 125 million viewers – the largest-ever American TV audience.

Television programs that combine entertainment with education have always been very popular. Special film-making techniques make it possible for us to see things, such as right inside a living colony of ants and animals that live in the dark, that we are unlikely to observe in everyday life.

Most of us enjoy fantasy as entertainment, and absurd antics in cartoon films, such as those featuring Mickey Mouse or Tom and Jerry, are old favorites. In addition, as technology improved rapidly after World War II, so it became possible to make TV programs with special effects, for example, Star Trek, so that impossible things seem to happen, transporting us to make-believe worlds.

The use of satellites in space to transmit TV pictures even allows us to receive pictures of events on the other side of the world as they happen. The widespread use of video also means that many more people can make their own recordings to show on the television screen. A series of channels devoted to different subjects is now offered by cable television. Music, sport, and natural history programs are just three of the specialities that we can see on cable TV at any time. And we can receive some programs being broadcast by television companies in other countries.

Regular radio broadcasting began in 1920 in the United States, and in ten years its popularity grew enormously. It became a major source of entertainment and news and the 1920s through to the 1950s were radio's golden age. New forms of drama, which told a story with sound alone, were invented specially for radio broadcasting. During World War II radio was a source of information and reassurance for the people of Europe, with regular broadcasts from war leaders such as Winston Churchill.

Radio disc jockeys often do much more than just spin pop records. Interviews with performers, commentary on the records, and light-hearted banter all form part of their repertoire.

With the advent of television, people probably listen to radio less today. Radio remains, however, very important to people wanting frequent news broadcasts, imaginative programs like plays, or background listening while doing something at home or driving a car.

William Shakespeare, probably the greatest playwright to write in English.

THEATER

Actors have been performing plays in theaters since the time of the ancient Greeks, and some of the most famous plays are the tragedies by the Greek writers Aeschylus, Sophocles, and Euripides. In Britain there were no proper theaters until the 1500s. William Shakespeare (1564–1616) is probably England's greatest playwright, and the Elizabethan and Jacobean period in which he lived can be seen as the great age of the theater in Britain. The past century has seen much powerful drama written and performed in the United States. Eugene O'Neill, who is widely regarded as America's finest playwright, attempts to look below the surface of everyday human life, often revealing great unhappiness.

SOME THEATRICAL TERMS

cabaret Entertainment performed while audience dines.

epilogue Speech made at the end of a play by one of the characters or by an actor representing the author.

farce Kind of comic play based on a series of hilarious improbable events. For example the farces of George Feydeau.

kitchen-sink drama Realistic plays of the mid-1950s about the lives of working-class people. For example Arnold Wesker's *Chicken Soup with Barley*.

melodrama Play with a sensational plot and exaggerated emotion. For example *The Bells* by Leopold Lewis.

mime Art of acting without words. Marcel Marceau is a famous mime artist.

morality play Religious drama of the Middle Ages popular in Western Europe.

music hall Kind of theater from the 1850s to World War I, which presented variety entertainment consisting of comic acts, acrobats, songs and dances.

mystery play Religious play of the 1300s and 1400s presenting a scene from the Bible. Also called a miracle play.

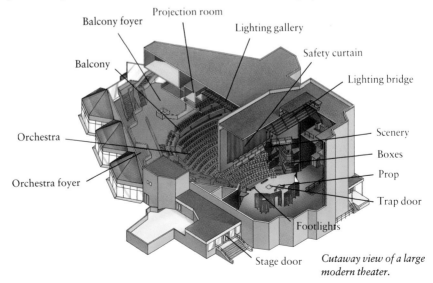

Balcony foyer
Projection room
Lighting gallery
Balcony
Safety curtain
Lighting bridge
Orchestra
Scenery
Boxes
Orchestra foyer
Prop
Trap door
Footlights
Stage door

Cutaway view of a large modern theater.

A production at the Drury Lane theater in the 18th century. David Garrick, manager of the theater, made many significant changes to theater conventions.

passion play Religious play about the Crucifixion performed on Good Friday in Middle Ages. A famous passion play is still performed every ten years at Oberammergau in southern Germany.

prologue Speech made at the beginning of a play by one of the characters or by an actor representing the author.

props, or **properties** Small objects needed on the stage to make a play realistic, such as cups, flowers, and newspapers, but not furniture or scenery.

repertory Collection of plays that a company performs in a season.

revue Theater entertainment popular since the 1890s and consisting of a series of songs, short acted scenes, and dances.

son et lumière Open-air entertainment at a place of historical interest. The history of the place is told over loudspeakers while relevant features are lit up.

theater-in-the-round Theater in which the stage is surrounded by the audience.

theater of the absurd Kind of drama of the 1950s portraying the absurd human existence on Earth, such as plays by Samuel Beckett, Harold Pinter, and Eugène Ionesco.

thriller Play with an exciting plot, usually including crime with murder.

tragedy Play in which the main character, or protagonist, is engaged in a great struggle which ends in his or her death or downfall.

vaudeville Play in which dialogue is interspersed with songs.

SOME GREAT DRAMATISTS

Beckett, Samuel (1906–1989), Irish dramatist and novelist, became famous for plays that express the absurdity of human existence including *Waiting for Godot* and *Endgame*.

Chekhov, Anton (1860–1904), Russian dramatist, whose plays include *Uncle Vanya*, *The Three Sisters*, and *The Cherry Orchard*.

Goethe, Johann Wolfgang von (1749–1832), German poet, dramatist, and novelist, wrote several plays, including *Egmont* and his most famous work *Faust*, a long poetic drama.

Molière (Jean Baptiste Poquelin, 1622–73), French writer of comedies and actor, ran a theater company for which he wrote many plays. The best include *The Bourgeois Gentleman, Tartuffe, The Misanthropist*.

O'Neill, Eugene (1888–1953), American dramatist, wrote a series of successful plays between 1920 and 1934, of which *Mourning Becomes Electra* is the best-known. His later plays include *The Iceman Cometh*.

Shakespeare, William (1564–1616), probably Britain's greatest dramatist, also an actor and a writer of beautiful sonnets. His 36 plays include historical dramas, such as *Henry V* and *Julius Caesar*; comedies, *A Midsummer Night's Dream* and *The Taming of the Shrew*; tragedies, *Hamlet, King Lear,* and *Romeo and Juliet*; and fantasy romances, *The Tempest*.

Movies

The first moving pictures came from an invention called the kinetoscope, built by Thomas Edison, in 1891. Shortly afterwards, Auguste and Louis Lumière built their cinematographe, which projected pictures from a piece of film on to a screen. Early films were black and white, movements were jerky and they had no sound. At first they showed only real events, but soon filmmakers began to invent their own stories and use actors. By the end of World War I (1914–18), Hollywood in California had become the film-making capital of the world, as it still is today. The first moving picture with sound was the *Jazz Singer* (1927).

Charlie Chaplin made film clowning an art.

SOME FILMMAKING TERMS

close-up Picture taken near the subject.
director Person who decides how filming and acting should be done.
dolly Mobile carriage to carry a camera.
dubbing Adding sound to a film.
freeze A shot held so that the action seems to stop.
flashback Interruption in the story of a film to recall a past event.
intercut shots Two related series of shots shown alternately, such as the heroine tied to the railway lines and the train approaching.
library shot Film taken from material already made and in stock.
long shot A shot taken from a distance.

pan Short for panoramic shot – a sideways sweep by the camera.
producer Person responsible for the general making of a film, apart from directing.
prop Short for property – an object used by an actor, such as a gun or a telephone.
rushes The day's shots, before editing.
scenario Scene-by-scene outline of a film script.
set Area prepared for a film scene, either in a studio or outside.
shooting Filming a scene.
take Part of a scene shot without interruption.
track in, track back Move a camera on its dolly toward or away from the subject.
zooming Using a variable lens to give the effect of tracking in or back.

ACADEMY AWARDS

Year	Best film	Best actor	Best actress	Best director
1927–28	*Wings*	Emil Jannings *(The Way of All Flesh* and *The Last Command)*	Janet Gaynor *(Seventh Heaven; Street Angel;* and *Sunrise)*	Frank Borzage *(Seventh Heaven),* Lewis Milestone *(Two Arabian Knights)*
1928–29	*The Broadway Melody*	Warner Baxter *(In Old Arizona)*	Mary Pickford *(Coquette)*	Frank Lloyd *(The Divine Lady)*
1929–30	*All Quiet on the Western Front*	George Arliss *(Disraeli)*	Norma Shearer *(The Divorcee)*	Lewis Milestone *(All Quiet on the Western Front)*
1930–31	*Cimarron*	Lionel Barrymore *(A Free Soul)*	Marie Dressler *(Min and Bull)*	Norman Taurog *(Skippy)*
1931–32	*Grand Hotel*	Frederic March *(Dr. Jekyll and Mr. Hyde),* Wallace Beery *(The Champ)*	Helen Hayes *(The Sin of Madelon Claudet)*	Frank Borzage *(Bad Girl)*
1932–33	*Cavalcade*	Charles Laughton *(The Private Life of Henry VIII)*	Katharine Hepburn *(Morning Glory)*	Frank Lloyd *(Cavalcade)*
1934	*It Happened One Night*	Clark Gable *(It Happened One Night)*	Claudette Colbert *(It Happened One Night)*	Frank Capra *(It Happened One Night)*
1935	*Mutiny on the Bounty*	Victor McLaglen *(The Informer)*	Bette Davis *(Dangerous)*	John Ford *(The Informer)*
1936	*The Great Ziegfeld*	Paul Muni *(The Story of Louis Pasteur)*	Luise Rainer *(The Great Ziegfeld)*	Frank Capra *(Mr. Deeds Goes to Town)*
1937	*The Life of Émile Zola*	Spencer Tracy *(Captains Courageous)*	Luise Rainer *(The Good Earth)*	Leo McCarey *(The Awful Truth)*
1938	*You Can't Take It With You*	Spencer Tracy *(Boys' Town)*	Bette Davis *(Jezebel)*	Frank Capra *(You Can't Take it with You)*

Gone with the Wind
*starring Clark Gable and
Vivien Leigh, broke all box-
office records.*

Year	Best film	Best actor	Best actress	Best director
1939	*Gone With the Wind*	Robert Donat *(Goodbye Mr. Chips)*	Vivien Leigh *(Gone With the Wind)*	Victor Fleming *(Gone With the Wind)*
1940	*Rebecca*	James Stewart *(The Philadelphia Story)*	Ginger Rogers *(Kitty Foyle)*	John Ford *(Grapes of Wrath)*
1941	*How Green Was My Valley*	Gary Cooper *(Sergeant York)*	Joan Fontaine *(Suspicion)*	John Ford *(How Green Was My Valley)*
1942	*Mrs. Miniver*	James Cagney *(Yankee Doodle Dandy)*	Greer Garson *(Mrs Miniver)*	William Wyler *(Mrs Miniver)*
1943	*Casablanca*	Paul Lukas *(Watch on the Rhine)*	Jennifer Jones *(The Song of Bernadette)*	Michael Curtiz *(Casablanca)*
1944	*Going My Way*	Bing Crosby *(Going My Way)*	Ingrid Bergman *(Gaslight)*	Leo McCarey *(Going My Way)*
1945	*The Lost Weekend*	Ray Milland *(The Lost Weekend)*	Joan Crawford *(Mildred Pierce)*	Billy Wilder *(The Lost Weekend)*
1946	*The Best Years of Our Lives*	Frederic March *(The Best Years of Our Lives)*	Olivia de Havilland *(To Each His Own)*	William Wyler *(The Best Years of Our Lives)*
1947	*Gentleman's Agreement*	Ronald Colman *(A Double Life)*	Loretta Young *(The Farmer's Daughter)*	Elia Kazan *(Gentleman's Agreement)*
1948	*Hamlet*	Laurence Olivier *(Hamlet)*	Jane Wyman *(Johnny Belinda)*	John Huston *(The Treasure of Sierra Madre)*
1949	*All the King's Men*	Broderick Crawford *(All the King's Men)*	Olivia de Havilland *(The Heiress)*	Joseph L. Mankiewicz *(A Letter to Three Wives)*
1950	*All About Eve*	Jose Ferrer *(Cyrano de Bergerac)*	Judy Holliday *(Born Yesterday)*	Joseph L. Mankiewicz *(All About Eve)*
1951	*An American in Paris*	Humphrey Bogart *(The African Queen)*	Vivien Leigh *(A Streetcar Named Desire)*	George Stevens *(A Place in the Sun)*

Year	Best film	Best actor	Best actress	Best director
1952	The Greatest Show on Earth	Gary Cooper (High Noon)	Shirley Booth (Come Back, Little Sheba)	John Ford (The Quiet Man)
1953	From Here to Eternity	William Holden (Stalag 17)	Audrey Hepburn (Roman Holiday)	Fred Zinnemann (From Here to Eternity)
1954	On the Waterfront	Marlon Brando (On the Waterfront)	Grace Kelly (The Country Girl)	Elia Kazan (On the Waterfront)
1955	Marty	Ernest Borgnine (Marty)	Anna Magnani (The Rose Tattoo)	Delbert Mann (Marty)
1956	Around the World in 80 Days	Yul Brynner (The King and I)	Ingrid Bergman (Anastasia)	George Stevens (Giant)
1957	The Bridge on the River Kwai	Alec Guiness (The Bridge on the River Kwai)	Joanne Woodward (The Three Faces of Eve)	David Lean (The Bridge on the River Kwai)
1958	Gigi	David Niven (Separate Tables)	Susan Hayward (I Want to Live)	Vincente Minnelli (Gigi)
1959	Ben-Hur	Charlton Heston (Ben-Hur)	Simone Signoret (Room at the Top)	William Wyler (Ben-Hur)
1960	The Apartment	Burt Lancaster (Elmer Gantry)	Elizabeth Taylor (Butterfield 8)	Billy Wilder (The Apartment)
1961	West Side Story	Maximilian Schell (Judgment at Nuremberg)	Sophia Loren (Two Women)	Robert Wise & Jerome Robbins (West Side Story)
1962	Lawrence of Arabia	Gregory Peck (To Kill a Mockingbird)	Anne Bancroft (The Miracle Worker)	David Lean (Lawrence of Arabia)
1963	Tom Jones	Sidney Poitier (Lilies of the Field)	Patricia Neal (Hud)	Tony Richardson (Tom Jones)
1964	My Fair Lady	Rex Harrison (My Fair Lady)	Julie Andrews (Mary Poppins)	George Cukor (My Fair Lady)

The hit musical My Fair Lady *transferred from the stage to the screen in the 1960s.*

Year	Best film	Best actor	Best actress	Best director
1965	*The Sound of Music*	Lee Marvin *(Cat Ballou)*	Julie Christie *(Darling)*	Robert Wise *(The Sound of Music)*
1966	*A Man for All Seasons*	Paul Scofield *(A Man for All Seasons)*	Elizabeth Taylor *(Who's Afraid of Virginia Woolf?)*	Fred Zinnemann *(A Man for All Seasons)*
1967	*In the Heat of the Night*	Rod Steiger *(In the Heat of the Night)*	Katharine Hepburn *(Guess Who's Coming to Dinner)*	Mike Nichols *(The Graduate)*
1968	*Oliver*	Cliff Robertson *(Charly)*	Katharine Hepburn *(A Lion in Winter)*, Barbra Streisand *(Funny Girl)*	Sir Carol Reed *(Oliver)*
1969	*Midnight Cowboy*	John Wayne *(True Grit)*	Maggie Smith *(The Prime of Miss Jean Brodie)*	John Schlesinger *(Midnight Cowboy)*
1970	*Patton*	George C. Scott *(Patton)*	Glenda Jackson *(Women in Love)*	Franklin J. Schaffner *(Patton)*
1971	*The French Connection*	Gene Hackman *(The French Connection)*	Jane Fonda *(Klute)*	William Friedkin *(The French Connection)*
1972	*The Godfather*	Marlon Brando *(The Godfather)*	Liza Minnelli *(Cabaret)*	Robert Fosse *(Cabaret)*
1973	*The Sting*	Jack Lemmon *(Save the Tiger)*	Glenda Jackson *(A Touch of Class)*	George Roy Hill *(The Sting)*
1974	*The Godfather Part II*	Art Carney *(Harry and Tonto)*	Ellen Burstyn *(Alice Doesn't Live Here Any More)*	Francis Ford Coppola *(The Godfather Part II)*
1975	*One Flew Over the Cuckoo's Nest*	Jack Nicholson *(One Flew Over the Cuckoo's Nest)*	Louise Fletcher *(One Flew Over the Cuckoo's Nest)*	Milos Forman *(One Flew Over the Cuckoo's Nest)*
1976	*Rocky*	Peter Finch *(Network)*	Faye Dunaway *(Network)*	John G. Avildsen *(Rocky)*
1977	*Annie Hall*	Richard Dreyfus *(The Goodbye Girl)*	Diane Keaton *(Annie Hall)*	Woody Allen *(Annie Hall)*

In the 1972 Oscar-winning movie Cabaret, *Joel Grey played the sinister Master of Ceremonies.*

Year	Best film	Best actor	Best actress	Best director
1978	*The Deer Hunter*	John Voight *(Coming Home)*	Jane Fonda *(Coming Home)*	Michael Cimino *(The Deer Hunter)*
1979	*Kramer Vs Kramer*	Dustin Hoffman *(Kramer Vs Kramer)*	Sally Field *(Norma Rae)*	Robert Benton *(Kramer Vs Kramer)*
1980	*Ordinary People*	Robert De Niro *(Raging Bull)*	Sissy Spacek *(Coalminer's Daughter)*	Robert Redford *(Ordinary People)*
1981	*Chariots of Fire*	Henry Fonda *(On Golden Pond)*	Katharine Hepburn *(On Golden Pond)*	Warren Beatty *(Reds)*
1982	*Gandhi*	Ben Kingsley *(Gandhi)*	Meryl Streep *(Sophie's Choice)*	Sir Richard Attenborough *(Gandhi)*
1983	*Terms of Endearment*	Robert Duval *(Tender Mercies)*	Shirley MacLaine *(Terms of Endearment)*	James L. Brooks *(Terms of Endearment)*
1984	*Amadeus*	F. Murray Abraham *(Amadeus)*	Sally Field *(Places in the Heart)*	Milos Forman *(Amadeus)*
1985	*Out of Africa*	William Hurt *(Kiss of the Spider Woman)*	Geraldine Page *(The Trip to Bountiful)*	Sydney Pollack *(Out of Africa)*
1986	*Platoon*	Paul Newman *(The Color of Money)*	Marlee Matlin *(Children of a Lesser God)*	Oliver Stone *(Platoon)*
1987	*The Last Emperor*	Michael Douglas *(Wall Street)*	Cher *(Moonstruck)*	Bernardo Bertolucci *(The Last Emperor)*
1988	*Rain Man*	Dustin Hoffman *(Rain Man)*	Jodie Foster *(The Accused)*	Barry Levinson *(Rain Man)*
1989	*Driving Miss Daisy*	Daniel Day-Lewis *(My Left Foot)*	Jessica Tandy *(Driving Miss Daisy)*	Oliver Stone *(Born on the Fourth of July)*
1990	*Dances With Wolves*	Jeremy Irons *(Reversal of Fortune)*	Kathy Bates *(Misery)*	Kevin Costner *(Dances With Wolves)*
1991	*The Silence of the Lambs*	Anthony Hopkins *(The Silence of the Lambs)*	Jodie Foster *(The Silence of the Lambs)*	Jonathan Demme *(The Silence of the Lambs)*

Daniel Day-Lewis played the author Christy Brown to win the Oscar for Best Actor in 1989.

255

Sports

Practicing sports gives people a chance to engage in mental or physical combat with one another, to improve their fitness and prowess, or just to exercise and have fun. The first organized sports were the Olympics, where athletes competed for crowns of laurels. Today, with huge money prizes and worldwide fame for the champions, sports are taken just as seriously as when they were first thought of as a training for warriors.

Discus-throwing was one of the pentathlon events in the ancient Greek Olympics.

Sports range from baseball to billiards, from boxing to chess. Dozens of different sporting activities can help to make us faster, stronger, more agile, or more skillful. The best sportsmen and sportswomen compete for prizes or to break sporting records, but most of us just play for fun. Schools recognize the importance of regular sporting exercise which keeps us fit and include physical education on the timetable. Early on, though, sports were not for amusement. More than 2,000 years ago athletic sports trained men for hunting or war.

Ancient Greeks were the first to hold sports festivals for friendly competition. The original Olympic Games began as early as 776B.C. Athletes raced one another on foot. They also boxed, long-jumped, and hurled the discus and javelin. Ancient Greece was the first home of what we now call track and field athletics. But Rome conquered Greece and in A.D.394 put an end to its Games.

Organized sports stayed almost unknown through Europe's Dark Ages, about A.D. 400–1000. Meanwhile, India or Persia invented chess, and horseracing flourished in the Middle East.

Left: *The Olympic stadium at Barcelona, site of the 1992 games.*

In the Middle Ages, Europe's main sports were archery contests and combat sports between knights fighting on foot or mounted. In the 1400s football began as a game where crowds brawled over a ball, and the Scots played an early form of golf. Germans rolled stones to knock over wooden clubs. The Dutch called the game skittles and took it to North America in the 1600s. In 1841 the original game, played with nine pins, was banned in Connecticut because of gambling. So the players added an extra pin, and tenpin bowling started.

257

Modern sports truly took shape only in the 1700s and 1800s. In the new Industrial Age millions of people gained the spare time and money to enjoy organized sports. This first happened in Great Britain, where the Industrial Age started. By the mid 1800s fast steam trains could carry sports teams to play far-off rivals. As sports became popular, organizations laid down rules for them. In 1863 the Football Association largely fixed the rules for association football (soccer). No one is quite sure how baseball developed, although it was probably based on an 18th century English game called rounders. After the Civil War, professional baseball teams were formed, and the National League was established in 1876. By 1900 sports and sports rules invented in Europe or North America had spread to countries around the world.

Some sports were old ones revived. Track and field athletics events reappeared in the modern Olympic Games, first held in Greece in 1896. German schools that taught physical fitness brought back gymnastics. New rules improved many old sports. (Boxers wear gloves and fight rounds with rests in between, thanks to rules laid down in 1867.)

Brand new sports appeared, too. In 1823 a boy at Rugby School, England, picked up a football and ran holding it. So rugby football was born. Rugby, in turn, led to American football. In the late 1800s old racket games gave

Martial arts, such as judo, karate, and kendo, were originally developed for combat, but have been refined for modern sports competition.

Steffi Graf was still a teenager when she won the tennis "Grand Slam" in 1988.

rise to badminton, squash, and lawn tennis. Figure skating dates from the 1860s and basketball from 1891. By 1900 the French were racing the newly developed cars and motorcycles.

Competition grew stronger once airplanes could whisk the world's best sportsmen and women to international contests anywhere on Earth. As standards improved, people broke old sporting records again and again. In 1896 the 1,500 meters (Olympic mile) was run in 4 minutes 33.2 seconds. By 1985 more than a minute had been lopped off that time. In 1896 the long jump record stood at under 21 feet (6.4 metres). Since then the distance has increased by nearly half as much again. In 1991, Mike Powell of the United States cleared a distance of 29 feet 4½ in. (8.95m). Year by year old records tumble to new world champions.

Since 1900 sports of all kinds have become ever more popular. Now, millions of us swim, run, skate, row, or play some form of ball game. Sports create good friendships and add excitement to life. Millions more watch ball games contests, and races on television or go to sports events in gymnasiums and in stadiums. Not only the fit and strong, but also the disabled, can derive pleasure from sporting effort and achievement.

ATHLETICS

Men's World Records

100 metres	9.86 sec	Carl Lewis (U.S.A.)	8.25.91
200 metres	19.72 sec	Pietro Mennea (Italy)	9.12.79
400 metres	43.29 sec	"Butch" Reynolds (U..S.A.)	8.17.88
800 metres	1 min 41.72 sec	Sebastian Coe (G.B.)	6.10.81
1,000 metres	2 min 12.18 sec	Sebastian Coe (G.B.)	7.11.81
1,500 metres	3 min 29.46 sec	Saïd Aouita (Morocco)	8.23.85
1 mile	3 min 46.32 sec	Steven Cram (G.B.)	7.27.85
2,000 metres	4 min 50.81 sec	Saïd Aouita (Morocco)	7.16.87
3,000 metres	7 min 29.45 sec	Saïd Aouita (Morocco)	8.20.89
5,000 metres	12 min 58.39 sec	Saïd Aouita (Morocco)	7.22.87
10,000 metres	27 min 08.23 sec	Arturo Barrios (Mexico)	8.18.89
Marathon*	2 hr 6 min 50 sec	Belayneh Dinsamo (Ethiopia)	5.17.88
110 metres hurdles	12.92 sec	Roger Kingdom (U.S.A.)	8.16.89
400 metres hurdles	47.02 sec	Ed Moses (U.S.A.)	8.31.83
3,000 m steeplechase	8 min 5.35 sec	Peter Koech (Kenya)	7.4.89
4 × 100 metres relay	37.50 sec	United States	8.7.91
4 × 400 metres relay	2 min 56.16 sec	United States	10.20.68
High jump	2.44 m (8 ft)	Javier Sotomayor (Cuba)	7.29.89
Pole vault	6.10 m (20 ft ¼ in)	Sergey Bubka (Russia)	5.8.91
Long jump	8.95 m (29 ft 4½ in)	Mike Powell (U.S.A.)	8.30.91
Triple jump	17.97 m (58 ft 11 in)	"Willie" Banks (U.S.A.)	6.16.85
Shot put	23.12 m (75 ft 10¼ in)	Randy Barnes (U.S.A.)	5.20.90
Discus throw	74.08 m (243 ft)	Jürgen Schult (E. Germany)	6.6.86
Hammer throw	86.74 m (284 ft 7 in)	Yuriy Sedykh (Russia)	8.30.86
Javelin throw†	91 m 46 cm	Stephen Backley (G.B.)	1.25.92
Decathlon	8847 points	"Daley" Thompson (G.B.)	8.8–9.84

Women's World Records

100 metres	10.49 sec	Florence Griffith Joyner (U.S.A.)	7.16.88
200 metres	21.34 sec	Florence Griffith Joyner (U.S.A.)	9.29.88
400 metres	47.60 sec	Marita Koch (E Germany)	10.6.85
800 metres	1 min 53.28 sec	Jarmila Kratochvilova (Czech)	7.26.83
1,000 metres	2 min 30.60 sec	Tatyana Providokhina (Russia)	8.20.78
1,500 metres	3 min 52.47 sec	Tatyana Kazankina (Russia)	8.13.80
1 mile	4 min 15.61 sec	Paula Ivan (Romania)	7.10.89
2,000 metres	5 min 28.69 sec	Maricica Puica (Romania)	7.11.86
3,000 metres	8 min 22.62 sec	Tatyana Kazankina (Russia)	8.26.84
5,000 metres	14 min 37.33 sec	Ingrid Kristiansen (Norway)	8.5.86
10,000 metres	30 min 13.74 sec	Ingrid Kristiansen (Norway)	7.5.86
Marathon*	2 hr 21 min 6 sec	Ingrid Kristiansen (Norway)	4.21.85
100 metres hurdles	12.21 sec	Yordanka Donkova (Bulgaria)	8.21.88
400 metres hurdles	52.94 sec	Marina Styepanova (Russia)	9.17.86
4 × 100 metres relay	41.37 sec	East Germany	10.6.85
4 × 400 metres relay	3 min 15.17 sec	USSR	10.1.88
High jump	2.09 m (6 ft 10¼ in)	Stefka Kostadinova (Bulgaria)	8.30.87
Long jump	7.52 m (24 ft 8¼ in)	Galina Chistyakova (Russia)	6.11.88
Shot put	22.63 m (74 ft 3 in)	Natalya Lisovskaya (Russia)	6.7.87
Discus throw	76.80 m (252 ft)	Gabriele Reinsch (E. Germany)	7.9.88
Javelin throw	80 m (262 ft 5 in)	Petra Felke (E. Germany)	9.9.88
Heptathlon	7,291 points	Jacqueline Joyner-Kersee (U.S.A.)	9.23–24.88

World best time (courses vary)   †New javelin

AUTO RACING
Ruling body Fédération Internationale de l'Automobile (FIA)
Major events and competitions Formula One – World Drivers Championship (based on points gained in individual grands prix: 9, 6, 4, 3, 2, 1 for first 6
Sports car racing – Le Mans

BASEBALL
Pitching distance 60 ft. 6 in. (18.4 m)
Side of "diamond" 90 ft. (27.4 m)
Max. length of bat 3 ft. 6 in. (1.07 m)
Diameter of ball 2¾ in. (7 cm)
Weight of ball 5–5¼ oz. (142–149 g)
Number per side 9 (substitutes allowed)
No. of innings 9 or more (played to finish)
Major organizations American League (A.L.), National League (N.L.)
Major competition The World Series

AUTO RECORDS
World Drivers Championship 5 JM Fangio (1951, 1954–57)
Championship Grand Prix wins 43 Alain Prost 1980–90
Grand Prix wins in season 8 Ayrton Senna
Land Speed Record 633.5 mph (1019.5 km/h) Richard Noble (GB) in *Thrust 2*, 1983
Water Speed Record 317.6 mph (511.1 km/h) Ken Warby (Aus.) in *Spirit of Australia*, 1978

WORLD SERIES RESULTS
1939–1991

1939 New York (AL) 4, Cincinnati (NL) 0	1966 Baltimore (AL) 4, Los Angeles (NL) 0
1940 Cincinnati (NL) 4, Detroit (AL) 3	1967 St. Louis (NL) 4, Boston (AL) 3
1941 New York (AL) 4, Brooklyn (NL) 1	1968 Detroit (AL) 4, St. Louis (NL) 3
1942 St. Louis (NL) 4, New York (AL) 1	1969 New York (NL) 4, Baltimore (AL) 1
1943 New York (AL) 4, St. Louis (NL) 1	1970 Baltimore (AL) 4, Cincinnati (NL) 1
1944 St. Louis (NL) 4, St. Louis (AL) 2	1971 Pittsburgh (NL) 4, Baltimore (AL) 3
1945 Detroit (AL) 4, Chicago (NL) 3	1972 Oakland (AL) 4, Cincinnati (NL) 3
1946 St. Louis (NL) 4, Boston (AL) 3	1973 Oakland (AL) 4, New York (NL) 3
1947 New York (AL) 4, Brooklyn (NL) 3	1974 Oakland (AL) 4, Los Angeles (NL) 1
1948 Cleveland (AL) 4, Boston (NL) 2	1975 Cincinnati (NL) 4, Boston (AL) 3
1949 New York (AL) 4, Brooklyn (NL) 1	1976 Cincinnati (NL) 4, New York (AL) 0
1950 New York (AL) 4, Philadelphia (NL) 0	1977 New York (AL) 4, Los Angeles (NL) 2
1951 New York (AL) 4, New York (NL) 2	1978 New York (AL) 4, Los Angeles (NL) 2
1952 New York (AL) 4, Brooklyn (NL) 3	1979 Pittsburgh (NL) 4, Baltimore (AL) 3
1953 New York (AL) 4, Brooklyn (NL) 2	1980 Philadelphia (NL) 4, Kansas City (AL) 2
1954 New York (AL) 4, Cleveland (AL) 0	
1955 Brooklyn (NL) 4, New York (AL) 3	1981 Los Angeles (NL) 4, New York (AL) 2
1956 New York (AL) 4, Brooklyn (NL) 3	1982 St. Louis (NL) 4, Milwaukee (AL) 3
1957 Milwaukee (NL) 4, New York (AL) 3	1983 Baltimore (AL) 4, Philadelphia (NL) 1
1958 New York (AL) 4, Milwaukee (NL) 3	1984 Detroit (AL) 4, San Diego (NL) 1
1959 Los Angeles (NL) 4, Chicago (AL) 2	1985 Kansas City (AL) 4, St Louis (NL) 3
1960 Pittsburgh (NL) 4, New York (AL) 3	1986 New York (AL) 4, Boston (AL) 3
1961 New York (AL) 4, Cincinnati (NL) 1	1987 Minnesota (AL) 4, St. Louis (NL) 3
1962 New York (AL) 4, San Francisco (NL) 3	1988 Los Angeles (NL) 4, Oakland (AL) 1
1963 Los Angeles (NL) 4, New York (AL) 0	1989 Oakland (AL) 4, San Francisco (NL) 0
1964 St Louis (NL) 4, New York (AL) 3	1990 Cincinnati (NL) 4, Oakland (AL) 0
1965 Los Angeles (NL) 4, Minnesota (AL) 3	1991 Minnesota (AL) 4, Atlanta (NL) 3

BASKETBALL

Court 85 × 46 ft. (26 × 14 m)
Height of baskets 10 ft. (3.05 m)
Diameter of baskets 18 in. (46 cm)
Circumference of ball 29½–30½ in. (75–78 cm)
Weight of ball 21–23 oz.(600–650 g)
Duration 40 min. actual play (2 × 20) plus periods of 5 min until result is obtained
Number per side 5 (usually up to 5 substitutes)
Ruling body Fédération Internationale de Basketball Amateur (FIBA)
Major competitions World championships (men and women) and Olympic Games

BILLIARDS AND SNOOKER

Table 12 ft. × 6 ft. 1½ in. (3.66 × 1.86 m)
Diameter of balls 2¹⁄₁₆ in. (5.25 cm)
Billiards red, white, spot white
Billiards scoring pot or in-off red 3, white 2; cannon 2
Snooker balls (value) black (7), pink (6), blue (5), brown (4), green (3), yellow (2), 15 reds (1 each), white (cue-ball)

BOWLS (FLAT GREEN)

Rink (max.) 132 × 19 ft. (40.2 × 5.8 m)
Bowls diam. (max.) 5¾ in. (14.6 cm) biased, weight (max.) 3½ lb. (1.59 kg), made of wood, rubber or composition
Jack diam. 2½ in. (6.35 cm), weight 8–10 oz. (227–284 g)
Ruling body International Bowling Board
Events singles (4 bowls each, 21 *shots* up), pairs (2–4 bowls each, 21 *ends*), triples (2 or 3 bowls each, 18 *ends*), fours
(2 bowls each, 21 *ends*)
World championships – every 4 years

BOXING

Professional
Ring 14–20 ft. (4.3–6.1 m) square
Gloves 6 oz. (170 g) fly to welter-weight,
8 oz. (227 g) light-middleweight and above
Duration 6, 8, 10, 12 or 15 (title) 3-min rounds
Ruling body World Boxing Council (WBC)
Amateur
Ring 16–20 ft. (4.9–6.1 m) square
Gloves 8 oz. (227 g)
Duration Three 3-min rounds (seniors)
Ruling body Amateur International Boxing Association

A boxing glove. The sport is banned in some countries.

BOXING WEIGHT LIMITS

Division	WBC lb.	WBC kg	AIBA lb.	AIBA kg	Division	WBC lb.	WBC kg	AIBA lb.	AIBA kg
Light-fly	—	—	105	48.0	Junior welter	140	63.50	140	63.5
Fly	112	50.80	112	51.0	Welter	148	66.68	148	67.0
Bantam	118	53.52	119	54.0	Junior middle	154	69.85	156	71.0
Feather	126	57.15	126	57.0	Middle	160	72.58	165	75.0
Junior light	130	58.97	—	—	Light-heavy	175	79.38	178	81.0
Light	135	61.24	133	60.0	Heavy	no limit		199	91.0

CHESS

Ruling body International Chess Federation

WORLD CHAMPIONS

1866–1894	Wilhelm Steinitz (Austria)
1894–1921	Emanuel Lasker (Germany)
1921–1927	Jose R. Capablanca (Cuba)
1927–1935	Alexander A. Alekhine (USSR*)
1935–1937	Max Euwe (Netherlands)
1937–1946	Alexander A. Alekhine (USSR*)
1948–1957	Mikhail Botvinnik (USSR)
1957–1958	Vassily Smyslov (USSR)
1958–1959	Mikhail Botvinnik (USSR)
1960–1961	Mikhail Tal (USSR)
1961–1963	Mikhail Botvinnik (USSR)
1963–1969	Tigran Petrosian (USSR)
1969–1972	Boris Spassky (USSR)
1972–1975	Bobby Fischer† (USA)
1975–1985	Anatoli Karpov (USSR)
1985–	Gary Kasparov (Russia)

*Took French citizenship
†Karpov won title when Fischer defaulted.

A chess board at the start of play.

Chess pieces: (from left) Pawn, Rook, Knight, Bishop, Queen, King.

CROQUET

Ball Court 35 × 28 yd. (32 × 25.6 m)
Players 2 or 4
Balls 4 (blue and black vs. red and yellow), $3\frac{5}{8}$ in.(diam 9.2 cm), weight 1 lb. (454 g)
Hoops 6 (twice each) plus *peg* diam $3\frac{3}{4}$ in. (9.5 cm)
International team competition MacRobertson Shield

CYCLING

Ruling body Union Cycliste Internationale
Major competitions *ROAD RACING* Tour de France, Olympic 62-mile (100-km) race.
TRACK RACING Olympics and world championships (sprint, pursuit, 1-km time trial, motor-paced)
Other cycle sports Six-day racing, cyclo-cross, cycle speedway, bicycle polo, time trials

EQUESTRIAN SPORTS

Ruling body Fédération Equestre Internationale (FEI)
Major competitions *SHOW JUMPING* world championships (men's and women's) every 4 years, alternating with Olympics; President's Cup (world team championship) based on Nations Cup results; 2-yearly European championships (men's and women's); King George V Gold Cup; Queen Elizabeth II Gold Cup
THREE-DAY EVENT (1. Dressage, 2. Endurance or Cross-country, 3. Show jumping) 4-yearly world championships and Olympics; 2-yearly European championships; Badminton Horse Trials
DRESSAGE Olympics and world championships

FENCING

Ruling body Fédération Internationale d'Escrimé (FIE)
Events Foil, épée, saber (men); foil (women)
Major competitions Annual world championships (including Olympics)
Duration of bout First to 5 hits (or 6 min) men; 4 hits (or 5 min) women

Track cyclists participating in a points race compete for the best position on the steeply sloped ends of the velodrome .

Fencers wear wire mesh masks, thick padded jackets and gloves. A 'hit' is recorded electronically in modern competitions.

FOOTBALL
Field 360 × 160 ft. (110 × 49 m)
Goals 20 ft. (6 m) high, 23 ft. 4 inches (7.1 m) wide, 10 ft. (3 m) off ground.
Ball Length 11 in. (28 cm), chort circum. 21¼ in.(54 cm), weight 14–15 oz (397–425 g)
Duration 60 min (4 × 15) playing time
No. per side 11 (unspecified no. of substitutes)
Scoring *Touchdown* 6 pts, *extra point* 1, *field goal* 3, *safety* 2

SUPER BOWL

Year	Winner	Loser	Site
1967	Green Bay Packers, 35	Kansas City Chiefs, 10	Los Angeles Coliseum
1968	Green Bay Packers, 33	Oakland Raiders, 14	Orange Bowl, Miami
1969	New York Jets, 16	Baltimore Colts, 7	Orange Bowl, Miami
1970	Kansas City Chiefs, 23	Minnesota Vikings, 7	Tulane Stadium, New Orleans
1971	Baltimore Colts, 16	Dallas Cowboys, 13	Orange Bowl, Miami
1972	Dallas Cowboys, 24	Miami Dolphins, 3	Tulane Stadium, New Orleans
1973	Miami Dolphins, 14	Washington Redskins, 7	Los Angeles Coliseum
1974	Miami Dolphins, 24	Minnesota Vikings, 7	Rice Stadium, Houston
1975	Pittsburgh Steelers, 16	Minnesota Vikings, 6	Tulane Stadium, New Orleans
1976	Pittsburgh Steelers, 21	Dallas Cowboys, 17	Orange Bowl, Miami
1977	Oakland Raiders, 32	Minnesota Vikings, 14	Rose Bowl, Pasadena
1978	Dallas Cowboys, 27	Denver Broncos, 10	Superdome, New Orleans
1979	Pittsburgh Steelers, 35	Dallas Cowboys, 31	Orange Bowl, Miami
1980	Pittsburgh Steelers, 31	Los Angeles Rams, 19	Rose Bowl, Pasadena
1981	Oakland Raiders, 27	Philadelphia Eagles, 10	Superdome, New Orleans
1982	San Francisco 49ers, 25	Cincinati Bengals, 21	Silverdome, Pontiac, Mich.
1983	Washington Redskins, 27	Miami Dolphins, 17	Rose Bowl, Pasadena
1984	Los Angeles Raiders, 38	Washington Redskins, 9	Tampa Stadium
1985	San Francisco 49ers, 38	Miami Dolphins, 16	Stanford Stadium, Palo Alto, Cal.
1986	Chicago Bears, 46	New England Patriots, 10	Superdome, New Orleans
1987	New York Giants, 39	Denver Broncos, 20	Rose Bowl, Pasadena
1988	Washington Redskins, 42	Denver Broncos, 10	San Diego, Stadium
1989	San Francisco 49ers, 20	Cincinnati Bengals, 16	Joe Robbie Stadium, Miami
1990	San Francisco 49ers, 55	Denver Broncos, 10	Superdome, New Orleans
1991	New York Giants, 20	Buffalo Bills, 19	Tampa Stadium
1992	Washington Redskins, 37	Buffalo Bills, 24	Metrodome, Minneapolis

GOLF
Ball Max. weight 1.62 oz. (46 g), min. diam. 1.68 in. (4.27 cm)
Hole Diam. 4¼ in. (10.8 cm)
No. of clubs carried 14 maximum
Ruling bodies Royal and Ancient Golf Club of St. Andrews; United States Golf Association
Major competitions Individual – Open, U.S. Open, U.S. Masters, U.S. PGA

GOLF RECORDS

Lowest round 55 A E Smith (G.B.) 1936
36 holes 122 Sam Snead (U.S.) 59–63, 1959
72 holes 255 Peter Tupling (G.B.) 1981
Most "Big Four" titles 18 Jack Nicklaus (U.S.)
Most British Opens 6 Harry Vardon (G.B.)
Most US Opens 4 Willie Anderson (U.S.), Bobby
  Jones (U.S.), Ben Hogan (U.S.), Jack Nicklaus
  (U.S.)
Most US Masters 6 Jack Nicklaus (U.S.)
Most US PGAs 5 Walter Hagen (U.S.), Jack
  Nicklaus (U.S.)

GOLF TERMS

big four The major individual tournaments: Open
and U.S. Open, Masters, and PGA.
birdie One under par for hole.
bogey One over par for hole.
dormie In match play, leading by numbers of
holes left.
double bogey Two over par for hole.
eagle Two under par for hole.
fairway Smooth turf between tee and green.
fourball Match in which pairs score their "better
ball" at each hole.
foursome Match in which pair play same ball,
alternately.

green Specially prepared surface in which hole is
situated.
handicap A shot allowance given to a player so
that he or she can play on equal terms with a
superior opponent; not used in professional
tournaments.
match play In which player or pair play each other
and winner is determined by holes won.
medal play In which number of strokes taken
determines winner.
par Standard score (assessed on first-class play)
for hole or holes.
putter Club used to hit ball when on green.
rough Unprepared part of course.
tee Starting place for hole, or peg on which ball is
placed.

*Above right: The three basic
types of golf club: woods,
irons, and putter.*

*Below: Gymnasts performing
on the asymmetrical bars
include a range of tucks, pikes,
and hand changeovers into
their routine.*

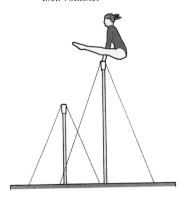

GYMNASTICS

Ruling body Fédération Internationale de Gymnastique
Events Men's – floor exercises, rings, parallel bars,
pommel horse, vault (lengthwise), horizontal bar; overall;
team; women's – floor exercises (to music), vault,
asymmetrical bars, beam; overall; team
Major competitions World and Olympic championships,
alternately every 4 years

HOCKEY, FIELD

Goals 12 ft. (3.66 m) wide, 7 ft. (2.13 m) high
Ball Circum. 9 in. (23 cm), weight 5½–5¾ oz. (156–163
g), made of cork and twine covered in leather
Duration of game 70 min. (2 × 35)
No. per side 11 (2 substitutes in men's game)
Ruling bodies Men's – Fédération Internationale de
Hockey (FIH); women's – Women's International Hockey
Rules' Board
Major competitions Olympic Games and World Cup
(4-yearly)

HORSE RACING
Major races
United States Kentucky Derby, Preakness Stakes, Belmont Stakes (Triple Crown); Washington International
England Derby, Oaks, St Leger, 1,000 and 2,000 Guineas (the 5 Classics), King George VI & Queen Elizabeth Stakes, Ascot Gold Cup; Grand National (steeplechase), Cheltenham Gold Cup (steeplechase), Champion Hurdle
Ireland Irish Sweeps Derby
France Prix de l'Arc de Triomphe
Australia Melbourne Cup, Caulfield Cup
South Africa Durban July Handicap

LACROSSE
Pitch 110 × 60 yd. (100 × 55 m) men; 120 × 70 yd.(110 × 64 m) preferred for women's international matches
Goals 6 × 6 ft. (1.8 × 1.8 m)
Ball Circum. $7\frac{3}{4}$–8 in.(19.7–20.3 cm), weight 5– $5\frac{1}{4}$ oz. (142–149 g) men; $4\frac{3}{4}$–$5\frac{1}{4}$ oz. (135–149 g) women
Duration 60 min. (4 × 15) men, 50 min. (2 × 25) women
No. per side 10 (13 substitutes) men, 12 (8 substitutes) women

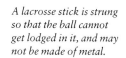

A lacrosse stick is strung so that the ball cannot get lodged in it, and may not be made of metal.

MOTORCYCLING
Ruling body Fédération Internationale Motocycliste (FIM)
Classes 50 cc, 125 cc, 250 cc, 350 cc (junior), 500 cc (senior), 750 cc, unlimited; sidecar
Major competitions World championships (based on points gained in individual grands prix), including Isle of Man TT
Other motorcycle sports Scrambling (motocross), trials, grasstrack racing

SOCCER
Pitch (field) 100–130 yd. (91.4–118.9 m) by 50–100 yd. (45.7–91.4 m)
Goals 8 yd. (7.3 m) wide, 8 ft. (2.4 m) high
Ball circum. 27–28 in. (68–71 cm)
weight 14–15 oz. (400–450 gm)
Duration of game 90 min. (2 × 45) plus 2 × 15 min. extra in certain cup games
Number per side 11 (1 or 2 substitutes, depending on competition)
Ruling body Fédération Internationale de Football Association (FIFA)

The FIFA World Cup, played for every four years, is the leading tournament for national soccer teams. More people play and watch soccer world-wide than any other team game.

SOCCER WORLD CUP FINALS

1930	Montevideo, Uruguay (100,000)	Uruguay 4	Argentina.................2
1934	Rome, Italy (55,000)	Italy........................2	Czechoslovakia 1
1938	Paris, France (65,000)	Italy........................4	Hungary 2
1950	Rio de Janeiro, Brazil (199,850)	Uruguay 2	Brazil......................1
1954	Berne, Switzerland (55,000)	W. Germany............3	Hungary 2
1958	Stockholm, Sweden (49,700)	Brazil......................5	Sweden....................2
1962	Santiago, Chile (69,500)	Brazil......................3	Czechoslovakia 1
1966	Wembley, England (93,000)	England...................4	W. Germany 2
1970	Mexico City, Mexico (110,000)	Brazil......................4	Italy........................1
1974	Munich, W Germany (75,000)	W. Germany............2	Netherlands..............1
1978	Buenos Aires, Argentina (77,000)	Argentina................3	Netherlands..............1
1982	Madrid, Spain (90,000)	Italy........................3	W. Germany 1
1986	Mexico City, Mexico (114,580)	Argentina................3	W. Germany 2
1990	Rome, Italy (73,603)	W. Germany............1	Argentina.................0

SPEEDWAY
Track 4 laps of 300–450 yd.(274–411 m) surface – red shale or granite dust
Meeting 20 races, 4 riders in race, each getting 5 rides
Scoring 1st 3 pts., 2nd 2, 3rd 1
Machines Brakeless 500 cc motorcycles
Ruling body Fédération Internationale Motocycliste (FIM)
Major competitions World Championship (individual), World Team Cup, World Pairs Championship
Most World Championship wins 6 Ivan Mauger (N.Z.)

SWIMMING AND DIVING
Standard Olympic pool 54.7 yd. (50 m) long, 8 lanes
Ruling body Fédération Internationale de Natation Amateur (FINA)
Competitive strokes Freestyle (usually front crawl), backstroke, breaststroke, butterfly; individual medley (butterfly, backstroke, breaststroke, freestyle), medley relay (backstroke, breaststroke, butterfly, freestyle)
Diving events Men's and women's springboard at 10 ft. (3 m), highboard at 33 ft. (10 m) (lower boards also used)
Major competitions Olympics and world championships
Major long-distance swims English Channel, Cook Strait (N.Z.), Atlantic City Marathon (U.S.)

SWIMMING MEN'S WORLD RECORDS

Freestyle

50 metres	21.81 sec	Tom Jager (U.S.A.)	24.3.90
100 metres	48.74 sec	Matthew Biondi (U.S.A.)	24.6.86
200 metres	1 min 46.69 sec	Giorgio Lamberti (Italy)	15.8.89

Breaststroke

100 metres	1 min 01.49 sec	Adrian Moorhouse (GB)	15.8.89

Butterfly

100 metres	52.84 sec	Pedro Morales (U.S.A.)	23.6.86

Backstroke

100 metres	54.51 sec	David Berkoff (U.S.A.)	24.9.88

WOMEN'S WORLD RECORDS

Freestyle

50 metres	24.98 sec	Yang Wenyi (China)	10.4.88
100 metres	54.73 sec	Kristin Otto (GDR)	19.8.86
200 metres	1 min 57.55 sec	Heike Friedrich (GDR)	18.6.84

Breaststroke

100 metres	1 min 07.91 sec	Silke Hörner (GDR)	21.8.87

Butterfly

100 metres	57.93 sec	Mary T. Meagher (U.S.A.)	16.8.81

Backstroke

100 metres	1 min 00.59 sec	Ina Kleber (GDR)	24.8.84

TABLE TENNIS

Table 9 × 5 ft. (2.74 × 1.52 m), 2½ ft. (76 cm) off floor
Net Height 6 in. (15.2 cm), length 6 ft. (1.83 cm)
Ball Diam. 1.46–1.5 in. (37–38 mm), weight 2.4–2.53 g
made of celluloid-type plastic, white or yellow
Bat surface Max. thickness 0.08 in. (2 mm) pimpled
rubber or 0.16 in. (4 mm) sandwich rubber
Scoring Best of 3 or 5 21-pt. games
Ruling body International Table Tennis Federation
Major competitions World championships, Swaythling
Cup (men's team), Corbillon Cup (women's team), all
2-yearly

TENNIS

Ball Diam. 2½–2⅝ in. (6.35–6.67 cm), weight 2–2¹⁄₁₆ oz.
(56.7–58.5 g) , made of wool-covered rubber, white or
yellow
Rackets No limits, wood or metal frames, strung with
lamb's gut or nylon
Scoring Best of 3 or 5 6-up sets, with tiebreaker at 6–6 (or
first to lead by 2); games of 4 pts. (15, 30, 40, game),
40–40 being *deuce* and 2-pt. lead required; tiebreaker
game usually first to 7 pts. with 2-pt. lead

Ruling body International Lawn Tennis Federation (ILTF)
Major competitions Wimbledon, Australian Open, US Open, French Open (the four constituting "Grand Slam"), Davis Cup (world team championship), Federation Cup (Women's World Cup), Wightman Cup (U.S. v GB women)

VOLLEYBALL
Court 59 × 29½ ft. (18 × 9 m)
Net height 7 ft 11.7 in. (2.43 m) for men, 7. ft 4 in. (2.24 m) for women
Ball Circum. 25.6–26.4 in. (65–67 cm), weight 9–10 oz. (260–280 gm)
No. per side 6 (6 substitutes)
Scoring Best of 3 or 5 15-pt. sets
Ruling body Fédération Internationale de Volleyball (FIVB)
Major competitions Olympics and world championships, alternately every 4 years (men and women)

WATER POLO
Pool 22–33 yd. (20–30 m) by 8¾–22 yd. (8–20 m), min. depth 1 m (1.8 m for international competitions)
Goals 9¾ × 3 ft. (3 × 0.9 m) for depths over 4 ft. 11 in. (1.5 m); for shallower pools, crossbar 7 ft. 10 in. (2.4 m) above bottom
Ball circum. 26¾–28 in. (68–71 cm), weight 14–16 oz. (400–450 gm)
Duration of game 28 min (4 × 7)
No. per side 7 (6 substitutes)
Ruling body FINA (see *SWIMMING*)
Major competitions as for *SWIMMING*

WEIGHTLIFTING
Ruling body International Weightlifting Federation (IWF)
Lifts *Snatch* (bar pulled overhead in one movement) and *(clean and) jerk* (bar raised to shoulders first, then driven aloft as legs are straightened); (non-Olympic) *bench press, squat, dead lift*
World championships Annual (including Olympics)
Classes – flyweight (114½ lb./52 kg limit), bantam (123½ lb./56 kg), feather (132¼ lb./60 kg), light (148¾ lb./67.5 kg), middle (165-1/4 lb./75 kg), light-heavy (181¾ lb. /82.5 kg), middle-heavy (198¼ lb./90 kg), heavy (242½ lb. /110 kg), super-heavy (over 110 kg)

WIMBLEDON CHAMPIONS
SINCE 1946

	men	*women*
1946	Yvon Petra (Fr)	Pauline Betz (U.S.)
1947	Jack Kramer (U.S.)	Margaret Osborne (U.S.)
1948	Bob Falkenburg (U.S.)	Louise Brough (U.S.)
1949	Fred Schroeder (U.S.)	Louise Brough (U.S.)
1950	Budge Patty (U.S.)	Louise Brough (U.S.)
1951	Dick Savitt (U.S.)	Doris Hart (U.S.)
1952	Frank Sedgman (Aus.)	Maureen Connolly (U.S.)
1953	Victor Seixas (U.S.)	Maureen Connolly (U.S.)
1954	Jaroslav Drobny (Cz.)	Maureen Connolly (U.S.)
1955	Tony Trabert (U.S.)	Louise Brough (U.S.)
1956	Lew Hoad (Aus.)	Shirley Fry (U.S.)
1957	Lew Hoad (Aus.)	Althea Gibson (U.S.)
1958	Ashley Cooper (Aus.)	Althea Gibson (U.S.)
1959	Alex Olmedo (Peru)	Maria Bueno (Brazil)
1960	Neale Fraser (Aus.)	Maria Bueno (Brazil)
1961	Rod Laver (Aus.)	Angela Mortimer (G.B.)
1962	Rod Laver (Aus.)	Karen Susman (U.S.)
1963	Chuck McKinley (U.S.)	Margaret Smith (Aus.)
1964	Roy Emerson (Aus.)	Maria Bueno (Brazil)
1965	Roy Emerson (Aus.)	Margaret Smith (Aus.)
1966	Manuel Santana (Sp.)	Billie Jean King (U.S.)
1967	John Newcombe (Aus.)	Billie Jean King (U.S.)
1968	Rod Laver (Aus.)	Billie Jean King (U.S.)
1969	Rod Laver (Aus.)	Ann Jones (G.B.)
1970	John Newcombe (Aus.)	Margaret Court* (Aus.)
1971	John Newcombe (Aus.)	Evonne Goolagong (Aus.)
1972	Stan Smith (U.S.)	Billie Jean King (U.S.)
1973	Jan Kodes (Cz.)	Billie Jean King (U.S.)
1974	Jimmy Connors (U.S.)	Chris Evert (U.S.)
1975	Arthur Ashe (U.S.)	Billie Jean King (U.S.)
1976	Bjorn Borg (Swed.)	Chris Evert (U.S.)
1977	Bjorn Borg (Swed.)	Virginia Wade (G.B.)
1978	Bjorn Borg (Swed.)	Martina Navratilova (Cz.)
1979	Bjorn Borg (Swed.)	Martina Navratilova (Cz.)
1980	Bjorn Borg (Swed.)	Evonne Cawley† (Aus.)
1981	John McEnroe (U.S.)	Chris Evert-Lloyd (U.S.)
1982	Jimmy Connors (U.S.)	Martina Navratilova (U.S.)
1983	John McEnroe (U.S.)	Martina Navratilova (U.S.)
1984	John McEnroe (U.S.)	Martina Navratilova (U.S.)
1985	Boris Becker (W. Ger.)	Martina Navratilova (U.S.)
1986	Boris Becker (W. Ger.)	Martina Navratilova (U.S.)
1987	Pat Cash (Aus.)	Martina Navratilova (U.S.)
1988	Stefan Edberg (Swed.)	Steffi Graf (W. Ger.)
1989	Boris Becker (W. Ger.)	Steffi Graf (W. Ger.)
1990	Stefan Edberg (Swed.)	Martina Navratilova (U.S.)
1991	Michael Stich (Ger.)	Steffi Graf (Ger.)

*Formerly Margaret Smith
†Formerly Evonne Goolagong

The first tennis rackets were wooden, with off-set, pear-shaped heads, strung with natural gut. Most modern rackets use synthetic materials – metal, carbon graphite, glass fiber, or ceramic.

All ice hockey players, but especially the goal minder, are padded for protection in this fast, rough sport.

WINTER SPORTS

Ice Skating
Ruling body International Skating Union (ISU)
World championships Annual (including Olympics)
Figure skating events Men's, women's single, pairs, (pairs) dancing (all with compulsory and "free" sections); two sets of marks, for technical merit and artistic impression
Speed skating events (on oval 400-m circuits) Men's 500, 1,500, 5,000 and 10,000 m; women's 500, 1,000, 1,500 and 3,000 m.

Ice Hockey
Rink Max. 200 × 100 ft. (61 × 30.5 m)
Surround Max. 4 ft. (1.22 m) high boards
Goals 6 × 4 ft. (1.83 × 1.22 m)
Puck Diam. 3 in. (7.62 cm), thickness 1 in. (2.54 cm) weight 5½ × 6 oz. (156 × 170 g), made of vulcanized rubber
Duration 60 min (3 × 20) playing time
No. per side 6 (max. 18 on team)
Ruling body International Ice Hockey Federation

Curling
Rink 138 × 14 ft. (42 × 4.27 m)
Houses (targets) Diam. 12 ft. (3.66 m), dist. between centers 114 ft. (34.75 cm)
Stones (max.) Circum. 36 in (91.4 cm), thickness 4½ in. (11.4 cm), weight 44 lb. (20 kg), made of granite or similar
No. per team 4 (2 stones each)
No. of *heads* (or *ends*) 10 or 12 (or time limit)
Ruling body Royal Caledonian Curling Club
World championships Silver Broom Trophy (annual)

Bobsleigh
Course Min. length 1,640 yd. (1,500 m), with at least 15 banked turns; agg. time for 4 descents
Events 2- and 4-man bobs
Ruling body International Bobsleigh Federation
World championships Annual (including Olympics)

Luge Tobogganing
Course 1,094–1,640 yd. (1,000–1,500 m); agg. time for 4 descents
Events 1- and 2-man luge, 1-woman luge; ridden in sitting position
Ruling body International Luge Federation
World Championships Annual (including Olympics)

Competitors in luge tobogganing descend the course feet-first aboard the lightweight skeleton toboggan.

Cresta Run

Course Unique to St. Moritz 1,326.6 yd. (1,213 m); agg. time for 3 descents
Event Single seater, ridden face down
Ruling body St. Moritz Tobogganing Club
Major competitions Grand National (full course, from Top), Curzon Cup (from Junction, 971 yd. or 888 m); Olympic event (full course) 1928 and 1948

Alpine Ski Racing

Events Downhill, slalom, giant slalom, combined
Downhill Vert. drop 2,625–3,281 ft. (800–1,000 m) men; 1,640–2,297 ft. (500–700 m) women
Slalom 55–75 gates men, 40–60 gates women; alternate gates, pairs of poles (13–16 ft., 4–5 m apart) have blue or red flags and are 2.5–49 ft. (0.75–15 m) apart
Giant slalom Min. 33 gates 13–26 ft. (4–8 m) wide, at least 33 ft. (10 m) apart
Ruling body Fédération Internationale de Ski (FIS)
Major competitions 2-yearly world championships (including Olympics, which has no combined title), annual World Cup (men's and women's, individuals scoring in 15 of 21 top international events, first 10 scoring 25, 20, 15, 11, 8, 6, 4, 3, 2,1 pts.), annual Arlberg-Kandahar

Ski-Bob Racing

Events Downhill, giant slalom, special slalom, combined
Ruling body Fédération Internationale de Skibob (FISB)
World championships Two-yearly (men's and women's)

Nordic Ski Competition

Events 9.3, 18.6, 31 miles (15, 30, 50 km) men's, 3.1, 6.2 miles (5, 10 km) women's; 4 × 10 km relay (men), 3 × 5 km relay (women); nordic combination (15 km cross-country and ski jumping, men's); men's 230 and 295 ft. (70 and 90 m) ski jumping (points awarded for style and distance)
Ruling body Fédération Internationale de Ski (FIS)
Major competitions 2-yearly world championships (including Olympics); 295-ft. (90-m) ski jumping and biathlon, annually

Biathlon

Course 12.4 miles (20 km), with 4 stops for target shooting men; 6.2 miles (10 km), with 3 stops, women
Events Men's individual and relay 2.5 × 4.5 miles (4 × 7.5 km)
Scoring On time, with 2-min penalties for shots missing target, 1-min penalty for hit in outer ring of target

INDEX

In this index the figures in **bold** denote main entries and those in *italics* denote illustrations in the book. In a work of this kind it is not possible to index every entry; otherwise the index would be almost as long as the book itself. For entries not found in the index, look in the relevant charts and alphabetically arranged glossaries.